The Success Ethic,
Education,
and the
American Dream

SUNY Series,
Education and Culture:
Critical Factors in the Formation of
Character and Community in American Life

Eugene F. Provenzo, Jr.
and Paul Farber,
Editors

The Success Ethic, Education, and the American Dream

Joseph L. DeVitis
and
John Martin Rich

State University of
New York Press

Published by
State University of New York Press, Albany

For information, address the State University of New York Press,
State University Plaza, Albany, NY 12246

Production by Bernadine Dawes • Marketing by Fran Keneston

Library of Congress Cataloging-in-Publication Data

DeVitis, Joseph L.
    The success ethic, education, and the American dream / Joseph L. DeVitis and John Martin Rich.
        p.   cm. — (SUNY series, education and culture)
    Includes bibliographical references and index.
    ISBN 0-7914-2993-8 (hard : alk. paper). — ISBN 0-7914-2994-6 (pbk. : alk. paper)
    1. Success.   2. Conduct of life.   3. Ethics.   I. Rich, John Martin.   II. Title.
III. Series.
    BJ1611.2D45   1996
    170'.973—dc20   96-3227
                                                                          CIP

To Leigh, Jeffrey and Suzanne

Contents

Acknowledgments

We wish to thank Jeanne Schrader, Sarah Supulski, and Vicky Vlach for their efficient word processing and cheerful dispositions throughout the preparation of this manuscript. We also appreciate the encouragement on the project from Eugene F. Provenzo, Jr., of the University of Miami; Paul Farber, of Western Michigan University; and Lois Patton, of SUNY Press. Finally, we owe Alan V. Hewat a debt of gratitude for his helpful copyediting.

Preface

The quest for success propels persons along diverse life paths. Beckoning is the American Dream. In this quest, informal education follows the blandishments of self-improvement formulas that promise wealth, mobility, status, and respect. Self-improvement literature, which began in America with Benjamin Franklin, proliferated in the nineteenth century and has since developed a number of different genres.

Our purposes are to explore, analyze, interpret, and critically evaluate the success ethics in terms of their impact on American culture and education, and also to formulate new models of the success ethic. Earlier studies provided nineteenth- and early twentieth-century embodiments of the success ethic and biographical material, but they neglected a number of important figures and offered largely uncritical presentations. This study seeks to overcome those shortcomings by identifying and exploring the contributions of these neglected figures and by critically assessing the different success ethics from three major perspectives: psychological, philosophical, and social. In addition, previous works have mentioned education only in passing; here we seek to uncover the influences of the success ethics on formal and especially informal education.

Richard M. Huber was the first scholar to identify three different forms of the success ethic in the self-improvement literature.[1] Our inquiry will not only reconsider and reassess these forms, but will explicate and fashion new ones. Earlier research overlooked such significant figures as Horace Mann, Jane Addams, Eleanor Roosevelt, Harry S. Truman, and others. An even more serious shortcoming is the relative lack of systematic and incisive evaluation from multiple inquiry perspectives and the grievous failure to assess the weaknesses and vulnerabilities of the various success ethics and their subsequent damage to the American Dream. Nor have previous works investigated the extent to which formal education deviated from the success ethics but still professed to fulfill them.

In its broadest sense, this book intends to weave a rich fabric of interdisciplinary material from the social sciences and popular culture in order to view education both within and beyond the narrower confines of schooling. In so doing, it focuses on those social and cultural problems, in C. Wright Mills's words, that "are of direct relevance to urgent public issues and insistent human troubles."[2] Mills further develops this central theme:

> The knowledgeable man in the genuine public is able to turn his personal troubles into social issues, to see their relevance for his community and his community's relevance for them. He understands that what he thinks and feels as personal troubles are very often not only that but problems shared by others and indeed not subject to solution by any one individual but only by modifications of the structure of the groups in which he lives and sometimes the structure of the entire society.[3]

Applying the spirit of Mills's use of the "sociological imagination," this volume seeks to "enable us to grasp history and biography and the relations between the two within society" as we attend to "the personal troubles of milieux" and "the public issues of social structure" in the world today.[4]

Given such wide-ranging purposes, the book's audience draws upon a broad potential readership. In particular, it should appeal to those public intellectuals who are interested in, and must grapple with, public controversies of vital concern that require multiple lenses of analysis. Such contextual critics are inquisitive about cultural and intellectual history as well as national and international issues whose solutions transcend circumscribed academic disciplines. The book's breadth, scope, and interdisciplinary thrust should prove stimulating and challenging to those individuals, both inside and outside classroom walls, who seek to explore the dialectic between personal and public discourse and practice.

A Look Ahead

The opening chapter is introductory, and provides an overview of the areas of investigation as we lay out the pursuit of the American Dream, both in its problems and potentialities. The American Dream is discussed and shown to be the goal of the various success ethics. We then examine why some citizens today are disillusioned with the American Dream and have given up pursuit of the success ethic and withdrawn from competition or else turned to crime and deviant behavior.

Chapter 2 reveals that the character ethic began with the works of Benjamin Franklin, prevailed in the nineteenth century, and has some twentieth-century exemplars. Influenced by the Protestant ethic, it extolled poverty because it supposedly would help produce the traits necessary for success. It was skeptical of talent and the values of higher education, but insisted on good character and the cultivation of such traits as perseverance, industry, frugality, sobriety, and the like. Besides Franklin, other character ethic writers were Henry Ward Beecher, Lyman Abbott, George H. Lorimer, and Horatio Alger (although Alger's stories are atypical in the emphasis on luck in getting ahead).

As will be shown in chapter 3, the mind power ethic appeared in the nineteenth century and persisted after the turn of the century; it differed from the character ethic in three respects. Though it carried on the success tradition and its attitude toward opportunity, it renounced the asceticism of the character ethic, it challenged its ethical principles, and it ignored the value of self-education. Prominent advocates were O. S. Marden, a writer in the 1890s who inspired President William McKinley, and Norman Vincent Peale.

Chapter 4 articulates the personality ethic, the third type of success ethic, which focuses on developing a charming presence and an attractive physical appearance, and on using manners to make a favorable impression. The objective is to get others to do what you want. An understanding of human relations pays off in profit-making situations; and though a knowledge of the product is important, the sales pitch is even more important. Dale Carnegie is a leading writer in this vein.

In chapter 5, the service ethic, the fourth success ethic, is introduced and explicated. It holds that the purpose of one's life and career is to provide service to one's fellows and to promote the public good. This type is benevolent, altruistic, self-sacrificing, indefatigable, nonmaterialistic, visionary, and a champion of public causes. Horace Mann, Jane Addams, and Eleanor Roosevelt are prime examples.

Chapter 6 shows that formal education had an ambivalent role in the success ethic. Though the McGuffey Readers and other early didactic material exemplified the character ethic, the first three success ethics were skeptical of higher education; instead, a "practical education" was urged. Yet the ideology of American education extolled the American Dream and sought to promote talent and foster social mobility (while often minimizing opportunity for women and other underrepresented groups). Also explored is the influence of such types of informal education as public libraries, correspondence courses, Chautauqua, vocabulary development, and brainstorming.

The next three chapters provide a penetrating evaluation of the success ethics and the American Dream from psychological, philosophical, and social perspectives. Chapter 7 uses studies by Freud, Adler, Jung, Horney, Fromm, and other psychologists to assess the deeper meanings of money, materialism, competition, and various other symbols in the success ethics.

In chapter 8, we present philosophical perspectives that represent leading ethical systems as sources for critically evaluating the success ethic and the American Dream. These perspectives are drawn from Aristotle, Kant, John Stuart Mill, Friedrich Nietzsche, Karl Marx, John Dewey, and some prominent theologians. Each system posits an alternate way of life that deeply challenges the success ethics and offers possibilities for rethinking and formulating compelling new ones.

Chapter 9, on social perspectives, provides an analysis and critique of the success ethics and the American Dream in light of social, political, and economic theories as they influence public policy decisions. The basis for the critique will be drawn from such figures as Herbert Marcuse, Robert N. Bellah, David Riesman, William H. Whyte, and Vance Packard.

Finally, chapter 10 offers a summary and conclusion. In so doing, it seeks to pull together what has been learned and to place it in a coherent perspective. It will also recommend desirable changes and new directions for the success ethic and the American Dream.

1

The Pursuit of
the American Dream

Historically, to be successful in this country meant that one could attain the American Dream. Though different models of success could be delineated by the late nineteenth century, success in America has usually meant making money and translating it into fame and status. But success meant not just being wealthy but achieving wealth and advancing beyond one's father in terms of occupation and income. It also meant continued advancement during one's working years and having a better job and more income at the end of one's career than at the beginning. America promised social mobility, and bettering oneself meant that one had to utilize money to gain increased social status. Those with discretionary income could use money as a social symbol for promoting mobility. These trends can be understood by exploring the emergence and development of the success ethic.

Growth of the Success Ethic

Puritanism and the Protestant ethic encouraged humans to be productive, to work hard, and to advance materially. Max Weber argued that the development of European capitalism could not be accounted for in strictly economic or technical terms but was largely the result of the ascetic secular morality associated with the emphasis in Calvinistic theology on predestination and salvation.[1] Since salvation is the focus of religious life, people are interested in knowing whether they are

1

among the chosen. Success in one's worldly calling is believed to be an almost infallible indication.

The Protestant ethic, according to Weber, regarded all work as a justified "calling" and, by treating persons in an individualistic and impersonal way, facilitated rational modes of behavior that allowed capitalistic enterprises to flourish. The maxims of action directed the believer to behave in the spirit of mature capitalism. By the term "the spirit of capitalism," Weber meant a set of attitudes and the belief that it is a good thing to make money even beyond the necessities, that one should maximize wealth without much consideration for the means as long as the means are efficacious. This, in turn, sanctioned competition and other business practices.

The elements in the Protestant ethic congruent with the capitalistic spirit are asceticism, a this-worldly orientation, and a compulsion to lead a well-ordered, systematic, impersonal, and individualistic life. Finally, Weber argued that capitalism, resting largely on hedonistic and material incentives, no longer needs the support of the Protestant ethic. The pursuit of wealth has become stripped of its religious and ethical meaning.[2]

Another salient influence on the success ethic was the ideal of continuous progress that grew out of the Enlightenment faith that through the use of "Reason" in all aspects of life, superstition, myth, dogma and all the shackles on the human mind would soon fall away, and the highest stage in human history would be ushered in. This same faith, although at times less connected with the use of reason and science, was found in nineteenth-century America in the drive of intrepid settlers to conquer a new frontier and tame a wilderness. America, many believed, was the land of opportunity, of vast untapped resources and unlimited possibilities for personal advancement, where even the most impoverished immigrant could hope to rise from his socioeconomic level.

American capitalism began with merchant capitalism based on the activities of businessmen who made profits through trade and commercial activity. As industrialization proceeded, it became based more upon an industrial capitalism in which businessmen made profits from manufacturing and production. Many inventions augmented the development of capitalism. British inventors in the eighteenth century created machines for the production of textiles, and these inventions found their way to America; the telegraph provided a communication link across the continent; and the use of Bessemer and open-hearth processes revolutionized steel production. Paralleling these inventions was the improvement of transportation by the steamboat and the building of a great network of canals, later to be followed by the railroads, eventually linking the Atlantic and Pacific coasts.

While the flood of immigrants between 1870 and 1910 provided a source of cheap, unskilled manpower for the ambitious capitalist, the schools were attempting to assimilate children into the dominant ethos of American culture. As industrial processes grew in complexity, the growth of bureaucratic organizations ensued, along with the need for a managerial class. In light of these changes, an expansion of secondary education was needed. The *Kalamazoo* case (1874) led to publicly supported high schools, and compulsory education laws were enacted, beginning in Massachusetts in 1852, and ending in Mississippi in 1918. Still, large numbers did not receive many years of formal schooling until the laws, after the turn of the century, were more firmly enforced, and until the passage of child labor laws.

In addition to its emphasis on the Protestant ethic, the industrial age recognized Social Darwinism, which held that social life was analogous to the human organism in its struggles with nature; hence, only those most fit will survive. Importance was placed on accumulating wealth however one could (which was accorded religious sanction through Calvinistic doctrine), production of goods, accumulating quantities of goods in the face of scarcity, and preparing oneself vocationally in order to compete successfully. With the expansion of the high school, on-the-job apprenticeship training shifted more to the schools, by instituting trade and industrial training.

Out of these dramatic technological and ideological changes came what Andrew Carnegie called "the gospel of wealth." This system of beliefs promoted a laissez-faire attitude toward the economy. At this time, the federal government did not regulate industry, except for tariff policies, and the states imposed few regulations. The gospel of wealth was built on the belief that government exists largely for defending property rights. The corollary to property rights was the acquisition of wealth by industry and thrift. Thus, the foundation of capitalist society consisted of individualism, private property, the accumulation of wealth, and competition.

The gospel of wealth became a formula that allowed Protestantism after the Civil War to reconcile its teachings with popular materialism. Sensitive to changing mores, Protestant leaders adapted to these developments in order for the church to retain a significant function. But with the growing prestige of science in modern thought, the formulas of the gospel of wealth were expressed increasingly in secular language.

The gospel of wealth retained the Christian concept of the individual as a moral agent. It emphasized freedom of action in the economic sphere and "rugged individualism." The control of the economy should be in terms of a natural aristocracy to be determined by the competitive struggle of the market, which eliminates the weak and incompetent and chooses those with initiative, vision, judgment, and organizing ability. As a result of these principles, industries became economic autocracies.

The government's functions were limited to maintaining order and protecting property. A more intrusive state is dangerous, it was argued, because political democracy does not place able men in power; politics fosters mediocrity. It was therefore important that a natural aristocracy of talent be arrayed against it.

How to account for poverty? It springs, according to this ideology, from laziness, vice, lack of thrift, and sometimes misfortune. Poverty is as inevitable as sin and is largely the result of it. The poor man should be given aid and charity, have his sins pointed out to him, and then be converted to Christianity. The gospel of wealth assumed that the poor would accept the leadership of the natural aristocracy. It overlooked possibilities for political action and the rise of labor unions.[3]

Rise of the American Dream

The ideal of success is found in the American Dream, which is probably the most potent ideology in American life. The ideas behind it were evident in the nineteenth century, but it was not formulated and designated as such until 1931, by James Truslow Adams. He spoke of

> that dream of a land in which life should be better and richer and fuller for every man, with opportunity for each according to his ability or achievement. . . . It is not a dream of motor cars and high wages merely, but a dream of a social order in which each man and each woman shall be able to attain to the fullest stature of which they are innately capable, and be recognized by others for what they are, regardless of the fortuitous circumstances of birth or position.[4]

Adams insisted that the American Dream had lured tens of millions to the nation's shores in the past century, to aspire not only for material plenty but to be able to grow to their fullest development unhampered by older civilizations and their social-class barriers. The Dream was not the product of a solitary thinker but evolved from the hearts and burdened souls of millions who came here from other nations. To make the Dream come true, he added, we must work together, no longer merely to build bigger, but to build better.[5]

Today, the American Dream has been formulated in terms of certain basic values and character traits. Americans generally believe in achievement, success, and materialism. This combination of values, in conjunction with equal opportunity, ambitiousness, and hard work and the means of attaining it, could be considered the American Dream. Among the core beliefs underlying the ideology is to work hard in order to succeed in competition; those who work hard gain success and are rewarded with fame, power, money, and property; since there is equal opportunity, it is claimed, those who fail are guilty of either insufficient effort or character deficiencies.[6]

A 1987 Roper survey of a nationwide cross section of 1,506 adults, with supplemental interviews among 148 black adults, found that Americans have distinct ideas about the American Dream; but when asked to name the individual that best exemplifies it, no one person stood out; in fact, 35 percent said they did not know. Family members, however, were cited most often (11 percent). Beyond family, Americans named John F. Kennedy (8 percent) and Abraham Lincoln (6 percent) most frequently, followed by Martin Luther King, Jr. (4 percent), Ronald Reagan (4 percent), and Lee Iacocca (4 percent).[7]

But lately the American Dream has been shrouded by doubt and pessimism as the economy falters and opportunities diminish. This is not a new development. The Dream in the 1930s became a record of unfulfilled promises and dashed hopes, characterized by John Steinbeck in *The Grapes of Wrath* and *Of Mice and Men* as illusion and tragedy. But the prosperity of the 1950s, a period of America's preeminence as a military and economic power, revived the Dream.

The American Dream in the 1990s is clouded and at a crossroads. Some perceive that the Dream is at stake, as reflected in public education and the rhetoric of equality of opportunity in current national reports on education. At risk in the decline of American schools is our leadership in technology and production, our economic prosperity, the loss of military security abroad, and the disintegration of civil and social order at home.[8] Others, in viewing the concept of equality of opportunity, find it to be equivocal, serving the interests of the powerful while placating the powerless. Thus, education can be equitable in offering beginnings to diverse individuals only if just principles first govern society.[9]

William Proefiedt notes two types of inequalities: per-pupil expenditures; and family income, which predicts school and career success. Yet some point out that efforts to create equality of conditions would abrogate individual freedom and destroy the connection between effort and reward so central to the American Dream. Schools should not reflect through financing, geography, tracking, and curricular structures the inequalities of the larger society. Proefiedt believes that the success ethic, on both an individual and national level, functions as a substitute for moral purpose in the schools.[10]

Vocational education has been an extension of the American Dream of getting ahead by hard work; it promises equality of opportunity and material success. Americans generally support vocational education despite research indicating that job placement and wage rates are not as high as once thought. As rigidity replaces innovation, programs become increasingly separate from the larger educational enterprise, and narrow skill training is substituted for general education among students who can least afford to be ill-prepared.[11]

Stephen Baldwin states that the American Dream includes adequate housing, education for one's children, and a secure retirement. Recent data indicate that achieving the Dream and succeeding in the labor market have become more difficult due to sluggish productivity growth, increased competition from abroad, technological change, and shifts in attitudes and expectations about roles of minorities and women.[12]

A special issue of *Fortune* magazine on "fixing" the economy claims that the United States needs a new economic agenda and politicians who face reality. The editors identify a host of areas that are deficient: productivity, jobs, trade, R&D, and taxes, as well as the budget, health care, infrastructure, regulation, and the environment.[13]

Of especial concern today is the decline of America's competitiveness internationally. A critical area is that of technology. Successful competition in technology requires managers with technological understanding; business traditions and financial incentives that encourage long-term investments; a well-educated work force; committed engineers and scientists; and institutions engaged in research and development.[14] America is paying an enormous price to boost its competitive position. Much of it has been initiated with borrowed funds, by selling off assets and laying off employees, or freezing workers' salaries. Worker output in Japan grew during the 1980s three times faster than in the United States.[15] "The past two decades is the greatest crisis of American industry by far," asserts business historian Alfred Chandler, Jr.[16] Industry had to restructure because of overdiversification and, while restructuring, "the competition was getting tougher." Germans and Europeans and Japanese would have given U.S. industry competition earlier if World War II had not intervened. Chandler observes that "It first hit us in the 1960s and our response was very poor."[17] What Americans must do, according to one report, is to "lift investments, bolster the competitiveness of small manufacturers and service companies, strengthen U.S. technology, and increase workers' skill at applying it."[18]

Kevin Phillips reports on the enormous concentration of wealth in the United States during the 1980s — most of it in the hands of the top one percent of the population.[19] He shows that the Gilded Age of the late nineteenth century and the 1920s were two other periods when Republican policy managed to concentrate vast wealth in the hands of a favored few. The top one percent of Americans during the 1980s increased their share of income by $100 billion to $150 billion a year. Thus, the 1980s "produced one of U.S. history's most striking concentrations of wealth even as the American dream was beginning to crumble not just in inner-city ghettos and farm townships but in blue-collar centers and even middle-class suburbs."[20]

Progress for women has been mixed. Though women have made progress in entering formerly all-male occupations, the infamous "glass ceiling" for women is not breaking; only three out of one thousand chief executive officers of the leading U.S. corporations are women.[21]

Though minorities have made some progress in the past generation, for many of them the American Dream is an unattainable ideal. Today the health of blacks in general has improved, more blacks are completing college, blacks are moving into better jobs, and more blacks are being elected to office. On the downside, the average income for blacks is 57 percent of whites' incomes, blacks are more likely than whites to use hard drugs, and 47 percent of the prison population is black, even though blacks constitute only 12 percent of the population.[22]

This situation is generally similar for Hispanic Americans. A study of the National Council of La Raza found that the majority of the nation's 20.1 million Hispanics made no significant economic gains in the 1980s. U.S. census data from 1979 to 1989 showed that nearly 27 percent of all Hispanic Americans lived in poverty in 1989, up from 25.7 percent in 1979. In comparison, about 31 percent of blacks and 10 percent of whites live in poverty.[23] However, the Center on Budget and Policy Priorities found that poverty among non-Hispanic whites has increased at a faster pace than it has for minorities. The number of impoverished whites increased 14 percent between 1989 and 1991.[24]

With unemployment 7.5 percent and higher nationwide during the recession of the early 1990s, and with not only blue-collar but middle-management persons seeking jobs and some job markets closed for the future, the common aspiration of advancing socioeconomically beyond one's parents is increasingly unrealistic for more and more youth. According to "The State of Working America," an analysis of U.S. economic trends issued by the Economic Policy Institute, younger workers have found in the last decade that the American Dream is fading for their generation.[25] Some have renounced their erstwhile dreams and are reluctantly resigned to lower living standards; others displace the American Dream by vicariously pursuing it through their sports heroes and other media personalities; and still others have become involved in crime.

Some people see specific threats to the American Dream. The Roper survey gave respondents a list of seventeen items and asked them to assess whether each item poses a severe threat, somewhat of a threat, or no threat at all to the American Dream. Those problems listed by a majority as posing a severe threat are illegal drugs (79 percent), crime (69 percent), diminishing quality of the education system (66 percent), deteriorating environment (57 percent), and federal deficits (57 percent).[26]

Some significant aspects of the American Dream, moreover, are no longer available to pursue. In American history, according to Robert Heilman, the Dream in action has been migration: from Europe to America, from society-at-large to utopian communities, and from the East Coast to various Wests. But the frontier has disappeared after being available to the Western world for half a millennium. The frontier — which by its existence seemed to legitimize all dreams — means space, space implies time, and time a future in which dreams can be realized. When horizontal mobility is closed, vertical mobility is substituted: instead of going to a new world of higher quality, one moves higher into the world as it is.[27]

But while a geographical frontier is no longer available, it could be argued that vast new "frontiers" are open through discoveries in sciences and technology, exploration of the solar system and the oceans, conquering of diseases and epidemics, new inventions, and creating new and imaginative forms in the arts. As for the economy, the 1920s, 1950s, and mid-1980s were periods of optimism about economic conditions and the American Dream. When the economy begins growing rapidly and jobs are more plentiful, some Americans will regain their buoyancy and optimism and rekindle their belief in the American Dream.

The Dream may be revitalized by great exemplars. Martin Luther King, Jr., in his memorable "I Have a Dream" speech, sought "to hew out of that mountain of despair a stone of hope":

> I still have a dream. It is a dream rooted in the American Dream. I have a dream that one day this nation will rise up and live out the true meaning of its creed: "We hold these truths to be self-evident that all men are created equal."[28]

David McCullough, author of the best-selling biography of former president Harry S. Truman,[29] concludes that Truman had his faults, both as a president and as a human being — but Truman knew who he was. "He's the ordinary fellow who achieves the extraordinary, again and again, all through life. And the reason I think we like [the Truman story] so much is that it's our story. We are the country of seemingly ordinary people who — with our freedom and opportunities — are going to do something extraordinary. That's the great story. That's the American Dream."[30]

Postscript

In *The Good Society* (1991), Robert Bellah and associates discuss the critical need to move beyond those persistent "distractions" that are entailed in the very idea of success in American life. Money, status, political influence, and social mobility all seem to have taken on an exclusive evaluative power of their own in a society rife with poverty and hopelessness. Are these so-called endowments the "proper measures of a good society"? Does the head-long pursuit of success drain our attention away from those we continue to neglect, and thereby constrict possibilities for everyone (including those who govern and thrive) in the long run?[31]

Similarly, it would seem that any notion of success played out in the unknowing fashion of Ayn Rand's egoistic protagonist, Howard Roark, in *The Fountainhead*, represses its own hollow prospects for the future: "I come here to say that I do not recognize anyone's right to one minute of my life. Nor to any part of my energy. Nor to an achievement of mine. . . . I come here to say that I am a man who does not exist for others."[32] Can we, as a nation and community, muster enough energy and imagination to bypass Roark's tragically self-contained, and thus pathetically limiting, cultural scaffolding?

2

The Character Ethic

The character ethic originated in eighteenth-century America, prevailed in the nineteenth century, and continued in various forms in the twentieth century despite stout competition from other success ethics. By 1800, the concept of character had begun to define a model type essential for maintaining the social order. It appealed to a burgeoning industrial nation undergoing large-scale social and economic changes by stressing ambition, hard work, self-reliance, and self-discipline. It would attract those who sought to advance economically and achieve success in a rapidly growing industrial society.

The character ethic represented a group of traits and a way of life considered to have significance and moral quality. Key words were associated with the concept of character: citizenship, duty, democracy, work, outdoor life, conquest, honor, morals, manners, integrity, and manhood.[1] Desirable character traits included perseverance, industry, frugality, sobriety, punctuality, reliability, thoroughness, and initiative.

Franklin as Self-Made Man

Called "the finest example in history of the self-made man,"[2] Benjamin Franklin (1706–90), a universal man during the Enlightenment, excelled as a statesman, printer, writer, scientist, and educator. The son of a tallow chandler and soap maker, he left school after two years of formal education at age ten to help his father. He was apprenticed two years later to his half-brother, James, a printer and publisher of the *New England Courant,* to which young Ben secretly contributed. He left this job after much disagreement and went to Philadelphia in 1723 to work as a printer. After a stay in London (1724–26), he returned and acquired an interest in the *Pennsylvania Gazette.* With Franklin as owner and editor, the periodical became popular after 1730, in particular for his common sense philosophy and language skills, which gained attention in *General Magazine* and in *Poor Richard's Almanac.* Franklin also established a circulating library, organized a debating club that became the American Philosophical Society, helped establish an academy that became a significant alternative to the Latin grammar school, and promoted civic reforms. He continued to extend his knowledge through study of foreign languages, philosophy, and science, and went on to make significant discoveries as an inventor and scientist, and vital contributions as a leading American statesman and founding father.

Many households in the colonies had no printed matter other than an almanac. Almanacs provided calendars, astrology, recipes, jokes, maxims, and poems. *Poor Richard's Almanac* (1732–57) was a great success from the beginning. Franklin's reputation spread beyond Philadelphia as he culled pithy and witty maxims from the aphoristic literature of the world and wove them into homespun American vernacular. The sayings of the fictional character, Richard Sanders, became proverbial wisdom repeated in the colonies and in Europe. The character epitomized homely charm, hard-headed practicality, and the drive for self-improvement.

In his "Advice to a Young Tradesman," Franklin stated some of his basic principles for acquiring wealth: Remember, that *time* is money. Remember, that *credit* is money. Remember, that money is of the prolific, generating nature. Money can beget money, and its offspring can beget more.[3] In "The Way to Wealth," which he peppered with maxims from Poor Richard, he reminded his readers that taxes are indeed heavy, but the ones from government we might more easily discharge if they were the only ones. "We are taxed twice as much by our *Idleness,* three times as much by our *Pride,* and four times as much by our *Folly....*"[4] Thrift is a key: "If you would be wealthy, think of saving as well as getting." And remember that "Creditors have better memories than debtors." There is no romanticized nobility in poverty. "Poverty often deprives a Man of all spirit and Virtue: 'Tis hard for an empty Bag to stand upright, as Poor Richard truly says."

In addition to thrift, industry is an essential character trait: "Sloth makes all Things difficult, but Industry all easy." As Poor Richard says: "He that rises late, must trot all Day, and shall scarce overtake his business at Night." "Plow deep, while Sluggards sleep." "Early to bed and early to rise makes a man healthy, wealthy, and wise." As Poor Richard says: "There will be sleeping enough in the Grave."

One must also guard against bad habits and dissipation: "Poverty wants some things, luxury many things, avarice all things." "Women and Wine, Game and Deceit, Make the Wealth small, and the Wants great." As for posterity, "If you would not be forgotten as soon as you are dead and rotten, either write things worth reading or do things worth writing."

About the year 1730, Franklin devised a plan for attaining moral perfection. He decided that good habits must be established and contrary ones broken before one can achieve any uniform rectitude of conduct. He drew up a list of virtues — thirteen in all — and decided he would master one at a time. He made a little book to record his progress, in which one page was allotted for each virtue, with seven columns for the days of the week. Franklin believed that by arranging the virtues in order, success in achieving some early virtues would help him to acquire other, later virtues. For instance, the acquisition of temperance would enable him to attain silence, i.e., control of his ears and tongue.

Franklin developed a list of desirable virtues and "annexed to each a short precept which fully expressed the extent I give its meaning. . . . 1. *Temperance:* Eat not to dullness; drink not to elevation. 2. *Silence:* Speak not but what may benefit others or yourself; avoid trifling conversation. 3. *Order:* Let all your things have their places; let each part of your business have its time. 4. *Resolution:* Resolve to perform what you ought; perform without fail what you resolve. 5. *Frugality:* Make no expense but to do good to others or yourself; i.e., waste nothing. 6. *Industry:* Lose no time; be always employed in something useful; cut off all unnecessary actions. 7. *Sincerity:* Use no hurtful deceit; think innocently and justly, and, if you speak, speak accordingly. 8. *Justice:* Wrong none so by doing injuries, or omitting the benefits that are your duty. 9. *Moderation:* Avoid extremes; forbear resenting injuries so much as you think they deserve. 10. *Cleanliness:* Tolerate no uncleanliness in body, clothes, or habitation. 11. *Tranquility:* Be not disturbed at trifles, or at accidents common or unavoidable. 12. *Chastity:* Rarely use venery but for health or offspring, never to dullness, weakness, or the injury of your own or another's peace or reputation. 13. *Humility:* Imitate Jesus and Socrates."[5]

Perhaps Franklin was most successful with *Humility*. He had not included it at first on his list, until a Quaker friend informed him that he was generally thought proud, especially in conversation; thereafter Franklin tried to forbear direct contradiction of others and positive assertions of his own. But the impulse he could not or did not regulate was sexual. According to a leading biographer, "In his morning litany he could pray to be kept from lasciviousness, but when night came lust might come with it."[6]

No doubt industry, frugality, and some of the other virtues contributed to Franklin's success, but some luck and a great deal of natural ability must be considered part of the equation. It may have been an element of luck that led to his apprenticeship as a printer, and his natural gifts enabled him to be creative in many areas. Undoubtedly, there were others beside Franklin in Philadelphia who were as industrious and frugal but whose accomplishments were slighter. Thus, the attempt to attribute success as a self-made man solely to the development of good character traits and following moral maxims may be only part of the story (to be discussed more fully later in the chapter).

Franklin's character trait approach has been an influential rationale for developing moral behavior, insofar as other character trait approaches have drawn upon and modified his thinking and applied it to new situations. But his approach assumes that the traits are consistent from one situation to another and stable over time. The trait approach does not envision an integrated individual interacting with others in a complex environment and engaged in purposeful behavior based on universalizable moral principles. The character trait approach, though usually not as detailed as Franklin's, was also a hallmark of the character ethic in the nineteenth century.

Character and the Inner-Directed Person

Capitalism grew rapidly in nineteenth-century America. This was a period of population growth, mobility, exploration, expansion of production, and accumulation of wealth in which, according to David Riesman, an inner-directed society developed out of which an inner-directed personality was shaped. This personality type, though outwardly an individualist, was not independent of the values and attitudes inculcated by parents. Inner-directed persons had their own internal gyroscope, created early in life, which helped them to cope with rapid change and sometimes violent upheaval; yet it still did not make them immune to the sway of mass movements and group ideologies.[7]

The nineteenth-century character ethic found more of a home in Jacksonian, as opposed to Jeffersonian, democracy. Jacksonian democracy promoted an egalitarian movement in American government and education. Andrew Jackson (1767–1845) joined a movement toward greater popular participation in government attacking privilege and monopoly and attempting to broaden opportunity in many areas of life. Jackson appealed to the farmer, the artisan, and the small business owner; he was viewed with suspicion and fear by those in established positions.

The literature of self-help was not a literature of business methods or techniques; it dealt instead with character. These writers considered poverty an asset because its demands would help produce the traits needed to succeed. Andrew Carnegie, in romanticizing his own childhood, claimed that without poverty society could not create self-made men, and therefore no social progress would be possible.[8] It was believed that opportunities were so abundant and open to all that each and every man could make of himself as he desired. But the wealthy would be deprived of the opportunity to develop strength of character. Instead of Calvinistic sin, one struggled against and overcame poverty.

Character is necessary and remarkable, but talent is not; having talent leaves one without the incentive or ability to develop character; it may lead to indolence and lack of discipline. Perseverance can accomplish far more then genius.

The character ethic held that it was better to come from rural origins. The stamina and grit of those who succeed were, as a rule, country bred. Of all the external influences on success, none was more important than the boy's mother, not because of any instruction in business but in shaping character. The young businessman was also advised to choose a good wife who would keep him from base morals. Moreover, marriage was preferred by employers and creditors over bachelorhood. One should earn money, and therefore one should not marry to obtain it; in any case, an heiress was likely to be extravagant and indolent. Despite the importance of these external influences, one could not be a self-made man and give these forces inordinate credit for one's character. Business skill could be developed, but no amount of business skill could compensate for a lack of desirable character traits.

A number of self-help writers were clergymen. Among them were Henry Ward Beecher, Lyman Abbott, and Horatio Alger. Most were

Protestants, as relatively few Catholics were among the business elite before 1900, and Catholic spokesmen opposed the movement's materialism. The doctrine of a secular calling provided a religious defense for worldly success. Such success could demonstrate that man might conquer his own base nature and overcome the limitations of his social environment.

The wealthy man was expected to live simply and observe moderation. The doctrine of the stewardship of wealth held that since God made the rich man's lot different than that of the poor, his money was merely placed in trust to be used in doing God's work, and must be applied to benefit others. McGuffey's *Second Reader* of 1844 insisted that "God gives a great deal of money to some persons in order to assist those who are poor." It was believed that the rich man's happiness flows from his benevolence to society.

The urge to advance was especially strong in regions transformed by the Industrial Revolution; therefore, it was not accidental that three out of every four nineteenth-century millionaires were natives of New England, New York, or Pennsylvania, and seventy percent made their fortunes in either banking, manufacturing, trade, or transportation.[9] The South was not a major participant in the character ethic because of economic disintegration and hurt pride, and its criteria of success differed sharply in terms of its reverence for the past and family background.

Andrew Carnegie (1835–1919), nineteenth-century exemplar of the character ethic, was born in Scotland and emigrated to the United States at thirteen, and settled in Allegheny, Pennsylvania. He grew up in poverty and received little more than a primary school education. First, he took a job in a cotton factory, and, a year later, became a messenger boy in a Pittsburgh telegraph office; his diligence led to promotion to an operator, and later to his employment with the Pennsylvania Railroad. During twelve years with that company, he was promoted to superintendent of the Pittsburgh division, and he introduced the first Pullman sleeping cars. Convinced by his railroad experience of the growing importance of the iron and steel industries, Carnegie resigned in 1865 and formed the Keystone Bridge Company. He was gifted with outstanding organizational ability, remarkable business acumen, and extraordinary ability to evaluate human potential. Carnegie built his steel company into a giant that survived the 1890s depression better than other firms. In 1889, he consolidated his holdings into the Carnegie Steel Company, and eventually dominated the industry. He became one of the wealthiest men in America and one its leading philanthropists.

Carnegie published a number of influential essays in various periodicals, some of which appeared in *The Empire of Business*.[10] He drew upon his long business career in advising young men about the road to business success. Young men should begin with the most subordinate positions. It is best to aim high and strive for the top, and to vow to reach the position with untarnished reputation. Three grave dangers, however, confront you: drinking to excess, speculation, and "indorsing" beyond one's means (lending one's name to help another gain credit). The man who expects to rise must do something exceptional. Sometimes one must violate regulations, whenever you are sure that doing so would be in the interest of your employer and you are willing to take responsibility for your actions. To become a partner, you must know the business of your department far better than the owners.

Agreeing with Franklin that one should start saving early, Carnegie recommends men to commence saving almost as soon as they begin to earn. Capitalists trust the person who saves, and will provide $1,000 credit for every $100 saved, and $50,000 for every $1,000. What is expressed is that you have acquired the business habits to create capital. But savings for its own sake is an ignoble aim unless you use your wealth to help society. Hoarding millions is avarice, not thrift. Thus, you should concentrate exclusively on the business in which you are engaged, and "put all your eggs in one basket and watch the basket."[11]

Opportunities abound, he claimed, for young men with certain desirable skills and character traits. Citing many of the leading industrial firms of his day, Carnegie maintained that they were founded and managed by mechanics who were "poor boys with natural aptitude." He also surveyed the officers of New York City banks and could not find a college graduate on the list. Those who have forged ahead have a head start on college graduates who are "learning a little about the barbarous and petty squabbles of a far-distant past, or trying to master languages which are dead; such knowledge as seems adopted to life upon another planet than this, as far as business affairs are concerned. . . ."[12] Carnegie recognized the need for college for those preparing for the learned professions, but college education, as it exists, seems fatal to success in the business world. But the doors to this world stand open to "the sober, frugal, energetic and able mechanic, to the scientifically educated youth, to the office boy and to the clerk. . . ."[13]

Carnegie believed he had discerned a causal relationship between poverty and human advancement: "Abolish poverty! but fortunately this cannot be done; and the poor we are always to have with us. Abolish poverty, and what would become of the race? Progress, development, would cease. Consider its future if dependent upon the rich. The supply of the good and great would cease, and human society retrograde into barbarism."[14]

Presumably, human misery and social degradation are warranted because of this assumed causal relationship. Studies of social mobility, however, have made it abundantly clear that the rags-to-riches story, despite spectacular and widely-publicized cases, is more of a symbol than a statistical actuality.[15] The top positions in American industry, even during the nineteenth-century expansion, were held by men with decided advantages. But there were enough men who had dramatically risen to keep hopes alive, if not for the top rung, at least for a middle-management position.

Carnegie was correct, however, that many business executives did not attend college. In the 1870s, 37 percent had some college study; in 1901–1910, 41 percent had.[16] In 1925, the figure rose to 51.4 percent, and in 1950, to 75.6 percent, and about one in five business executives had graduate study.[17]

In an article that was novel for its time, Carnegie expostulated that the millionaire, other than bequeathing a modest and independent living for those dependent upon him, should hold wealth in a sacred trust for the people.[18] "To try to make the world in some way better than you found it, is to have a noble motive in life. Your surplus wealth should contribute to the development of your own character and place you in the ranks of nature's noblemen."[19] Carnegie lived by his principles, and supported many philanthropies — public libraries, colleges, endowments for peace — totaling some $350 million.

Not a character ethic exemplar like Carnegie, Elbert Green Hubbard (1856–1915) was an author and publisher who was influential through his self-help writings. Hubbard visited England in 1892 and met William Morris, whose Kelmscott Press deeply impressed the young American. In 1895, after writing several novels, he founded, near Buffalo, the Roycroft Press, modeled on Morris' firm. He published a series of monthly booklets titled *Little Journeys,* consisting of biographies laced with his own comments, and the *Philistine,* an experimental magazine that, unexpectedly, attracted a large circulation; at its inception, in 1895, it consisted of contributions from many authors, but it was written exclusively by Hubbard from 1899 to his death. One of the 1899 issues contained his most famous story, "A Message for Garcia." Its publication and other works created a great demand for Hubbard as a lecturer, and his Roycroft establishment attracted many visitors.

When war erupted between Spain and the United States, it was necessary to communicate with Garcia, leader of the insurgents, in order to gain cooperation. President McKinley sought Rowan, an explorer and investigator, to find Garcia and to deliver a letter. Rowan landed in Cuba, traversed a hostile country, and delivered the letter.

The point is, Hubbard insists, that it is neither book-learning nor instruction in this or that matter, "but to be loyal to a trust, to act promptly, concentrate their energies: do the thing — 'Carry a message to Garcia!'"[20] But the average man shows his inability to concentrate on a thing and do it. Slipshod assistance and half-hearted work seems to be the rule; it is an incapacity for independent action, an infirmity of will. Advertise for a stenographer and nine out of ten who apply can neither spell nor punctuate.

We hear much maudlin sympathy for the "down-trodden denizen of the sweatshop" and the "homeless wanderers searching for honest employment," and with it much criticism of those in power. Employers, however, have to weed out the "incompetent and unworthy." "Self-interest prompts every employer to keep the best — those who can carry a message to Garcia."[21]

Hubbard added emphatically: "My heart goes out to the man who does his work when the 'boss' is away, as well as when he is at home. . . . Civilization is one long anxious search for just such individuals. Anything that such a man asks shall be granted; his kind is so rare that no employer can afford to let him go."[22]

It is estimated that Hubbard's tract reached forty million copies, with translations into forty or fifty languages and dialects.[23] While the tract may resemble some complaints of today's business community about the inadequate preparation of high school graduates for the work force, its immense popularity at the turn of the century deserves some explanation. First, Hubbard's tract was timely for business and industry leaders who were under attack by Populists and from the Left, as in Thorstein Veblen's *Theory of the Leisure Class,* and from Protestantism's social gospel movement. Some credit must also go to Hubbard for promotion, and for producing and distributing huge numbers of copies. The text was written in language understandable to the masses, with their limited reading skills and formal education. Its simple formulas could be readily applied, and its vivid maxims and colorful stories engaged and captivated its readers.

Another widely read author, and one still referred to today, Horatio Alger (1832–99) graduated from Harvard Divinity School, assumed the ministry of a Unitarian church in Brewster, Massachusetts, in 1864, and two years later resigned his pulpit, and within a year had published his first successful novel, *Ragged Dick, or Street Life in New York.* The hero, a bootblack, through pluck and luck rises to become a wealthy man. The pattern set in *Ragged Dick* varied very little in more than one hundred Alger books published during the next thirty years. His stories, while they exhibit some features of the character ethic, atypically place much emphasis on luck in getting ahead. For instance, Ragged Dick rescues a child who has just fallen in the water. The grateful father hires the lad and starts him on the way to fame and fortune. In *Luck and Pluck,* John Oakley's rightful inheritance is restored to him by recovering a will that his wicked stepmother had hidden. Though in Alger's day he only had four bestsellers, in the first twenty years after his death a revival occurred in which an estimated seventeen million copies of his books were sold. The boom ended in 1926 when his publisher stopped issuing his works.

In 1899, George Horace Lorimer (1867–1937) became editor of the *Saturday Evening Post* and began to shape it into one of the leading periodicals of its time. He increased its circulation from 1,800 in 1898 to one million in 1908, to more than three million at the time of his retirement in 1937, and was able to attract leading American writers to its pages.

In 1902, Lorimer first published a series of articles in the *Post* that were based on Franklin's Poor Richard, and that were subsequently published as a book titled *Letters from a Self-made Merchant to His Son.*[24] It became a best seller in the United States, England, and Germany, and was more widely circulated than any book of American authorship since *Uncle Tom's Cabin.*

Lorimer's hero, John Graham, a pork baron, is a fictionalized version of Chicago meat packer Philip Armour, for whom Lorimer worked before becoming editor of the *Post.* The letters are discourses to his son, Pierrepont, who, during the series, attends Harvard, goes to work for his father's company, and acquires the qualities of a successful businessman.

The character ethic's skepticism of higher education's efficacy is evident, as well as a preference for learning through experience in social life and the marketplace. Education is about the only thing you can have as much of as you are willing to haul away, Graham tells his son. Some get it from newspapers and public libraries; others from professors and parchment. Though he is anxious that his son be a good scholar, he is more concerned that he "be a good clean man" — and this can be gained more from classmates than professors. He worries that his son may acquire undesirable habits at college (taste for sporting clothes and cigarettes).

He wants his son to form good mental and physical habits in college. College pays if it trains a boy to think more quickly than the other fellow. "It's the fellow who knows enough about practice to test his theories for blow-holes that gives the world a shove ahead, and finds a fair margin of profit in sharing it."[25] Here we have sort of a Jamesian pragmatism.

Poverty never spoils a man, but prosperity often does. One first has to manage one's money by adjusting spending to what your earning capacity will be. It is best to let a boy follow his own bent and see if he has chosen the wrong business. One starts in a firm at the bottom. "Life isn't a spurt, but a long, steady climb."[26] Persistent, plain work is good; the only undignified job is loafing. In fact, ". . . the meanest man alive is the one who is generous with money that he has not had to sweat for. . . ."[27] Make it a rule to take the first job offered and use it for bait. "You can take a minnow with a worm, and a bass with your minnow."[28] Persistence is necessary. "A man's got to keep company a long time, and come early and stay late and sit close, before he can get a girl or a job worth having."[29]

Certain business skills are important. A businessman should have something to say, say it, and stop talking. Say less than the other fellow and listen more than you talk. A salesman is one part talk and nine parts judgment. "You've got to have the scent of a bloodhound for an order, and the grip of a bulldog on a customer."[30] Never threaten, show courtesy and consideration, stay close to your employees, and do not forget your own weaknesses when criticizing others." Back up good looks by good character yourself, and make sure that the other fellow does the same."[31]

Thus, it can be seen that many features of the character ethic were exhibited in this popular work: the importance of humble origins, hard work, self-reliance, learning through experience, and the development of good character traits weighs more heavily than specific business skills. How are the traits to be learned? Presumably through social interaction, everyday experiences, and learning on the job. But in doing so the boy needs to keep uppermost the homilies, aphorisms, and rules articulated in order to test and apply them in everyday experience. Formal education, perhaps because of its classical nature, is perceived as of questionable importance and at times an impediment in achieving success. Hard work and good character are sufficient for business success; specific business knowledge, talent, employment opportunities, and job discrimination are overlooked.

Russell Herman Conwell (1843–1925), lawyer, lecturer, and clergyman, grew up in Massachusetts, and, after being admitted to the bar, moved to Minneapolis, where he founded the *Minneapolis Daily Chronicle*. A few years later, he moved to Boston to continue his law practice, and founded the *Somerville Journal*. He revived a Baptist church in Lexington and became its minister in 1879. Conwell was called upon three years later to perform the same service with the Grace Baptist Church in Philadelphia. His successful efforts led to the opening of the Baptist Temple in 1891, the establishment of three hospitals, and the founding of a night school in 1884 that became Temple College in 1888, with Conwell serving as its first president.

Conwell delivered his lecture, "Acres of Diamonds,"[32] initially in 1861, and continued to modify it until 1915. The lecture brought him widespread fame, and he became a noted speaker on the Chautauqua circuit.

The lecture opens with a tale conveyed by an Arab guide about Ali Hafed, a Persian who owned a large farm with orchards, grain fields, and gardens. An old priest told him that if he had a diamond mine, he could place his children upon thrones. Ali Hafed, consequently, felt poor because he was discontented, and therefore sold his farm, left his family in charge of a neighbor, and departed in search of diamonds. After lengthy wanderings through the Middle East and Europe to no avail, he despairingly threw himself into the sea and was washed away. But the man who purchased Ali Hafed's farm inadvertently discovered some magnificent diamonds on the land.

Conwell then conveys other tales with the same message before imploring his audience to seek wealth in their own backyard. He insists that one ought to become wealthy, and it is a duty to do so. Ninety-eight out of every one hundred rich men in America are honest. They are trusted with money, conduct great enterprises, and find many people to work for them — all because they are honest men. Conwell reminds his audience that money is power and one ought to be ambitious to acquire it. But how do we respond to the theology student's claim: "The love of money is the root of all evil?" True, Conwell avers, the idolatry of money and hoarding it is evil, but those who find purposes for wealth and invest it are wise.

Moreover, "there is not a poor person in the United States who was not made poor by his own shortcomings, or by the shortcomings of some one else. It is all wrong to be poor, anyhow."[33] Thus, one need not be troubled by materialistic urges because "the foundation of godliness and the foundation principle of success in business are both precisely the same,"[34] Conwell insists in a true Calvinistic spirit. It is undesirable for children to inherit money; rather, they are better served by an education, Christian and noble character, and a good name. In seeking wealth you should look in your own neighborhood, find out what people need, and fulfill those needs. Remember that the great inventor sits next to you, or you are that inventor. "The really great man is a plain, straightforward, every-day, common-sense man."[35] You need to put your whole mind into any task and persist until it is completed. Thus, "if you wish to be great at all, you must begin where you are and what you are."[36]

Conwell's "Acres of Diamonds" is a diffuse, desultory, highly embellished lecture that was strengthened by exceptional rhetorical skills. Conwell's biographer spoke of "astonishing proof of his [Conwell's] power to move and sway."[37] He delivered the speech more than six thousand times and it eventually earned its author over eight million dollars.

The sports world has generated divergent values, from "winning at all costs" to the character ethic model. An exceptional exemplar of the latter model, Amos Alonzo Stagg (1862–1965), was an all-around athlete but is best remembered as a highly influential coach of a national pastime, the game of football. He began playing and coaching football when it was similar to rugby, and did not retire until the game had been almost completely transformed, with many of the changes stemming from his own innovations.

Stagg is widely recognized as "one of the game's greatest coaches."[38] He was elected in 1951 to the Football Hall of Fame, and was one of the first men chosen and the only one honored as both a player and a coach.

Youngsters from his background had to be satisfied with a grade school education, with many stopping at the third or fourth grade. But he realized the handicaps his father had suffered with a limited formal education and therefore aspired to attend high school; yet, since his hometown of West Orange, New Jersey, had no high school, he sought to attend the one in Orange, which exacted a fee from nonresidents. Here he began a lengthy process of working to finance his education, from tending furnaces to beating carpets. It was his assistant principal who suggested that he should attend college; but upon investigating, he found that he could not pass the Yale entrance examinations and therefore decided to attend Phillips Exeter Academy to better prepare.

He passed the Yale entrance examination but was disturbed that during the exam a boy nearby asked him the answer to one question, and Stagg looked at him in "shocked amazement." Stagg found himself an unheated garret room but no work at first, and suffered from a starvation diet and soon fell ill. Not only did he not drink, smoke, or use profanity, but he felt uncomfortable in the presence of anyone who did.

He decided to concentrate on baseball because of the demands of his studies and part-time work, but he did make the freshman football team. At first there were no coaches or trainers. Stagg pitched for five seasons (one in which he was a graduate student), and six National League teams offered him pitching contracts before his last season, but he rejected all offers because of his loyalty to Yale, and because of the corrupt level of the professional game. He was proud that, despite his impecunious state, he never borrowed money from anyone in his life, as the fear of debt was great for someone "who was at close grips with poverty." Stagg had done religious work through the Y.M.C.A. since his freshman year, and planned to enter divinity school; but the time required to fulfill the student secretary job he held did not permit him to do so, and he took graduate courses instead.

Stagg was selected in 1889 for the first All-American football team, and also became an assistant coach while still playing ball. He coached in Springfield, Massachusetts, for a while before being invited, at age twenty-nine, to become head coach at the newly founded University of Chicago, where he remained for forty-one years. To his chagrin, upon taking up his new post he found that there was no football field and only thirteen players suited up for the first practice, thereby forcing him to activate himself (allowed under the rules of the day). He demanded respect. "To my face, I was Mr. Stagg; but about 1899, I began to be the Old Man when one student spoke of me to another. I was still a young man, even by a collegiate yardstick, and inwardly I resented the title. I find it quite satisfactory now." [39] He believed in military obedience on the football field: "A player must obey orders like a soldier, act swiftly and surely on his own in an unforeseen contingency." [40] He was demanding, especially with his weaker teams: "I tried to meet this weakness in part by drilling the squad by the hour on their knees, bellies, all fours, rolling over and getting up quickly, to teach them where the ground was and what it felt like. . . . When the linemen failed to suit me I made them crawl eighty yards on their knees." [41] He added that "The boy who is worth his weight in gold is he who is always in every play and every game up to his neck, and I will forgive him if he falls short of All-American brilliancy."[42] University of Illinois Coach Zuppke once told his class in coaching that Stagg did not swear at his players, "but he calls this man a jackass, then that man a jackass, then another a jackass. By the end of the workout there are no human beings left on the field."[43] Stagg recognized that everyone loves a winner, but "It is not necessary to cheat or buy players in order to produce a team of which a school may be proud. A college with brains and courage, however small, does not need to hire a squad of mercenaries to wear its uniform."[44]

Football was a strange game when Stagg first entered it. If the ball was not fumbled away, it could be kept indefinitely. A Princeton vs. Yale game in 1881 resulted in Princeton holding the ball for the entire first half and moving it only a few yards; in the last half, Yale did the same thing. As for rules, a goal was equal to four touchdowns.[45] The game was transformed over the years, in large part by Stagg's remarkable innovations: the backfield-in-motion play, option pass play, unbalanced line, onside kick, and numerous others.[46]

Stagg's long tenure at the University of Chicago abruptly halted on his seventieth birthday, when President Robert Maynard Hutchins decided to abolish football. Hutchins's action caused a near riot on campus, which Stagg himself was called in to quell. Stagg coached at College of the Pacific until he was eighty-four; then he became an assistant coach at Susquehanna University, helping his son, Amos, Jr., who was head coach, followed by his final job as kicking coach at Stockton Junior College. He lived to the age of 102, and could not have resented being widely known as the "grand old man of football."

At one time in America, many boys aspired to be President when they grew up. But Harry S. Truman (1884–1972) never entertained the idea until relatively late in life. Truman symbolizes the American Dream — the opportunity for someone from humble origins, through ambition, hard work, and perseverance, to rise to the top. Our interest in Truman is in the extent to which his traits exemplify the character ethic.

Truman's rise to public prominence was very slow; he had been a late bloomer all along. He had not found his political career until he was nearly forty, and did not marry until thirty-five.[47] He grew up on a farm near Independence, Missouri, graduated from high school in 1901, and expected a chance for more education; but with the loss of the family farm, it was necessary to bring in income. He took a job as timekeeper on a railroad construction outfit and, after the job ended in ten months, worked at the *Kansas City Star*. He later went to Kansas City, Missouri, and became a bank clerk, but returned to the family farm after five years. He had joined the National Guard, and World War I gave him the opportunity to sail to France as a first lieutenant of artillery. He was a capable officer, and was promoted to captain. Upon his return he married Elizabeth Virginia (Bess) Wallace. Truman established a clothing store in Kansas City with an army comrade, but the store failed in the economic downturn of 1920–21, and he was left with about $20 thousand in debts. He refused to declare bankruptcy, and paid back every penny. He once wrote that it took "work, work and more work" to get satisfactory results.[48]

In Independence, people read books, listened to music, and discussed ideas at supper.[49] Young Truman reported that as a youth, "I always had my nose stuck in a book, a history book mostly. Of course, the main reason you read a book is to get a better insight into the people you're talking to. There were about three thousand books in the library downtown, and I guess I read them all, including the encyclopedias. I'm embarrassed to say that I remembered what I read, too."[50] Besides his love of history, he was impressed with Franklin's *Autobiography*, and noted that "you'll find a good deal in there about how to make good use of every minute of your day and a lot of horse sense about people."[51] He found little use for textbooks, but usually enjoyed school, was generally well-liked by his teachers, but did not receive the highest grades or win any prizes upon graduation.[52]

As for honesty, "I was taught that the expenditure of public money is a public trust and I have never changed my opinion on that subject. No one has ever received any public money for which I was responsible unless he gave honest service for it."[53] He also reported that in the Senate "there were bribes all over the place," and at any one time he could have "picked up a dozen fortunes."[54] But a statesman, he believed, should be an "honorable man."

As a boy, he attended the First Presbyterian Church, and at eighteen, joined the Baptist Church, which he attended for the rest of his life. He was unimpressed with people who paraded their religious beliefs, and believed that "religion is something to live by and not talk about."[55]

He once told a reporter that "Three things ruin a man: Power, money, and women. I never wanted power, I never had any money, and the only woman in my life is up at the house right now."[56] Truman was seen by his Senate colleagues as pleasant and conscientious but bland. He made no pretense in any way of being superior, nor did he seek the limelight, flattery, or a following. "He did not want to be the President."[57]

Truman believed that one should make plans and follow through on them. "Keep working on a plan. Make no little plans. Make the biggest one you can think of, and spend the rest of your life carrying it out."[58] As a corollary, one of Truman's strongest traits was his decisiveness. In describing his decision to drop atomic bombs on Japan, he said that the bombs ended the war and saved half a million soldiers on both sides from being killed and a million more from being maimed. Truman made the decision by himself.[59] During the Berlin blockade, Truman faced the issue with caution and firmness. Some recommended that the Allies force their way into Berlin; others questioned whether American forces should remain in that city. Truman insisted, "We stay in Berlin, period." In making his decision, he consulted none of the White House staff nor any political advisers.[60] He was never troubled by hindsight and believed it was a waste of time. "I have always believed," he said, "that right will prevail in the end. It has been a policy with me to get the facts and then make a decision. That decision should be made in the public interest as conditions then prevailing require. If the facts available justify a decision at the time it will also be correct in future time."[61]

Was Truman's belated success largely a matter of luck rather than living by the character ethic? "You asked about being lucky, and I'd say, yes, I have been. To have gone as far as I did — a lot of it has to be luck." But as Merle Miller, Truman's oral biographer, added: "Mr. President, you may have been lucky, but you never . . . there's no point in your life when you seem to have trusted to luck." Truman agreed that he was "always out there pushing."[62] As Truman stated in his *Autobiography:* "Opportunity — what is opportunity? Define it and go on from there."[63]

One of Truman's leading biographers ventures that World War I was a great dividing line between the old century and the beginning of something new. Truman's outlook, tastes, and habits had been shaped by a world that preceded 1918. Much that came later never appealed to Truman.[64] This interpretation is consistent with the notion that the character ethic is predominantly based on nineteenth-century values.

Another feature of the character ethic is that one must continue to develop one's attitudes and abilities in order to reach the top. This is evident in Truman, who persisted into the late 1930s enjoying racial jokes and using epithets to characterize different minority groups[65] but became the president who integrated the armed forces and recognized Israel as an independent state. His early small-town, parochial views, and his limited knowledge of foreign affairs widened and deepened, so that he was able as president to grasp and act decisively on world problems.

Truman was ambitious but not torn by ambition. As David McCullough concludes, "He [Truman] held to the old guidelines: work hard, do your best, speak the truth, assume no airs, trust in God, have no fear. . . . He never had a doubt about who he was, and that too was part of his strength, as well as the enjoyment of life he conveyed."[66]

Opportunity and Social Mobility

Could one be assured of advancement by closely following the character ethic? How adequate is the ethic for explaining social mobility? As viewed historically, industrial societies have demonstrated higher rates of mobility than agrarian societies, for two reasons: industrial societies tend to assign status on the basis of achievement rather than ascribed characteristics; the percentage of upper- and middle-status positions increase as society industrializes. Technological innovation or organizational change creates more new jobs at the higher than the lower levels of the occupational structure. For example, from 1940 to 1970, professional and technical jobs for men increased 192 percent, while jobs for farm laborers dropped by 75 percent.[67] The arrival of large numbers of immigrants at the turn of the century provided a major source of semiskilled and unskilled labor, enabling native-born youth to take skilled manual and white-collar positions.

The nineteenth-century vision of an open society led to a belief in opportunities virtually unlimited for those who possessed the right traits. In such a society, opportunities were thought to be limited only by one's ability and imagination. But no actual society is ever totally open or closed. Many Americans may have exaggerated the opportunities for mobility, as the westward push of the frontier and the growth of a new industrial economy caused people to view America as the land of opportunity. One might expect greater social mobility to have occurred in the United States in recent decades than in other developed countries, but comparative studies show only moderate differences among such nations.[68]

Studies of intergenerational mobility indicate that almost forty percent of the sons of blue-collar workers have white-collar jobs, while almost thirty percent of sons born into blue-collar families have a blue-collar occupation. When occupational categories are defined more narrowly, about eighty percent of sons show at least some upward social mobility in relation to their fathers.[69] But social mobility over a single generation usually involves incremental rather than dramatic changes. The idealistic notion of character ethic proponents that with the right traits one can rise in one's lifetime from poverty to the top of the occupational ladder is not borne out by research. Movements from the bottom to the top of the occupational structure, or the reverse, are quite rare. Father-to-son mobility steps are typically quite small, and only rarely does a son obtain a job much higher or lower than his father's in occupational prestige.[70]

The character ethic evidently addressed white boys whose ancestry was Western European, with no consideration given to the impediments to advancement faced by women and minorities. Whites have higher overall occupational standing than blacks and Hispanics, and slightly higher educational achievement. Significant differences in income also exist among whites, blacks, and Hispanics. Historically, the wealthiest and most powerful Americans have been of English ancestry.[71] Gender also has a significant effect on social position. Women generally have less income, wealth, occupational prestige, and educational achievement than men do.[72]

The earnings of high school graduates are about two-thirds of those of college graduates. Some studies have estimated that individual ability accounts for twelve to forty percent of the difference in earnings between high school and college graduates.[73] On-the-job training tends to raise earnings, but its influence is difficult to separate from the influence of formal education.

A study by Christopher Jencks and co-authors found that a bachelor's degree can be expected to add an average of thirty to forty percent to a man's lifetime earnings. (Women were not included because of insufficient data.) But for those who do not attend college, Jencks said, economic success is not affected by whether they complete high school or drop out at the legal minimum age. The study also found that intelligence, as measured by I.Q. tests, has little effect on an individual's economic success. A fifteen-point difference in intelligence test scores will, on average, produce only a fourteen percent difference in lifetime earnings — a small gap compared to the overall earnings gap between wealthy and poor Americans. Jencks also concluded that family background is responsible for forty-eight percent of the variance in men's occupational status.[74] Various other studies show conflicting and inconsistent results, but the prevailing opinion is that education accounts for sixty percent of earnings differentials, and factors such as family background and I.Q. account for forty percent.[75]

Rates of return also can be estimated according to intended occupation. McMahon and Wagner report an expected return of 14 percent for physicians and dentists. An undergraduate engineering degree is expected to yield 25.5 percent, and a master's in engineering another 12 percent. An undergraduate degree in elementary or secondary teaching is expected to return 12.3 percent and a master's degree another 0.8 percent.[76]

In an earlier study, which, presumably, he no longer accepts, Jencks, in a sense, concurred with Horatio Alger and Dale Carnegie, respectively, that luck and personality make the biggest difference in getting ahead, accounting for three-fourths of the variations in income.[77] While personality will be discussed at length in chapter four, a word here about luck. There will always be a measure of chance and unexplained variation: being at the right place at the right time, working in growth industries or for prosperous firms, having supervisors who recognize and reward ability, living in economic growth areas of the country, and the like. Since the American economy is difficult to predict, chance, to some degree, will affect mobility.

Blue-collar workers today are a minority in America's labor force, with white-collar workers constituting six out of ten employees. "Downsizing" has become addictive as corporations strive for greater efficiencies. The economy is generating white-collar jobs at only half the rate of past recoveries because industries such as real estate, banking, and aerospace have had financial crises. While blue-collar workers bear the brunt of most recessions and their unemployment rate is twice that of white-collar workers, the critical difference between them is that the blue-collar layoff is usually temporary, while the white-collar worker who loses a job is likely never to regain it. Thus, an inordinate number of careers are cut short.[78]

Postscript

In conclusion, the character ethic fit well the ideology of many Americans in the nineteenth and early twentieth centuries. A reconstructed character ethic for America today, however, would need to assess more fully a panoply of changing socio-cultural conditions: parental influence on mobility, the cultivation of native ability, the role of higher education in advancement, a sustainable theory of professional development, a plan to show how workers can learn to comply with justifiable codes of ethics, the development of workable plans for women and minorities to advance, and explication of how one can organize to ratify legislation designed to promote desirable economic policies. While the original character ethic stressed the individual's own efforts as the primary impetus for change, a reconstructed one would envision working in concert through voluntary associations and large and small-scale organizations to achieve shared purposes.

Such an end-in-view might lead to concrete visions of a more communitarian nature, though that futuristic perspective would need to take into account the decidedly individualistic tradition of American culture and the more competitive features of its success ethic. In a curious sense, Americans today seem reticent about completely abandoning the character ethic, yet they also appear reluctant to rely on its received forms when they are steeped solely in rugged individualism. According to Frances Moore Lappé and Paul Martin DuBois:

> In the last century, major community decisions — which companies came to town, where businesses located, which production technologies they used — were decided by a few people responding to the market. Today, with a greater population density, and with the growing awareness of the hazards of current technologies, more people are asking whether they feel safe leaving the future of their communities to chance, or in other people's hands.[79]

3

The Mind Power Ethic

The mind power ethic in American thought and practice appeared in the nineteenth century and persisted into the twentieth century, for reasons peculiar to the secular and spiritual ethos that pervaded the United States at that time, and which continue into the present. Americans were grappling with balancing burgeoning advances in science and technology with the old-time religion they had been taught as children. They continued to be pragmatic in spirit, seeking after "what works" and solutions that might proffer "quick-fix" panaceas. Their nation was still seen as a land of opportunity, even if they were beginning to view the older character ethic and its moral principles with increasing skepticism. Accordingly, this chapter focuses on those social thinkers and movements that emphasized the power of mind and will as the fulcrum for success and self-improvement at a time when Americans began to turn inward in their search for the assumed realities of the American Dream.

The Influence of Psychology and Pragmatism

Pragmatism, particularly that offered by the influential psychologist-philosopher, William James, epitomized the myriad intellectual and practical movements that enabled Americans to mold this new world of flux and transition into "the shape of mind-cure [that) gives to some of us serenity, moral poise, and happiness, and prevents certain forms of disease as well as science does, or even better in a certain class of persons."[1] James's *The Varieties of Religious Experience* (1902) bespoke a peculiarly American response to individual forms of mental healing that might result in richly diverse ways of achieving willful success stories. Indeed, less philosophical merchants of mind power would attenuate James's examples into all manner of secular and spiritual admixtures.

In the late nineteenth century, psychology was beginning to legitimate a whole host of success writers, who extolled the new language of scientism. "Auto-suggestion," the "unconscious," "inferiority complex," "psychosomatic disorder," among other terms, became familiar bywords to lay persons who were unfamiliar with the often secret, labyrinthine world of psychoanalysis. A New Thought movement had emerged, linking the ancient idealistic platitudes of the Stoics with the modern intrapsychic paradigms of Sigmund Freud, Alfred Adler, Carl Jung, and others. (It is interesting and noteworthy that Freud and Jung made their celebrated journey to lecture at Clark University in Worcester, Massachusetts, in 1909.)

New Thought: Its Labyrinthine Paths

A proverbial congeries of people from all walks of life participated in the New Thought movement, whether by attending mental-healing lectures in auditoriums or reading about the "miracles" of mind power in popular magazines. Their interests were widely diverse, covering secular and spiritual concerns as varied as the Happy Thought Coffee House of Honolulu and the first Congress of the International New Thought Alliance, which devoutly believed that "he who trusts in the divine return has learned the law of success."[2] The low-income denizens of the Coffee House's soup kitchen were informally instructed to believe that "thought is the most powerful force in the world. It constructs all cities, all works of art, all machinery, all invention, all institutions and all states. . . . It literally builds the body, molds the features, forms the character, controls the health, shapes the circumstances, and makes the fortune and the happiness or unhappiness of the individual."[3]

More religious proponents of New Thought advocated belief in the overriding principle of Pure Spirit. For them, the essential nature of Spirit resides in the Universal Mind. Ergo, since everything is mental, the only reliable instrument for signifying reality is mind power. In an appropriately pragmatic twist, we can thus become whatever our mental attitude brings us to believe.[4] Some New Thought spiritualists also added a considerable dose of humanitarianism to their cauldron of ideas: One Spirit, One Mind equated with love for all humankind.[5] Hellfire and brimstone had given way to a religion of warmth and optimism: "All we must do is to plug into the divine power plant and our bodies will refresh themselves with health, our lives bubble over with happiness, and our pocketbooks expand with the plumper paychecks of success."[6]

In both spiritual and secular terms, perhaps Prentice Mulford put it best in this 1880s rendition of New Thought:

> Your every thought is a force, as real as a current of electricity is a force. . . . Set the magnetic power of your mind persistently in the desire and *demand* of the best of every thing; and the best will, by an inevitable and unerring law, eventually come to you. . . . THOUGHT IS FORCE, GOD COMMANDS, MAN DEMANDS.[7]

Mulford was also among the first New Thought advocates to challenge the asceticism of the older character ethic. He admonished against Ben Franklin's maxim of "early to bed and early to rise, makes a man healthy, wealthy, and wise." Instead, Mulford proffered a "plea for laziness" in this form:

> The physical degeneracy of a portion of the American people is owing to an excess of industry. . . . My friends term me lazy. That does not trouble me. I laugh as I behold them rushing by, wearing out body and soul in the chase after dollars. . . . Therefore, as long as I can afford it, I shall choose the better part and be lazy.[8]

However, Mulford did warn captains of industry to manage their businesses confidently and with full responsibility, and, above all, to avoid failures. Plainly, he saw no merit in being poor, and he considered material wealth as a rightful good that all humans should seek in abundance. According to Mulford's "law of justice and compensation," we should reasonably take "all we can sensibly and honestly"; and, "in giving, we should release our thoughts and material possessions only in proportion to a just return."[9] In secular Darwinian and Freudian terms, Mulford's views largely recapitulated the Gilded Age theme of enlightened self-interest.

The prototypal exponent of "success" through mind power in the Gilded Age was Orison Swett Marden, editor of *Success* magazine and author of more than forty-five books on the success ethic. Bridging the competing values of the character ethic and mind power, Marden extolled the virtues of both philosophies. Writing primarily in the 1890s, he personally inspired President William McKinley.

Marden asserted that the Creator did not intend for human beings to be poor or to suffer; rather, they were made for prosperity, happiness, and success. According to Marden's formula for success, one no longer should strain to acquire necessities; instead, one should learn to attract luxuries. He held that morals had no real connection with money-making ability. The law of attracting money is amoral and like attracts like. That is to say, a very bad man may obey the law of accumulation and acquire a fortune (though Marden added the non-sequitur that honesty is always the best business policy). In the process, he virtually ignored the roles of self-education and formal education as means for success.

For Marden, it is not laziness that impedes success, but diffidence, worry, and discouragement. When people worry they defraud themselves; thus, one needs both freedom from fear and self-confidence to release money-making powers. Marden recommended that one should visualize oneself radiating magnetism and picture oneself as gregarious, unselfish, generous, and tolerant.

The New Thought movement lent a decided impetus to the success of *Success* magazine's circulation and the career of O. S. ("The Doctor") Marden by the early 1900s. By that time, its staff consisted of two hundred employees and distribution had topped 300,000.[10] In the meantime, Marden personally circulated widely among New Thought groups in New York City's cultural center.

The mind power message in Marden's mature ideas seems startling in its boldness and simplicity; his thought system encapsulated divine, natural, material, and mental law in one fell swoop:

> Everything in man's life, everything in God's universe, is based upon principle — follows a divine law, and the law of prosperity and abundance is just as definite as the law of gravitation, just as unerring as the principles of mathematics. It is a mental law. Only by thinking abundance can you realize the abundant, prosperous life that is your birthright; in other words, according to your thought will be your life, your supply, or your lack.[11]

Akin to a hydraulic system, Marden's supply line mined the law of attraction. He exhorted his readers to saturate themselves with the idea of success, thinking it constantly and living with its vibrations at the core of one's being. Presaging future success writers such as Norman Vincent Peale, Marden suggested that his subscribers memorize and repeat certain stanzas of poetry that opined the glory of divinity and success: "God is my Father. He has wealth untold; His wealth is mine, health, happiness and gold." [12]

In the final analysis, Marden postulated that mental healing directly influences one's body as well as one's mind. Optimism brings wealth; cheerful thoughts improve one's cell life; and abiding attention to the principles of attraction, affirmation, and visualization of positive thinking bodes well for one's pathways to success. Indeed, Dr. Peale had already met his "post-life" alter-ego in the good "Doctor" Marden, i.e., their thought patterns and prescriptions ran largely in tandem, if several decades apart.

Forming an intellectual and practical bridge between Marden and Peale were the success books of Napoleon Hill, whose *Think and Grow Rich* (1937) still sells briskly in the self-help section of many popular bookstores. Stressing the power of mind and will to storm most any external bastion of restraint, Hill applauds America as a splendid land of unfettered freedom and opportunity for those who would be content, like Horatio Alger, to rise slowly up the ladder of success. Echoing Mulford's plea for moderation in personal industry and labor, Hill argues that "riches begin with a state of mind, with definiteness of purpose, with little or no hard work." [13] Implicit in Hill's statement of success is the overarching and persistent assumption that material wealth is among the most enviable of human aspirations. Positive thinking becomes the primary source of that brand of success: "You may as well know, right here, that you can never have riches in great quantities unless you work yourself into a white heat of desire for money." [14] According to Hill's methods of repetition and visualization, one must picture the exact amount of money one wishes to acquire and continue to repeat that amount to oneself (preferably at bedtime and upon awakening the next day) if there are to be any "realistic" chances for success.

In his concluding remarks, Hill somewhat tempers his materialist aims with a cautionary mentalistic note:

> You have absolute control over but one thing, and that is your thoughts. . . . If you must be careless with your possessions,

let it be in connection with material things. *Your mind is your spiritual estate!* Protect it and use it with care to which divine royalty is entitled.[15]

In concrete light of his spiritual suggestions, Hill held imaginary meetings each evening with such great minds as Luther Burbank, Andrew Carnegie, Charles Darwin, Thomas Edison, Ralph Waldo Emerson, Henry Ford, Abraham Lincoln, Napoleon, and Thomas Paine, so that he might re-pattern his own life in their image:

> My purpose was to rebuild my own character so it would represent a composite of the characters of my imaginary counselors. Realizing, as I did, early in life, that I had to overcome the handicap of birth in an environment of ignorance and superstition, I deliberately assigned myself the task of voluntary rebirth through the method I have described above.[16]

Of course, Hill did not bother to fret about the blatantly mystical quality of his own teachings.

Positive Thinking: Norman Vincent Peale

Both from his pulpit as a Methodist pastor and in his thousands of speeches and programs, Dr. Norman Vincent Peale preached the gospel of mind power to a large following among the American bourgeoisie. In 1932, he assumed the ministry of the Marble Collegiate Church in Manhattan, one of the oldest evangelical institutions in the country. Peale published two books during the 1930s, a best seller in the 1940s, and *The Power of Positive Thinking* in 1952, the titan of money-makers, which by 1956 had exceeded every book but the Bible as the all-time nonfiction best seller. In contrast to the character ethic literature, many of Peale's works are written for those facing middle age and "mid-life crisis."

Peale also carried on the semi-mystical, semi-scientist treatment of the mind power success ethic that had been popularized previously. His *The Power of Positive Thinking* purports to teach "a hard, disciplinary way of life, but one which [presumably] offers great joy to the person who achieves victory over himself and the difficult circumstances of the world."[17] Peale thus appears to believe that the mental power for problem solving exists almost entirely within the person, i.e., that the solutions to life's problems are already within oneself if one simply heeds the call to Peale's parsimonious and divine prescriptions. As with most models of therapeutic healing, Peale focuses on changing the individual, with little regard for altering the wider social environment that might be restraining him or her.

Though he does not acknowledge Carl Jung or Alfred Adler, Peale pinpoints human dysfunctionality as caused by "the malady popularly called the inferiority complex."[18] He suggests that faith through prayer and imaging power can eventually conquer such fleshly incapacities if the individual practices his techniques fervidly and sincerely. His basic message is that the way you think can create failure and unhappiness, but it can also bring you success and happiness. Those who think negatively get negative results; therefore, believe and you shall succeed. Specifically, he recommends emptying the mind at least twice a day of fears, hatred, guilt, and other negative feelings and filling it with positive, happy, optimistic thoughts.

Happily, according to Peale, one need not be a genius to succeed. He lists his rules for success in a series of simple credos and provides anecdotes for overcoming inadequacy and learning to practice faith. His formula is to (1) PRAYERIZE, (2) PICTURIZE, and (3) ACTU-ALIZE.[19] Peale asks the reader to continually repeat and meditate upon such biblical sayings as "if God be for us, who can be against us." Thus, he seeks to overcome the lack of self-confidence that stems from a deep sense of inadequacy and insecurity. All things are possible for those who believeth. For example, he relates the story of the woman who sold vacuum cleaners from door to door who learned to recite: "'If God be for me, then I know that with God's help I can sell vacuum cleaners.'" Using the other laws simultaneously, she announced: "God helps me sell vacuum cleaners." Naturally, Peale concludes: "Who can dispute it?"[20] Consequently, he asks that you stamp an indelible image of success on your mind, and always picture that success, no matter how bad conditions are at the moment. This is the law of visualization. Never entertain a failure thought; expel it by increasing positive affirmation. Peale again concludes by asking us to affirm aloud: "God is now giving me success. He is now giving me attainment."[21]

Perhaps Peale kept his lessons and examples as simple as possible because he was appealing to everyday people in everyday situations in life, love, and work. He wanted the Willie Lomans of the world of struggle and tragedy to become the Ross Perots of the universe of happiness and success. Indeed, salespersons and executives represented the principal audience for his practical guides to functional and spiritual maintenance. As Donald Meyer so aptly puts it:

> Peale's readers are offered power for meeting the trials of a world which is already there, already shaped, not to be changed, already accepted by them as the fit and proper scene for their proof of themselves.[22]

In modern psychological terms, Peale's positive thinking model may possibly have a relation to self-efficacy theory. Self-efficacy refers to an individual's judgments regarding his or her ability to succeed at a task. According to Albert Bandura, self-efficacy judgments affect the task one selects, his effort and persistence, and the level of performance. "People avoid activities that they believe exceed their coping capabilities, but they undertake and perform assuredly those they judge themselves capable of managing."[23]

Peale, however, seems unable to envision peace of mind without the sanction of material success. He also leaves his readers the distinct impression that positive thinking alone is sufficient for success. Yet, if the truth be known, the positive thinking approach may mislead those with serious psychological problems, as they are unlikely to benefit and may be harmed by failing to seek proper psychiatric care.

Above all else, Peale ignores essential features of the human condition. Paul Tillich, for one, observed that the principal existential concern is that of the courage of self-affirmation in the face of nonbeing. Courage has both an ethical and an ontological dimension. The ethical dimension expresses concrete action and signifies that one cares enough to decide to pursue a course of action despite opposition. The ontological dimension consists of affirming oneself in spite of the threat of nonbeing. The basic human anxiety is awareness of nonbeing, one's finitude, which is an irremovable part of one's being. It must be courageously faced, so that it does not become a form of pathological anxiety.[24]

Spiritual Success: Eddy and Schuller

In the late nineteenth and early twentieth century, Mary Baker Eddy's peculiarly pragmatic blend of Christianity and scientism fostered another new wave of mind power through spirituality. Originally associated with Phineas Quimby's mental healing movement and experiments in homeopathic medicine, Eddy diverged from those paths to create a more distinctively religious form of salvation. "For Mrs. Eddy, however, God, or Life, was not in matter; matter had no independent positive existence; and man's true being was not that of a material organism. The belief of life in matter was, for her, an error which science must correct."[25] Literally and figuratively, she became a Joan of Arc of spiritual force, seeking to render Christian Science as the most legitimate version of both Christianity and science as such.

According to Mrs. Eddy, the physical and material world, as one of artificiality and destruction, is inimical to the pure world of God and Spirit. As she envisions it, "The term Science, properly understood, refers only to the laws of God and to His government of the universe, inclusive of man."[26] Rather than practice what she considered deficient forms of mesmerism, she established her Mother Church in Boston to propagate rigid, doctrinaire religious teachings which she would spread throughout the fleshly world. No philosophic thinker herself, Mrs. Eddy derived her notions primarily through intuition and revelation.

For Christian Science, the true and only path to salvation is through complete acceptance and affirmation of Jesus Christ. Through His transfiguration comes a full spiritual awakening in the more insufficient selfhoods of human beings. As Mrs. Eddy understands it, "Nothing aside from the spiritualization — yea, the highest Christianization — of thought and desire, can give the true perception of God and divine science, that results in health, happiness, and holiness."[27] In essence, she equates material existence with a deathly sleep; to accept the life of Spirit is to be reborn to reality. Her ultimate purpose is not simply to heal physical illness, but to cleanse corrupt humans from sin and evil itself. "Admit the existence of matter," she writes, "and you admit that mortality (and therefore disease) has a foundation in fact. Deny the existence of matter, and you can destroy the belief in material conditions."[28]

Since the essential etiology of disease is seen to be in the erroneous acceptance of material life, Mrs. Eddy views mental and physical healing as similarly deficient. Only revelation and spiritual sense can save us from our corporeal incapacities. Thus, "the proof of healing is not the destruction of the bone, but its restoration to normal formation and functioning."[29] In this sense, she sets up an oddly pragmatic form of possibility: if prayer and Christian Science doctrine works, perhaps it is right, after all. Of course, no causal connections could be proven, one way or another.

Nevertheless, Christian Science came under wide attack and biting ridicule. Mark Twain's satirical example in his *Christian Science* is a humorous case in point. In his book, Twain imagines himself being treated by a Christian Scientist practitioner when he has just fallen off an Alpine cliff. A messenger tells him he is being given "absent treatment" by the practitioner, who claims that Twain is in fine health. Twain's shock and disbelief is apparent:

> "Did you tell her I walked off a cliff seventy-five feet high?"
> "Yes."
> "And struck a boulder at the bottom and bounced?"
> "Yes."
> "And struck another one and bounced again?"
> "Yes."
> "And struck another one and bounced yet again?"
> "Yes."
> "And broke the boulders?"
> "Yes."
> "That accounts for it; she is thinking of the boulders. Why didn't you tell her I got hurt, too?"
> "I did. I told her what you told me to tell her: that you were now but an incoherent series of compound fractures extending from your scalplock to your heels, and that the comminuted projections caused you to look like a hatrack."
> "And it was after this that she wished me to remember that there was nothing the matter with me?"
> "Those were her words. . . ."
> "Does she seem to be in full and functionable possession of her intellectual plant, such as it is?"
> "*Bitte?*"
> "Do they let her run at large, or do they tie her up?"[30]

Meanwhile, H. L. Mencken leveled his criticism of Christian Science more succinctly: "[It] is the theory that since the skyrockets seen following a wallop on the eye are an illusion, the eye is one illusion and the wallop another."[31]

Despite such assaults on its assumptions of truth, Christian Science lives on in contemporary America. However, its celebration of spiritual success has not been without competitors. In the 1980s and 1990s, from his "The Hour of Power" telecast at the Crystal Cathedral in Garden Grove, California, Dr. Robert Schuller has appeared as a smiling new sword carrier for the blissful righteousness and healing balm of the Beatitudes. His *The Be (Happy) Attitudes* (1985) sets forth another menu of positive principles for effective living in light of precepts gleaned from the Sermon on the Mount. At bottom, Schuller is a more direct descendant of the practical ideas and prescriptions of Dr. Peale, as opposed to the more rarefied, structured dogma espoused by Mrs. Eddy.

Like Peale, Schuller insists that external factors have little to do with achieving personal happiness. Indeed, he skirts over problems of *financial* poverty in order to concentrate instead on issues of *occupational, intellectual,* and *emotional* poverty. To avoid occupational poverty, one must chart goals toward professional success and strive to reach those aspirations. To ward off intellectual poverty, one must acknowledge that one is not an expert on everything, i.e., that one will someday need help from other intellectual sources besides oneself. To suppress emotional poverty, we all "need to be needed," and we must grant that "success starts when I dare to admit I need help." In a soothing, if questionable, rendering of financial poverty via a softened version of Social Darwinism, Schuller muses: "Poverty handled in a pleasant, positive manner is an opportunity to involve good and generous people in our dreams, for often the strong welcome an opportunity to help the weak." [32]

Along with seeking help for their problems, Schuller recommends that human beings take on the humble cloak of the poor in spirit. For they are blessed in their openness to their predicament. In a real way, he is beseeching us to convert our problems into success through the sheer force of mind power and the adoption of the Holy Spirit. "God particularly pours out His blessings upon those who know how much they need Him. The *promise* is joy. The *principle* is to ask God for help, admit we cannot do it alone. The *problem,* of course, that stands in the way of our crying out to God is the problem of an *unholy pride.*" [33] Thus, only errors in human judgment forestall us from the ultimate fulfillment of our dreams of happiness and success. Revivifying Peale's central message, Schuller reminds us that we can change our lives if we but change our attitudes.

How, according to Schuller, does God help us change our attitudes, and thus our lives? He gives us courage, a sense of calm, companionship, compassion, and a new set of commitments. Given the possibility of this bountiful harvest of presents, Schuller continues to smile down upon those still in the darkness: "And that's why the people that mourn are really comforted. Believe it or not, they're happy." [34] Of course, not everyone believes and, presumably, that is why they are not happy. Relentlessly, but sweetly, Schuller urges those who are still unhappy to unravel the potential riches in the simple, yet powerful, word "meek": M (mighty), E (emotionally stable), E (educable), and K (kind).[35] If one does not succeed on that sure-fire formula, the problem is either a failure of pride or perhaps an inability to be correctable. For Schuller, both are doubtless one and the same.

In the end, Schuller is asking us to become more Christ-like in our attitudes and behavior. We should be disciplined and controlled; we should resist temptation; and we should be open to help and helping through our sensitive, unselfish, born-again spirit.[36] We can all become "pure in heart" if we take Schuller's four-step plunge: (1) wise up; (2) clean up; (3) give up; and (4) take up.[37] This practical and spiritual recipe for success requires us to strip away any negative thoughts and emotions that block pure faith and obscure the need to reach out for God's help. Only He can open up human renewal projects that fulfill dreams and call us to greatness. Personal victory comes to those who are prepared, positive, perseverant, forgiving, prayerful, and stronger for having passed through the shadows of darkness.[38] Ultimately, Schuller concludes that we should travel like Christ through life's tragic phases and be reborn.

Psycho-Cybernetics and Self-Renewal: Maxwell Maltz

Born and raised on New York City's Lower East Side, Maxwell Maltz, M.D., eventually made it uptown to become one of America's pioneering practitioners of plastic surgery. From the 1940s through the 1970s, he took his "magic scalpel" and wielded its seemingly incandescent power for clients eager to ward off frustration and hopelessness. While not acknowledging Peale's obvious spiritual similarities, Maltz clearly undertook a distinctively secular search for "creative living for today" in a manner that would echo Peale's even more profitable psychic remedies. Maltz's most representative works include *Psycho-Cybernetics* (1960), *The Magic Power of Self-Image Psychology* (1964), and *The Search for Self-Respect* (1973).

For Maltz, the productive force of psycho-cybernetics can be synthesized in simple terms: "You combat your fearful tendencies by refocusing on your past successes, making your happy moments live again in your imagination, over and over, fortifying your sense of self-esteem, so that you can reverse your orientation toward failure and build in yourself the courage to act constructively."[39] Thus, a potpourri of success imagery, healthy morsels of emotional tonality and active living, and the cooling ventilation of peace, tranquility, and self-respect make for psychic survival in Maltz's eyes.

Such a recipe for success requires certain core goal builders and the ready seizing of life's opportunities for advancement. In Maltz's formula, one moves from "constructive thinking" to "constructive imaging" and then to "constructive action" over a specific fourteen-week period. Each of his goal builders is to be pursued for six days, with one day off for relaxation. Creative "mirror watching" is central to any success in this process, one in which the person focuses on the image within which propels her onward and upward. Negating frustration and self-flagellation, the mirror watcher peers at herself with "kind eyes," forgives herself past mistakes, and "seeks to cook up a nourishing feeling of self-respect."[40]

Indeed, the building of self-respect is Maltz's prime mover in goal construction. One must grasp this motivation assiduously, even to the point of writing the word SELF-RESPECT on the mirror of one's bedroom or bathroom, preferably with an erasable pencil or lipstick. In the same fashion, Maltz instructs his readers to inscribe these other motivational phrases on their omnipresent mirrors: UNDERSTANDING, SINCERITY, DEFEAT UNCERTAINTY, OVERCOME RESENT-MENT, NO EMPTINESS, OPPORTUNITY, FORGIVENESS, FRIEND, PRISON, TRANQUILITY, CLOCK, RESPONSIBILITY, INTEGRITY, and SURVIVAL.[41]

Their translation into happiness is not difficult to decode. *Understand* yourself well and benignly. Face up to reality with *sincerity*. *Defeat uncertainty* so as not to paralyze yourself. *Overcome resentment* in order to alleviate your anxieties. *Get rid of emptiness* and rise above apathy. Wake up to *opportunity* so you can explore life to its fullest. *Forgive* yourself of your failures and limitations and move on to life's vast offerings. Look at yourself as a *friend* with rich capacities for living well. Tear down *prison* walls that constrain your confidence. Afford yourself enough *tranquility* to find relief from life's harshness. Throw out your retirement *clock*, which simply kills time, and instead adopt a constructive lifestyle. Attack life usefully and purposefully, with *responsibility* and *integrity* in your actions. Accept yourself no matter what calamities befall you because your *survival* is at stake.[42]

Maltz's emphasis on imaging is remindful of Peale's mind-power approach to the challenges and precipices of modern civilization. It is one which has been put to pragmatic use in arenas as disparate as the corporate office and the gridiron. In the words of Mean Joe Greene, the Pittsburgh Steeler football great of the 1970s:

> When I dream at night, . . . I visualize techniques. Some of 'em are just ungodly. It's just cat quickness; run over a guy, hurdle him, jump six feet, put three or four moves on him so he freezes. No flaws in those moves. Perfect push and pull on the guard, jump over the center. Another blocker, slap him aside. Block the ball when the quarterback throws it, catch it and run 99 yards. . . . The only thing that ever matched the dreams I had was the Super Bowl.[43]

Like Peale's, Maltz's own peripatetic schedule of lecture tours insured that he spoke to Everyman and Everywoman in a common language invitingly laced with the scientistic sounds of psycho-cybernetics. In fact, he often peppered his success manuals with informal dialogs between himself and the myriad cab drivers, bus boys, maids, and concierges he met along the byways to best-seller status.

Offering a rather superficial makeover of the sheer realities of life, Maltz afforded a facile transcendence of everyday woes for those seeking solace and a "quick fix" to deeper psychic dilemmas. His was hardly a world filled with existential *angst,* nor was his philosophical quest riddled with much suffering or doubt.

Postscript

Regardless of the many arguments offered by both the secular and spiritual proponents of the mind power ethic, it would seem dangerous and foolhardy to adopt their prescriptions and proposed solutions for success in any unquestioning fashion. To become enmeshed in any single panacea for life's manifold problems does little more than constrict one S capacities for challenging existing realms of knowledge and valuation and, therefore, restricts one S full growth potentiality. Formulas for success, whether material or spiritual, maintain "success" definitions on more or less their own terms, often irrespective of evidence to the contrary.

None of the main figures treated in this chapter affords us a genuinely dialogic and integrative approach to self-help forms of success through mind power. In sporadic bits and pieces, they tend to serve up only quasi-informative illustrations and cases for readers. The latter should be careful to scrutinize their work for normative consequences and critical implications. Unfortunately, they do not beseech us to question their own authority; nor do they qualify their arguments based on the reader's own life experience and perceptual interpretation and understanding. Those individuals who forsake their ability to look beyond the answers proffered may be at risk from such self-help interventions.

In chapters 7, 8, and 9, we will reconsider the arguments of the mind-power advocates with a view toward marshaling more acute and concerted critique from various psychological, philosophical, and social perspectives. Those chapters will recapitulate mind-power assumptions from the vantage points of multidimensional factors and variables. Such a reconsideration will take into account the full range of forces that lead individuals to adopt recipes for success through mind power and how they might profit, or be led astray, by its teachings.

4

The Personality Ethic

By the early twentieth century, particularly by the 1920s, a new wave of success was beginning to make its presence felt in various guises. Sometimes its figures surfaced fictitiously, like Gatsby along the shores of Long Island Sound. At other times, its stormy rebellion turned into conformity, as was often the case with real-life flappers in SoHo. Whatever their form, exponents of the personality ethic focused on developing a charming presence and attractive physical appearance. They tended to show less concern for manners as an expression of morals and more concern for the impression that manners make on other people. Their singular objective was to get others to do what they wanted. Much of the early literature on personality power was directed at salesmen; but by the late 1920s, it focused as well on those in manufacturing. Indeed, the personality ethic would appeal to many individuals in a changing society caught up in trading off old and new brands of individualism.

The personality ethic holds that opportunities are abundant, and that more business leaders and executives are needed. Advancement does not depend on luck, but on making something of oneself and not blaming circumstances for one's condition in life. Thus, its effects were politically conservative, since the failure of upward mobility does not lie in social and economic conditions. "Personality is the quality of being Somebody" — a definition repeated in many manuals of the day. But to be somebody, one had to be oneself. And, ironically, even the many self-help manuals insisted that one should not follow another's advice, but be oneself.

Such old-time assets as rural origins, an influencing mother, and higher education were unnecessary for advancement in the personality ethic. In fact, a classical or liberal arts education could do more harm than good. One could always educate oneself through public libraries and correspondence courses, since formal education usually ignored the most important part of one's education: human relations. Proponents of the personality ethic emphasized that an understanding of human relations paid off in profit-making situations; and though a knowledge of the product was helpful, the sales pitch was even more valuable.

Some advocates of the personality ethic were more interested in justifying material success than warning against the dangers of avarice; they, therefore, saw service as an expression of love for others and money as the measure of that service. Writers in this vein addressed adults, not youth (in contrast to the character ethic writers), and saw no need to lace their material with spiritual uplift. Instead, they wrote to convey the psychological principles of success they observed in the marketplace.[1]

In short, the personality ethic provided advice on how to manipulate people and develop an attractive personal and physical appearance. As cultural historian Christopher Lasch has noted, "The captain of industry gave way to the confidence man, the master of impressions." Personality success manuals differ from earlier ones "in their frank acceptance of the need to exploit and intimidate others, in their lack of interest in the substance of success, and in the candor with which they insist that appearances . . . 'winning images' . . . count for more than performance, ascription for more than achievement."[2] This chapter traces various historical and contemporary versions of those images and image-makers, from small-town transactions on Main Street to sleight-of-hand corporate takeovers on Wall Street.

Winning People Over: Dale Carnegie

No one contributed more to the perpetuation of the personality ethic than Dale Carnegie. In 1912, he initiated a course in public speaking that by 1985, thirty years after his death, had graduated three million people around the world and enrolled approximately two thousand new students weekly. His lecture, "How to Win Friends and Influence People," was published in 1936 as a book.[3] It appeared on the *New York Times* best-seller list for ten years. The book has been translated into more than thirty languages, and more than seventeen million copies had sold worldwide by 1989.

Born to country farmers in rural Maryville, Missouri, in 1888, Carnegie attended the State Normal School in Warrensburg, where he gained a reputation as a stellar debater. Leaving college before graduation, he became a salesman for the International Correspondence Schools and Armour and Company. Beckoned by the idea of becoming a Chautauqua lecturer and perhaps even an actor, he matriculated at the American Academy of Dramatic Arts in New York City in 1911. When his thespian ambitions failed him, he convinced the director of the Young Men's Christian Association at 125th Street to hire him as a lecturer in public speaking. Carnegie never looked back at failure again.[4]

Carnegie's mammoth bestseller, *How to Win Friends and Influence People,* originated from a panoply of sources, some academic but most an assortment of practical folk psychology and lessons drawn from countless interviews with famous people whom he thought anyone would like to emulate. Carnegie acknowledged his admiration for Alfred Adler, William James, and, most of all, H. A. Overstreet's *Influencing Human Behavior* (1925). At all times, Carnegie spoke to the common man and woman in everyday language: "Dealing with people is probably the biggest problem you face, especially if you are a business man. Yes, and that is also true if you are a housewife, architect, or engineer."[5]

With this presupposition in mind, he clearly states his view of human nature, which undergirds his prescriptions for success: "Of course you are interested in what you want. You are eternally interested in it. But no one else is. The rest of us are just like you: We are interested in what we want."[6] What to do about it? People want to feel good about themselves; therefore, in order to get ahead, you have to show interest in them, make them feel important, smile, remember their names, and talk in terms of their interests. To win people to your way of thinking, you should avoid arguments, show respect for others' opinions, admit your mistakes, be a good listener, and be sympathetic with others' ideas. To change people, one should begin with praise and call attention to others' mistakes only indirectly, talk about your own mistakes first, and ask questions instead of giving direct orders. These and related rules of conduct were designed to make the other person happy about doing the thing you suggest.

Equally clearly, Carnegie forfeits the moral development and hard work prescribed as necessary by the character ethic. He cites a director of a large rubber company, who claims that one rarely succeeds unless he has fun doing something.[7] Indeed, Carnegie quotes approvingly one of his student's remarks: "I find that smiles are bringing me dollars, many dollars every day."[8] Carnegie also downplays formal education and technical ability alone; rather, he seeks technical knowledge combined with the capacity "to arouse enthusiasm among men." Evidently his model requires the transformation of personality in whatever way necessary to make the sale, clinch the deal. In effect, one is left with no self or personality apart from whatever the market demands. Throughout his work Carnegie seldom deals with "any form of human activity not associated with the making and selling of goods. Nor is there anything resembling criticism of the structure or practices of enterprise in America."[9]

Dinner with Jesus: Bruce Barton

In the 1910s and 1920s, the journalist and advertiser Bruce Barton boldly served up Jesus Christ as the answer to how to sell ourselves as salesmen and industrial giants. He did so using the cloak of service as a vehicle to material success. And no servant could be imagined as more powerful than Jesus, either in Barton's vision or the eyes of a majority of the American public.

Integral to Barton's success motif was the pure potency of simplicity: be brief and use words that everyone knows. His best-seller, *The Man Nobody Knows* (1925), portrayed Jesus in terms starkly befitting the personality ethic: He was strong, successful, and a great business leader. According to Barton, Christ was no dour savior; rather, He was a smiling, cheerful, radiant person who liked to please people. In other words, He had all the qualities necessary to super-salesmanship.[10]

Barton saw his own mission as that of making business flourish throughout the world. He viewed business enterprise as radiating God's work on earth; thus, it was only understandable that he would want to augment the Almighty's bountiful harvest.[11] Those who could not fathom his work may well have considered Barton a huckster. Yet such skepticism did not forestall his success; he represented Manhattan's "silk-stocking" district in Congress from 1937 to 1941. Though he lost his bid for the Senate, still others thought that he should run for the Presidency. In the end, Barton decided against campaigning for the White House, thus leaving us to wonder forever whether divine discontent ensued thereafter. Using Barton's own logic, we can assume that Jesus smiled.

Fictional Prototype: Willy Loman

Perhaps no fictional portrait in American letters and literature more acutely epitomizes the personality ethic, its tantalizing promises, and its ultimate pitfalls than the life of Willy Loman, the main character in Arthur Miller's celebrated drama, *Death of a Salesman* (1949). For Loman, personality, in the form of being well liked, is considered all-important in winning the day. Indeed, he views it as more significant than education and knowledge, mental healing, or good moral character. Yet Willy's pure and simple faith in the success ethic and the power of personality inexorably leads to his demise:

> Willy Loman's values are very much those of contemporary society — the American Dream that the rest of the world mimics — and his downfall derives both from his personal failure in relation to his values and from the failure of the values themselves. . . . [He] articulates through the way he lives and dies the latent self-destructiveness of a society in which the false promises of advertising corrode not only our business lives but our personal relationships. His only hubris is in believing the propaganda of a success-oriented society.[12]

After thirty-five years as a hosiery salesman, living in Brooklyn but covering much of New England by car, Loman's commissions stop and he is fired unceremoniously from his job. He is exhausted, tormented, hallucinatory, and suicidal. His sons ridicule his unrealistic, worn-out ambitions; only his caring, dutiful wife seems to offer understanding for his plight. Close to death, Willy cannot give up his life of appearances even as it overwhelms him.

Willy's whole life and relations with the world are played out as if he had attended a super sales seminar with Dale Carnegie as his mentor. Loman continually visualizes the United States as "the greatest country in the world," i.e., a vast landscape of opportunities waiting for those, like his wayward son Biff, who exude "personal attractiveness" and athletic prowess.[13] Willy thus admonishes Biff in the splendid ways of this seemingly glory-filled universe: "The man who makes an appearance in the business world, the man who creates personal interest, is the man who gets ahead. Be liked and you will never want."[14] In a word, one's ability to smile and one's flair for making personal connections become the essential ingredients for success.

Indeed, Willy himself was initially attracted to a sales career because he envisioned that he would "put on his green velvet slippers" and "pick up his phone and call the buyers, and without ever leaving his room."[15] In fact, no profession more necessitates personality power than does salesmanship. It also implies selling oneself and being loved in return. Nevertheless, Willy's dream turned into a sheer nightmare, even as he fought to stay awake at the wheel. He eventually lost his way in an overgrown industrial society run amuck, yet he had only an illusory dream to bank upon in the first place. At his funeral, his best friend puts Willy's life and death in the best possible light:

> Nobody dost blame this man. You don't understand: Willy was a salesman. And for a salesman, there is no rock bottom to the life. He don't put a bolt to a nut, he don't tell you the law or give you medicine. He's a man out there in the blue, riding on a smile and a shoeshine And when they start not smiling back — that's an earthquake. And then you get yourself a couple of spots on your hat, and you're finished. Nobody dost blame this man. A salesman is got to dream, boy. It comes with the territory.[16]

Political Prototypes: Selling One's Sunny Side

The power of personality, the ability to appear at one with the American people, the capacity to communicate an image of sincerity above and beyond any ideological banners — all these characteristics seem to have merged in the politics and presidencies of Dwight D. Eisenhower and Ronald W. Reagan. Historian Norman Graebner describes Eisenhower's charm in fitting fashion:

> The Eisenhower personality overshadowed the Presidency itself. The traditional duties and obligations of office appeared inconsequential when contrasted with the warm and easy smile, the beaming face, the informal, simple and unpretentious manner that captured the imagination of people everywhere. . . . His image was that of a well-meaning man standing at the center of American life.[17]

Gary Wills depicts Reagan in similar ways:

> He is, in the strictest sense, what Hollywood promoters used
> to call "fabulous." We fable him to ourselves, and he to us.
> We are jointly responsible for him. He is aware of his own
> prototypical status, yet that awareness neither galls us nor
> discommodes him. It is simply "All-American" in his eyes for
> him to be all America; so, in his eyes, he is. His vast claims are
> made in ways that convey modesty, not megalomania.[18]

Their roots were carved out of a national landscape that mythologized
how young men could climb up the ladder of success from rural back-
woods and seemingly humble origins. Born in 1890 in Denison, Texas,
and raised in Abilene, Kansas, Eisenhower learned from the stern tute-
lage of his father, who ran a creamery, and from the admixture of
fundamentalism and pacifism bred by his mother. The Eisenhower
family, which included five other sons, lived right across the railroad
tracks. As a youth, Ike liked to dramatize the heroes of Abilene's cowboy
past; and he read Zane Gray's Western novels by candlelight (his favorite
adult reading as well). In 1911, Ike left Abilene to attend the United
States Military Academy at West Point, New York, where he graduated in the top third of his class.[19]

That same year, Ronald Reagan was born in the small town of
Tampico, Illinois, and later grew up in nearby Dixon, the son of an
alcoholic salesman and a literary-minded Disciples of Christ mother.
Young Reagan's life centered around church activities, being a life-
guard, and studying as little as possible at Eureka College, where he
was more active in campus politics and football. He became a radio
announcer in Davenport and Des Moines, Iowa, recreating baseball
games from memory and imagination, before moving on to Hollywood's screen studios.[20]

In their political careers, both Eisenhower and Reagan were masterful
merchandisers of advertising, advance teams, and public relations;
indeed, they may well have been among the most public-relations-
conscious Presidents in modern American history. Eisenhower's aides
talked about the White House as a "sales office" and often spoke of
government in advertising metaphors:[21]

> Eisenhower's television style, assiduously cultivated by profes-
> sionals, had become technically perfect. Television, in fact,
> provided party managers with the perfect medium for maintaining

the Eisenhower image, for what mattered was not the intellectual content of his speeches, but the sincerity and warmth
which he communicated to the public.[22]

Thus, the inimitable slogan, "I like Ike," epitomized Eisenhower's sunny
image of success and popularity. Reagan also made special use of
"hidden persuaders" in the media and technological society:

> The spokesman for rugged individualism was programmed
> more than any major candidate up to that time, with tech-
> niques — psychiatry, conformity-enhancers, group dynamics
> — that were anathema to conservatives. Social engineering
> was a swearword on the right. Yet Reagan was the first
> candidate to be engineered by professionals at that arcane
> calling.[23]

The Eisenhower and Reagan presidencies were notable for their
penchant to foster harmony and smooth working relations, to delegate
duties and details to a staff that would guard their bosses from confu-
sion (as much as possible), to keep company disputes at a minimum,
and, above all, to relegate higher forms of abstract thought to the
ashbin. At the same time, both Presidents would pace themselves to
assure that their personalities would shine in those "decisive moments"
when media and policy action seemed important. With such arrangements in hand, few appeared to mind when Ike played golf or Ronnie
rode his golden palomino. Indeed, such activities simply added luster
to their sunny-side, all-American personas.

Sherman Adams, Eisenhower's ill-fated White House Chief of
Staff, claimed that Ike was "not much of a reader. He was impatient
with the endless paperwork of the Presidency and always tried to
get his staff to digest long documents into one-page summaries."[24]
(Similarly, Reagan tended to work from cue and index cards.) Yet,
as Ike learned at West Point, the European front, and the Philip-
pines, a good general "always visits his troops to inspire them" and
"to infect those around him with [a] 'nothing is impossible' feeling."[25]
Akin to Dale Carnegie, Eisenhower had a politician's knack for
remembering names, calling mere acquaintances "my friends," and
using film stars (Robert Montgomery was his favorite) to model his
media techniques.[26] Again, like Carnegie, he honed the ability to lead
"the people by moving in the direction toward which they were
already inclined."[27]

Following the cultural lead of Carnegie and Eisenhower, Reagan promoted an attitude of cheer and hopefulness. In 1980, in his first successful Presidential campaign, he proclaimed: "Our optimism has once again been turned loose. And all of us recognize that these people who keep talking about the age of limits are really talking about their own limitations, not America's."[28] It was "Morning in America" again, when Disneyland was seen as real. Yet Wills gleans the stark power of Reagan's sunny appeal: "He casts a surface unity over elements that have long been drifting apart — religious beliefs away from religious posturing, conservative nostalgia from capitalist innovation, interdependence from nonconformism. He spans the chasm by not noticing it. He elides our cultural inconcinnities."[29]

Interestingly enough, it may have been the mind power gospel of the likes of William James and other secular healers that presaged Reagan's eventual ascendancy. In James's brand of "healthy-mind" psychology, unhappiness, and pessimism are the chief roadblocks to personal success and national progress.[30] Reagan attacked Jimmy Carter and Walter Mondale for their "gloom and doom" politics, which projected sinful images of despair and malaise, while upholding the mind power and personality ethics and their hopeful message that Americans should once again "feel good" about themselves. In 1984, Reagan and George Bush ran on the slogan, "America is Back." James might not have smiled completely, but he would have admitted that Reagan's sunny healthy-mindedness had obviously worked for him, if not for the country's present and future generations.

Prophetic Prototype: Billy Graham

The smoothly successful career path of evangelist Billy Graham paralleled those of Eisenhower and Reagan. They were contemporaries of heart and temperament who preached similar themes of Christian Americanism and fervid anti-Communism. Beginning with Eisenhower, Graham befriended presidents for four decades, no matter what their religion or how religious they were. He was also among the first televangelists to use the electronic media with a politician's sophisticated gift for cadence and timing. In fact, the Billy Graham Evangelistic Association would become a worldwide apparatus for redemption and salvation, operating out of Charlotte, North Carolina.

As Peter Steinfels puts it, the primary reasons for Graham's phenomenal success grew out of "his country-boy charm and his dramatic good looks . . . as well as his cheerful disregard for theological and political differences." In a word, this powerful man with "the profile for which God created granite" had Eisenhower's "uncanny ability to smooth over conflicts." Whether he agreed or disagreed with his friends or enemies, Graham would still call them "terrific fellows" with "great vision" and "tremendous charisma." Those terms could apply with equal ease to Pat Robertson or Bill Clinton in Graham's tasteful lexicon.[31]

A sincere, yet clever, prophet of human vulnerability, Graham has been able to preach dogmatic fundamentalist certitudes without appearing overly rigid in the process. That is, his message has always been absolutistic, but he has diligently delivered it in such a way as to seem friendly and non-threatening. Even his skeptical listeners have been less than willing to change their television channels; his converts simply cannot resist his charm and power:

> Beautifully groomed, beautifully assured, brilliant in profile, beautifully tonic, Graham comes to his audiences, a man who on the plain evidence of his personal appearance is equipped to meet all the requirements of the American cult of happy, healthy living, popularity, and self-assurance.[32]

Donald Meyer has also analyzed the special audience that is drawn to Graham's personality power:

> [Their] folk culture has been overlaid by mass culture. They have been infected, and now they are ready for someone to neutralize, to de-value, to discount the cult of personality for them. . . . Because of what he is, because he himself is a vibrant full-color personality, he can give good conscience to those afraid to discount and dismiss the cult directly for themselves.[33]

Paradoxically, Graham continues to preach apocalyptic visions of hellfire and brimstone while exuding the optimistic tone and style of a soothing grandfather. With consummate grace, he learned to eschew Elmer Gantry's crass road to success for the more accommodating rhythms of politicians like Eisenhower and Reagan.

Faces of Industry: Personality Counts

Throughout the 1920s, 1930s, and 1940s, Americans of all ages were inundated by popular pamphlets, self-help manuals, vocational guides, and other forms of success literature that extolled the virtues of a winning personality in the struggle for corporate ascendancy. This section of the chapter focuses on several typical examples in the literature which appealed to college youth and working adults. The section concludes with a present-day model of success through personality, though the proffered example also exhibits how "personality counts" can lead to "personality corrupts."

By the 1940s, Science Research Associates had published a lengthy series of occupational monographs; one, by Paul W. Chapman, *Your Personality and Your Job,* summarized and typified the usual strain of thought and advice articulated in much of the literature in this genre. Chapman was then dean of agriculture at the University of Georgia and formerly a consultant to the United States Office of Education. His particular manual was widely distributed in school guidance offices across the country. In the first few pages of his small monograph, Chapman attempts to unravel why one succeeds or fails. Having sifted through countless studies from both business and education, he claims that personal characteristics provide the best answer to that query. Chapman's citations from various industrial and academic institutions are worth repeating at some length in order to convey an appropriate flavor for how he depicted the impact of personality.

For example, Chapman cites an oft-quoted Carnegie Foundation study to this effect: "Technical training counts for only 15 percent in the success of an individual, while personal qualities count for 85 percent." According to a study of 4,400 persons conducted by the Harvard Bureau of Vocational Guidance, personality factors were the principal cause for job dismissal in sixty-six percent of the cases. Moving on in similar vein, Chapman acknowledges a now-classic survey of graduate engineers five years out of Purdue University, which showed that those rated highest in personality earned greater incomes than those rated highest in intelligence.[34]

Chapman proceeds to gather "factual comments" from a variety of employers to glean those personal characteristics most in demand by them. Many are related to appearance, agreeableness, cheerfulness, cooperativeness, enthusiasm, stability, self-control, and sociability. The following negative traits are to be avoided if one hopes to advance or keep one's job: nervousness, moodiness, pessimism, sarcasm, suspiciousness, jealousy, bossiness, egotism, arrogance, shyness, argumentativeness, tactlessness, and even soberness. Evidently, one must practice the proverbial golden mean with a modicum of confidence and vitality, though without undue boastfulness. To bolster personality, Chapman recommends that those in need seek the self-help aid of the likes of Napoleon Hill and his *Mental Dynamite: The Philosophy of American Achievement;* Margery Wilson, author of *Charm* and originator of correspondence courses on women's personality improvement; and Dr. Doncaster G. Humm, a psychologist whose *Temperament Test* directed industry to test workers for jobs that supposedly fit their personalities.[35]

Other everyday men and women read the work of Eugene J. Benge, a self-styled "hu-management engineer" and the author of *Manpower in Marketing, You — Triumphant,* and other volumes in personality development. Benge tended to mimic Dale Carnegie's lines, both in spirit and in his equally devout passion for list-making:

1. Develop anew the genuine smile.
2. Become interested in people as individuals, in their hopes and aspirations.
3. Be a good listener. Get people to talk about the things they want to talk about.
4. Praise when praise is due.
5. Don't take your friends and loved ones for granted; tell them the things that you appreciate about them.
6. Do small acts for others without expectation of benefit to yourself.
7. Observe the minor courtesies.
8. Speak well of others behind their backs. Speak ill of no one.
9. Refrain from gossip or scandalmongering.
10. Take active part in the discussions and activities of groups to which you belong.
11. Look for some good in everyone — it's true.
12. Talk about positive things and avoid the negative.[36]

Benge also encouraged Americans to exercise their "extrovert actions" as much as possible, inasmuch as they are "too prone to engage in the introvert types of things." To assist us beyond the perils of introversion, he created yet another suggestion list of extrovert activities:

Play bridge
Dance
Ice or roller skate
Bowl
Competitive sports
Pool or billiards
Church work
Amateur plays
Choral singing
Club or society activity
Boy or girl scout leader
Committee work for a Chamber of Commerce
Community activities in your city or town
Group work with members of your own family
Debating or public speaking[37]

In many ways, Benge's extroverted character exhibited the same kinds of personality attributes that David Riesman and his associates would later describe in *The Lonely Crowd* (1950) as characteristic of the "other-directed" person. Outward striving for success, paying close attention to others' signals, and, above all, wanting to be well-liked — these conformist attitudes were fast becoming the ruling yardsticks by which to measure one's progress in the American way of life. Being people-oriented, even a "glad-hander," was quickly taking on a trademark status in our culture's socialization process — in the family, the school, and the workplace. Inevitably, such social skills also meant that the manipulation of other people's wants for one's own wishes and desires would no longer be considered beyond the pale of social etiquette.[38]

These social trends had been forecast several decades earlier by the radical behaviorist, John B. Watson, who abruptly left academe for the greener fields of Madison Avenue and Ipana toothpaste advertisements. Watson epitomized the interlocking web of business, media, and scientism in America's other-directed society. For the behaviorist, Watson admitted, "would like to develop his world of people from birth on, so that their speech and their bodily behavior could equally well be exhibited freely everywhere without running afoul of group standards."[39] Social manipulation had thus become a ready enterprise once individual and group adjustment were synonymous terms.

Relentlessly, the personality ethic's burgeoning use of advertising and other media techniques ushered in a new wave of moral relativism and a "public relations morality":

Unlike hard work or honesty [of the character ethic], the techniques for messaging other people were not absolutes, good in themselves. They were good only if they achieved the desired results. Profit was exploited by controlling the responses of man; truth was something found in public opinion polls.[40]

The modern American industrial revolution has thus been "concerned with techniques of communication and control. . . . It is symbolized by the telephone, the servo-mechanism, the IBM machine, the electronic calculator, and modern statistical methods of controlling the quality of products; by the Hawthorne counseling experiment and the general preoccupation with industrial morale."[41] Making people more productive by making them happy in their work also undergirded the use of training groups (T-groups) in mid-twentieth-century America. While attempting to change group members' attitudes and ways of doing things on the job, T-group leaders focused on employees' "outer workings," i.e., their relations with other people in the organization.[42] Training groups implied that human relations models could supply effective solutions for most human problems, especially in the workplace. The method was first developed by the National Training Laboratories at Bethel, Maine, in 1947, and still exists today.

Of course, many persons molded by the personality ethic do not necessarily prize learning, either intrinsically or extrinsically, as a primary ambition on their road to success. Deal-making, glad-handing, and glamorous connections — those outer signs of success — have been even more prominent at the twilight of the Reagan era. Perhaps the rise and fall of RJR Nabisco and F. Ross Johnson, its erstwhile former president and chief executive officer, best personifies the short-lived effervescence of wealth and power and some ultimate prospects for destruction in the personality ethic today. Johnson's personal triumph and tragedy has been chronicled in the bestseller *Barbarians at the Gate* (1990), by Bryan Burrough and John Helyar.

Only an average academic student in college in the late 1940s, Johnson excelled as an extracurricular leader and organizer. At General Electric in Montreal, he began his career as a salesman because he surmised that was "where the good parties are." Early on in his corporate ventures, he mastered "the hundred-dollar golf game," while wining and dining his clients at the most expensive restaurants. Johnson also honed his "flip, wisecracking," even profane, sense of humor while cavorting around town with his Merry Men, a raucous band of young businessmen who gave each other such nicknames as "El Supremo," "The Fonz," and "Vice President of Worry." For extra measure, Johnson added an illustrious stable of ex-athletes to his entourage, including former New York Giant football stars Frank Gifford and Alex Webster.[43]

After a decade in New York City, as CEO of Standard Brands from 1973 to 1983, Johnson became more fascinated with glitz and the pure power of personality. No character ethic to restrain him, no scars from the Depression to haunt him, he was a "Broadway Joe or Reggie Jax, an iconoclastic superstar, television-age man" of business and extroversion writ large. On ascending the presidency of Nabisco, he quickly decided to sponsor the Dinah Shore golf tournament while augmenting his celebrity circle ("Team Nabisco") to include Gerald Ford, Bob Hope, and Oleg Cassini, among others. No shy wallflower, Johnson admitted that most of his successful business moves were made from "boldness" and "opportunism."[44]

Emblematic of the "Game of Greed" that marked the culture of the 1980s, Johnson was at the vanguard of those captains of industry who put buyouts above productivity in their day-to-day strategies. As mentioned earlier, he forgot, or never learned, the cardinal lessons of the character ethic. Nor did he care for the psychological sublimations sometimes required by the mind-power ethic. When Johnson and Nabisco floundered, their downfall was due largely to his own maverick ways, which discouraged teamwork and careful organizational planning. Ultimately, Johnson had not mastered *all* the nuances of the personality ethic in his headlong plunge to power.

Postscript

The failure of the personality ethic, as will be seen in subsequent chapters, can be assessed on broadly philosophical grounds. At root, advocates of personality power propound blatant and subtle forms of ethical egoism, i.e., the view that one need not behave morally if doing so does not promote one's interest and not doing so does. Yet ethical egoists impair their own advantage by promulgating their doctrine, which encourages others to act exclusively in their own interests. Surely, ethical egoists who seek their own advantage must persuade them to do otherwise. But in order to be an ethical doctrine, it must apply to others; thus, ethical egoism, when carried out in practice, is reduced to individual egoism, which is not an ethical doctrine at all. Then again, many of the popularizers of the personality ethic never pause long enough to ask an even more central question: What is the purpose of life?

5

The Service Ethic

From the mythical City on the Hill of the Puritan era through the civil rights revolutions in contemporary times, the American Dream has been propagated, and partially realized, by those who fostered an ethic of service to larger groups, institutions, and communities beyond themselves. Though visible throughout American history, the service ethic and its exemplars were particularly prominent from the middle 1800s through the mid-twentieth century — a strikingly transformative period marked by increasing urbanization, industrialization, immigration, and internationalism.

The term "service ethic" is linked to humanitarianism, and refers to those individuals and movements that emphasize "any type of disinterested concern and helpfulness . . . for people who are in distress."[1] It is perhaps noteworthy and revealing that, in American culture, the service ethic has usually been perceived as a secondary ideal, compared to some other success ethics:

> . . . it is striking that failures to follow the standards of concern and helpfulness have not been defended as legitimate in themselves; they have been interpreted as *deviance from* a criterion which is not basically challenged, or "justified" in terms of other, allegedly more vital values.[2]

John Steinbeck put the matter in starker terms in *Cannery Row* (1945):

"It has always seemed strange to me," said Doc. "The things we admire in men, kindness, and generosity, openness, honesty, understanding, and feeling are the concomitants of failure in our system. And those traits we detest, sharpness, greed, acquisitiveness, meanness, egotism, and self-interest are the traits of success. And while men admire the quality of the first, they love the produce of the second."[3]

Historically, advocates of the service ethic in America have propounded an abiding faith in human potentiality and in the capacity of the country to continue to make progress in solving national problems, whatever they might be and however difficult their solutions. This progressive ideology implies a corollary belief in the essential malleability of the American character and its susceptibility to being molded in presumably "better" directions. In many of the case examples highlighted in this chapter, the service ethic summons America away from older, once dominant, conceptions of rugged individualism and toward more communitarian mosaics of social responsibility. Historian Vernon L. Parrington has aptly captured these fundamental tensions in our national psyche:

At the beginning of our national existence two rival philosophies contended for supremacy in America: The humanitarian philosophy of the French Enlightenment, based on the conception of human perfectibility and postulating as its objective an equalitarian democracy in which the political state should function as the servant to the common well-being; and the English philosophy of *laissez-faire,* based on the assumed universality of the acquisitive instinct and postulating a social order answering the needs of an abstract "economic man."[4]

Many proponents of the service ethic would locate themselves solidly in Parrington's humanitarian camp.

At the same time, some critics of the service ethic have assailed its advocates' thoughts and actions on several grounds: (1) that they assumed a naive belief in human perfectibility and societal progress; (2) that a psychological need for power over others, however camouflaged or subtle, might lie at the root of their seemingly altruistic impulses; and (3) that many of their social reforms may actually have yielded cultural mechanisms of political manipulation and social control. Thus, this chapter presents the lives and work of numerous exemplars of the service ethic from the dual standpoint of depicting the main currents of their social philosophies and practices, and taking note of some of the major claims of their social critics.

The Common School Movement: Horace Mann

After the Revolutionary War, the responsibility for education was turned over to the states, because the new United States Constitution did not specifically mention education. In the early nineteenth century, many people resisted the idea of public support for common schools (i.e., schools under state auspices designed to teach a common body of knowledge to students from different social backgrounds). The wealthy did not think they should be required to pay for the education of working-class children, and they argued that property should not be taxed to support schools. Moreover, they contended that education had long been a family matter, not a public concern. Some people also feared that public education would conflict with parochial schools.

An argument about human nature was advanced as well: human ability is widely variable and traits are unevenly distributed; hence, most people cannot profit from schooling. Furthermore, it was argued, children of the poor who were educated at taxpayers' expense were likely to lose their initiative and become indolent. Besides, if the poor were forced to attend school, they would not be free to work. Not everyone thought this way, of course, and some exponents of the service ethic rose up to demand improvements in education.

One of the reformers was Horace Mann (1796–1859), a young, respected lawyer and state senator in Massachusetts who gave up a promising political career to pursue his broad humanitarian interests. His role as secretary to the Massachusetts State Board of Education was to assess school conditions and attempt to overcome any inadequacies. Mann discovered dereliction of school committees in performing duties, unqualified teachers, high rates of student absenteeism, substandard school facilities, an absence of libraries, and widespread public apathy.

His relentless drive toward educational and social service stemmed largely from the "stern mandate of duty" which Mann carried throughout much of his adulthood. As a youth, he had imbibed sturdy doses of Yankee Puritanism, leavened by the "pristine and uncorrupted tenets of modesty, simplicity, sobriety, and kindness." Later he learned to shun material success and the personal pursuit of pleasure in his single-minded dedication to molding moral harmony and social stability. Thus, the fulfillment of duty became Mann's life work, though he tended "to appeal to an individualistic sense of duty, honesty, and responsibility," rather than any collectivist vision of radical social reform:

> As a legatee of Puritanism, he was prepared and conditioned for an ascetic life devoted to duty, but having discarded the aggressive sanctions of his theology, he assumed more of the stance of a martyr than a conqueror.[5]

Mann tirelessly crisscrossed the state appealing to people's vested interests. He promoted education as necessary for a republican form of government; as an instrument for equalizing opportunity; and as a means for improving industry and conquering vice, crime, and poverty. Mann issued twelve annual reports that influenced public opinion not only in Massachusetts, but throughout the nation and abroad. He opposed sectarian teaching in the common schools, and established the first public normal school for teacher preparation in 1839. Although bitterly attacked by his opponents, by the time he resigned in 1848, the common schools had been founded in many states. Five years later, he became president of Antioch College in Yellow Springs, Ohio, one of the more progressive institutions of higher learning in the United States at the time. In his last address to the graduating class in 1859, the year of his death, he urged Antioch's graduates to heed his parting words: "Be ashamed to die until you have won some victory for humanity."[6]

Traditionally, consensus historians have characterized Mann's contributions to common schooling as evocative of democratic and meritocratic aspirations and achievements. According to Lawrence Cremin, "Common schools increased opportunity; they taught morality and citizenship; they encouraged a talented leadership; they maintained social mobility; they promoted social responsiveness to social conditions."[7] Such historical interpretations especially extolled the presumed power of common schools in reaching the burgeoning immigrant population in America's depressed urban areas.

In the last several decades, revisionist historians have viewed Mann's influence in more conflictual terms, arguing that "the common schools were designed from the very beginning as agencies through which the prosperous and propertied could control and contain the poor."[8] For example, in his historical analysis of early school reform in Massachusetts, Michael Katz has shown that relatively few working-class children attended common schools.[9] Even more pointedly, Colin Greer blames the common school movement for what he considers to be a legacy of programmed failure:

> The failure of many children has been, and still is, a learning experience precisely appropriate to the place assigned them and their families in the social order. They are being taught to fail and to accept this failure.[10]

In a related sense, Mann's frequent letters to *The Boston Globe* argued that the common schools would act as a crime-preventive measure (he typically depicted Irish immigrant families as slovenly and irresponsible).

Still other interpreters have weighed Mann's impact in more individualistic ways which defy any simplistic appraisal. For instance, Richard Pratte explains the many vagaries surrounding common schooling thusly:

> The essential point is that any social order creates support for those who profit from it, creates anxiety among those who do not understand it, and creates hostility and conflict among those who feel threatened by it. . . . We should be careful not to hold the initial proponents of such schooling responsible for the much later employment of their design.[11]

Toward Social Salvation: The Social Gospel Movement

Traditional assumptions of predominantly Protestant America have focused on change from the limited vantage point of individual personal conversion. "American religion has an individualist emphasis. Much Protestant teaching has been exclusively concerned with the virtues, activities, and relationships of individuals rather than of groups and institutions."[12] Personal salvation has often taken precedence over social action and social reform. As with many helping strategies, ministerial projects for change have also tended to subordinate the need to alter surrounding social and cultural constraints, which impede individual change. The Social Gospel movement tilted the image and inclinations of salvation in radically different directions.

Several early nineteenth-century church leaders weaned their flocks away from purely individualistic notions of salvation. A congregationalist preacher in New England, Lyman Beecher (1775–1863), peppered his sermons with stern calls to both moral piety and social reform. An orthodox Calvinist, his missionary efforts in trans-Appalachia, which he christened the "Christianizing of the West," were marked by unfortunate nativistic zeal, as was his influence in founding the African Colonization Society, in 1817. Beyond revivalism, Beecher urged his "congregations toward corporate action in the newly created voluntary reform societies, and direct political involvement through lobbying for the passage of needed moral legislation."[13] In 1804, Beecher published a manuscript which fit those aims precisely, *The Practicability of Suppressing Vice by Means of Societies Instituted for That Purpose.*

Beecher retained certain elements of the character ethic when it came to extolling the virtues of success through hard work. Indeed, he insisted that "the rich were successful because of their moral superiority over the immoral poor."[14] Accordingly, he was not ready to lead any pleas for nationwide anti-poverty programs that might redistribute the wealth. Instead, he hoped that Christianity itself was moving the world onward and upward. Like many harbingers and stalwarts of the Social Gospel, Beecher naively grasped the magic urn of inevitable progress.

Horace Bushnell (1802–1876) succeeded and surpassed Beecher on the cheery road to societal perfectibility. With his organic model of development, coined as the "Christian theory of socialization," Bushnell stripped away Calvinist beliefs in the moral depravity of infants and children. A Congregationalist minister in Hartford, Connecticut, he viewed the human race as reflective of heavenly providence and headed unceasingly in that direction, if only "divine seeds" would be nurtured lovingly on earth. Thus, he urged the establishment of caring Christian families that could form the basis for an unfolding evolution among other social institutions in industry, government, and education. Naturally, Bushnell acknowledged that such evolutionary change would take a long time, indeed; yet he believed that "there is no other kind of national advancement which is legitimate or safe."[15] In this conservative view, his appeal would dovetail, if rather more softly, with later hard-core devotees of Spencerian Social Darwinism.

The more ameliorative social gospel of Washington Gladden (1836–1918) moved American Christianity beyond the narrow confines of atomistic individualism and laissez-faire Social Darwinism. The Congregationalist Gladden served congregations in Springfield, Massachusetts, and Columbus, Ohio, for much of his ministerial career. More than his predecessors, he recognized the necessity of human interdependence in an increasingly complex world. He was also ever mindful that "a new appreciation of the sacredness of personality issued in new motivations to serve, minister, and cooperate in public endeavors in order to realize the love of both God and man."[16] Gladden would turn religious salvation in the concrete direction of correcting the sins of competition and corporate greed engineered in the Gilded Age. He sought fervidly to apply Christian precepts to contemporary social issues ranging from conflict between labor and management to the appropriate place of socialism in the economic and spiritual order.

Echoing Bushnell's vision of the child as a spark of God's grace, Gladden extended its evolutionary thrust so that "the kingdom of Heaven is the leaven which should permeate the whole society, ultimately bringing total human existence into harmony with Christ's spirit."[17] Consequently, he attempted to enliven his ministry with all sorts of secular activities, from athletics to photography, in an effort to make daily life sacred. Eventually, Gladden would seek to educate social workers in the social gospel of treating all persons as brothers and sisters in full and equal humanity and spirituality, in the name of Jesus Christ.[18] In fact, he defined sin as the "placing of selfishness or self-will above the claims of love and duty."[19]

Amplifying the Golden Rule as a moral and communitarian yard-stick, Gladden preached an ethic of service and social responsibility that placed *duties* above individual rights:

If [Americans] could be taught from infancy to think that citizenship rests upon duties rather than upon rights, and that when in a democracy, as in a family, duties are faithfully performed, rights may be trusted to take care of themselves.[20]

While pinpointing private property as a principal barrier to social intercourse, he chastised the robber barons of his day for placing their self-interest ahead of common democratic interests. Those captains of industry were also taken to task for failing to create an equitable wage system and for neglecting to ensure safe, comfortable working conditions in their factories. Gladden had similar unkind words for bureaucrats and politicians who worked to enrich themselves rather than the public welfare.

Caught up in the heady Progressivism of his times, Gladden encouraged the secular marriage of Christianity and social science in order to help solve the mounting social ills that hampered the full evolutionary flow toward human perfectibility. Like Jane Addams and other reformers, he recommended that sociology be used for such purposes; and he defined that newly established academic discipline in terms of an explicit service ethic, as "the social relations of man to man and the duties growing out of those relations."[21] Gladden argued that sociology and Christianity could become partners in service to humankind in several mutually rewarding ways:

> (1) Sociological studies of vice, crime, pauperism, and ignorance could provide valuable information that Christians needed to document the scope of America's social problems; (2) Christians could gain some useful hints from the suggestions of social science as to the means necessary to rid society of its social ills; and (3) sociology could help elucidate some of the more important truths of theology and thus give the Christian gospel a scientific foundation.[22]

More a prolific popularizer than a weighty theorist, Gladden wasted little time trying to disentangle the warranted or unwarranted justification for his religo-scientific wedding.

The zenith of Social Gospel thought was reached in the work and writings of the Baptist theologian Walter Rauschenbusch (1861–1918). A scholar at the Rochester (New York) Theological Seminary, he sought to interpret the kingdom of God as "a regeneration and reconstitution of social life," in tandem with the growth of academic and popular Progressivism. While retaining the earlier Social Gospel's emphasis on evolution and progress, he wanted to unleash Christianity's moral power in the critical service of social and economic change. And while Gladden had never completely accepted socialism as a viable solution, Rauschenbusch contended that, without it, the American Dream would become a long-forgotten vestige of our national mythology. However, he insisted that his brand of socialism would be "religiously inspired" and appropriate to the radical spiritual roots of primitive Christianity.[23]

For Rauschenbusch, early Christianity evoked an impassioned quest for social justice within collectivity. For modern men and women, the new journey required them to serve Christ by building a social order consonant with His powerful and passionate vision. Like other Progressivist critics, Rauschenbusch especially enlisted the aid and service of those from the professional and academic classes, urging them "to take the side of the poor in most issues."[24] He focused on many of the same questions as Gladden, but appealed in more scholarly and eloquent language to the intellectual elites, whom he expected to be in the vanguard of social change. In his *Christianizing the Social Order* (1912), he spoke of this "new type of Christian" as one who is willing to fight for the crucial goals of justice, liberty, and fraternity against an economic system that often represses each of those ideals."[25] In eschatological terms, Rauschenbusch would come to refer to that repressive social order as the Kingdom of Evil.

In the end, with Gladden, Rauschenbusch also attempted to wed Christianity to modern science. He put the matter bluntly: "Theology ought to be the science of redemption and offer scientific methods for the eradication of sin."[26] In essence, he was searching after a unity of the Kingdom of God with ongoing human development. And though he detested Herbert Spencer's politics, he still clung to his evolutionary model. Thus, according to Cecil Greek, "The social gospelers' need to have dominion over nature and the world in order to bring about social salvation depended so heavily on a knowledge of God's scientific laws that they soon became virtual captives of science."[27]

For others of its critics, the Social Gospel movement would come to symbolize, on the one hand, a valiant antidote to the harsh realities of an industrial age; on the other hand, those same critics would contend that the movement was led astray by its own self-propelled social optimism. Reinhold Niebuhr (1892–1971), who is discussed more fully later in this text, for one perceived "the impending disintegration of modern civilization, and for just that reason he [did] not tie Christianity to any particular social success."[28] In its predilection toward the secularization of religion, the Social Gospel had begun to submerge sin, substituting cultural neurosis in its place. Nor did the movement address directly such important social issues as racism, sexism, and segregation. Those central features of the American dilemma would be left to the likes of Martin Luther King, Jr., and the women's movement of the 1960s and 1970s.

The Settlement House Movement: Jane Addams

Perhaps the most famous social worker in American history, Jane Addams (1860–1935) grew up in Cedarville, Illinois, the daughter of a wealthy banker and mill owner. In 1881, she graduated from Rockford Seminary; for a decade thereafter, she struggled with depression and the young adult's existential concern for charting a life that would be meaningful in thought and action. Driven by her father's charitable giving and moral piety, Addams "could no more be content with mere good works" than she could "accept a religion of beauty detached from rigorous standards of personal conduct." According to cultural historian Christopher Lasch, she chose social work as a vocation because it "ideally resolved the conflict; it combined good works with the analysis not only of the conditions underlying urban poverty but also one's relation to the poor."[29]

In 1889, Addams and her friend Ellen Gates Starr bought a large brick mansion on Chicago's near West Side, calling it Hull House and establishing it as a social settlement for the surrounding immigrant neighborhood. Hull House would become a lively center for community activities, including the alleviation of housing, health, environmental, and educational problems. Initially, Addams founded Hull House on the "presumption that life could be improved by sharing the advantages of learning with people who had not had the opportunities for study associated with a secure, American middle-class way of life."[30] Later, she would permit neighborhood residents more involvement in decision-making activities. In the process of teaching and learning, Addams regularly invited a host of illustrious Progressive thinkers from the University of Chicago to assist her effort to bridge the gap between the social sciences and social living. Those academic notables who visited Hull House included John Dewey, Richard T. Ely, and George Herbert Mead.

Addams harbored a deistic faith in human potentiality, especially in the power of social relationships. Shunning the rugged individualism which had once been ingrained in the American Dream, she cherished Hull House as a vehicle for "expressing her instinctual revulsion from the prospect of a lifetime . . . of whist."[31] Historian Richard Hofstadter has interpreted such craving for activism as endemic to the Progressive era. It was a tenuous age in which many intellectuals felt that they had been displaced from status and power, thus allowing them to forge a greater identity with those Americans who were less powerful.[32]

Traditionally, consensus historians have credited Addams with influencing Progressive movements toward democracy and participation in American society.[33] Some recent revisionist historians, however, have criticized Addams's approach on the ground that she ostensibly fostered social control rather than social liberation. In his analysis of the "new radicalism" in Progressivism, Lasch concludes that Addams and other liberal reformers tended to practice a psychology of cultural adjustment. For example, he cites Addams's penchant for seeking to engender "healthful relations" among all humankind, especially immigrant populations.[34] Similarly, Paul C. Violas has focused on Addams's "new middle-class ideology" in his claim that she encouraged "acceptance of a compulsory corporate state in which the individual would be simply a part of the greater collective unity."[35]

In any case, there seems to be little doubt that Addams exemplified the service ethic in its starkest possible form in early twentieth-century America. Her very works and deeds embodied the moral belief that "only when inquiry and action were joined . . . would there be achieved a fuller, more overtly avowed, and actually lived recognition of the rootedness of social ethics in the individual conduct and ideals that defined personal experience."[36]

Responsibility and Relationship: Eleanor Roosevelt

Anna Eleanor Roosevelt (1884–1962) enjoyed a remarkable career as a humanitarian and political activist. The niece of Theodore Roosevelt, she was married to Franklin D. Roosevelt for forty years, until his death in 1945. However, she spent an eventfully rich life, filled with responsibilities and triumphs, in her own right. While her husband was governor in Albany, she taught history and literature at the Todhunter School for Girls in New York City. Following her devotion to state politics in New York and social issues in the White House, she became a delegate to the United Nations General Assembly in 1945, chairing its Social, Humanitarian, and Cultural Commission, which drafted the Universal Declaration of Human Rights.

Throughout her long and fruitful life, Roosevelt would be challenged to service by the intertwined themes of responsibility and relationship. In many ways, the wellsprings for her growth are remindful of Nel Noddings' eloquent description of ethical caring: "The source of ethical behavior is . . . in twin sentiments — one that feels directly for the other and one that feels for and with that best self."[37] Giving in relationships was the true secret of Roosevelt's success. As a young child, she considered herself a shy ugly duckling and was touched deeply by any suffering she observed around her. As an adolescent, she had "painfully high ideals and a tremendous sense of duty entirely unrelieved by any appreciation of the weaknesses of human nature."[38]

In her early years of marriage and politics, Roosevelt imbibed that sense of social responsibility in strenuous fashion:

Duty was perhaps the motivating force of my life, often excluding what might have been joy or pleasure. I looked at everything from the point of view of what I ought to do, rarely from the standpoint of what I wanted to do. There were times when I almost forgot that there was such a thing as wanting anything.[39]

Roosevelt would carry that service ethic with her, if in somewhat modulated tones, in her tenure as the most active First Lady in American history. Wherever she journeyed, from India to West Virginia, she sought to help people help themselves. She stood up to racist Senators and callow United States Representatives who used smear tactics against young people in the American Youth Congress. She boldly befriended African Americans in all walks of life, from Marian Anderson to Mary McLeod Bethune. She visited the sick and infirm at hospitals across the world, trying to negate the image of the "ugly american."[40]

For Roosevelt, the American Dream was personified in a life of service and dedication to others, not in keeping up with the Joneses or impressing others with one's power, beauty, or material wealth. She felt more at home in mud huts than on polo grounds because she felt more needed in the former. No speculative philosopher, Roosevelt could communicate instead with concrete individuals and empathize with their feelings at a deep level of understanding:

One curious thing is that I have always seen life personally; that is, my interest or sympathy or indignation is not aroused by an abstract cause but by the plight of a single person whom I have seen with my own eyes. It was the sight of a child dying of hunger that made the tragedy of hunger become of such overriding importance to me. Out of my response to an individual develops an awareness of a problem to the community, then to the country, and finally to the world.[41]

To some of her intellectual critics, Roosevelt's uncritical allegiance to New Deal liberalism made her appear somehow quaint, patrician, and well-worn. However, her sense of ethical caring called forth an ultimate ethic of virtue couched in concrete situations and concrete lives. In an era when women were still supposed to stand meekly in the background, she combined unconditional personal regard with a visceral public vision. In contemporary terms, she had exquisitely captured the guiding message that Noddings refers to in today's fractured world: "Everything depends . . . upon the will to be good, to remain in caring relation to the other."[42]

Practical and Spiritual Education: Mary McLeod Bethune

One of seventeen children born to former slaves, Mary McLeod Bethune (1875–1955) was raised near Mayesville, South Carolina, and educated at Scotia Seminary in Concord, North Carolina, and Moody Bible Institute in Chicago. After teaching at several private black schools, she left her husband to fulfill a lifelong dream in Daytona Beach, Florida, in 1904: the creation of her own school for young black females (The Daytona Literary and Industrial School for Training Negro Girls). In Bethune's mind, her mission was clear and persistent, i.e., "to work for racial uplift through the education of the race."[43] Especially for black women, such education "was also about . . . being trained to be morally and spiritually effective in the world."[44]

In all her educational practices, Bethune advocated a necessary interplay of mind, heart, and hand; and that trinitarian ideal was amply displayed in her school's many achievements. In order to raise money for her fledging institution, she followed the lead of Fisk University's highly successful Jubilee Singers in forming a youth choir which performed at wealthy white hotels in the resort areas in and around Daytona Beach. Bethune also constructed a makeshift truck garden across from the campus, from which she sold produce. As an outgrowth of her work, Daytona founded its first hospital for blacks and the first practical nursing school in the entire state. As part of her school's outreach efforts to illiterate laborers in the nearby turpentine camps, Bethune also started a normal school for future teachers. In 1923, Bethune's institution merged with Cookman Institute, a men's college in Jacksonville; seven years later the combined school was named Bethune-Cookman College in her honor.[45]

In part, Bethune was practicing a pedagogy of accommodation and social control akin to that of Horace Mann, Booker T. Washington, and Jane Addams, particularly in terms of her original emphasis on manual training and community service. Agricultural arts and personal hygiene did play significant roles in her early curriculum; however, as her institution matured, pre-professional studies would become more prominent. For both herself and her students, Bethune, like Addams, felt "the need to rise above the limitations of their time and place" in order to provide "a call from God to put their lives in service to the poor and ignorant."[46]

Politically, Bethune was active in black voter registration drives through the women's club movement. In 1935, she founded the National Council of Negro Women, remaining as its president until 1949. She also served as an officer or board member for a whole host of educational and political organizations, including the National Association for the Advancement of Colored People, the National Council of Women of the U.S.A., the National Urban League, the Commission for Interracial Cooperation, the Commission for International Cooperation, the Southern Conference Educational Fund, the Highlander Folk School, and the Planned Parenthood Federation of America.[47] In this respect, Bethune's incorporation of power roles placed her among the mythical "talented tenth" of African Americans so extolled by W. E. B. DuBois.

In 1935, President Roosevelt appointed Bethune, who was friendly with his wife Eleanor, to the position of special assistant on racial issues; four years later, she was named the director of black affairs for the National Youth Administration. At the federal level, Bethune "presented the public image of a woman who was so affable that even southern whites could hardly be offended by her approach, but who, at the same time, clearly expressed a vision of racial equality."[48]

Despite the manifest reality of Bethune's myriad service accomplishments, biographer Rackham Holt has attributed her considerable success, in part, to her yearning for power over others: "Mary realized the need for and the importance of power in a spiritual sense. She, too, wanted to have power over men and women."[49] Whatever the reason, Bethune also succeeded through her gentle, yet insistent, use of both a pragmatic and inspirational philosophy: "Deeds of help and hope and respect for others will produce, without panic, or repression, or injustice to any man, the loyalty we seek."[50]

The March Toward Freedom: Martin Luther King, Jr.

In contemporary times, no one person represented the essence of the service ethic as dynamically and forcefully as Martin Luther King, Jr. (1929–1968), whose eloquent crusade of nonviolent civil disobedience spurred the American civil rights movement from 1955 to 1968. Heavily influenced by folk and slave preaching, which he learned from his father and grandfather, King grew up in comfortable middle-class surroundings in Atlanta, Georgia. He attended Morehouse College, Crozer Theological Seminary in Philadelphia, and Boston University's School of Divinity, where he earned his doctorate.

An eager student of the Social Gospel, especially of Rauschenbusch, King wrote his dissertation on Paul Tillich and Henry Nelson Wieman, liberal post-Social Gospel Protestant theologians. The Baptist King criticized the rarefied abstractions in their religious outlook; he preferred the more concrete Personalism taught by his mentors, Edgar Brightman and L. Harold DeWolf. However, King himself was always much more an ardent preacher than a systematic philosopher. Accordingly, he was perhaps even more influenced by the popular sermons and homiletics of the likes of Harry Emerson Fosdick and Robert McCracken.[51]

King's reading of Thoreau and Gandhi also led him to invoke the practices of nonviolent protest early on in his public career. Tying civil disobedience to Christian morality, his passionate activism was seen in the "sit-ins" of 1960, the Freedom Ride of 1961, and the decisive demonstrations organized by his Southern Christian Leadership Conference. From Albany, Georgia, to Birmingham and Selma in Alabama, Southern blacks eventually brought their struggle for freedom to the North, culminating in inner-city Chicago by 1966. Such black protest led to the enactment of the Civil Rights Act of 1964 and the Voting Rights Act of 1965.

In oxymoronic terms, King viewed himself as a humble preacher, yet one who cast himself in the image of Moses:

> King saw clearly the meaning of the gospel with its social implications and sought to instill its spirit in the hearts and minds of black and white in this land. He was a man endowed with the charisma of God, he was a prophet in our own time. . . . Like the prophets of old, he had a dream, a dream grounded not in the hope of white America but in God.[52]

If many Americans, in their quest for competitive achievement and material wealth, had tainted the ethical core of that dream, King had placed himself in the redemptive role of a voice of personal deliverance and social salvation.

Seeking to transform the conscience of all Americans, King was sometimes viewed as too moderate by more militant blacks and as too radical by mainstream white society. Nevertheless, his gifts as a conciliator won him easy access to the Kennedy and Johnson administrations.

By 1967, his courageous opposition to the Vietnam war would alienate him from most elements of the latter, and from some factions within the civil rights movement itself. Shortly before his assassination in Memphis, where he was leading a demonstration as part of a sanitation workers' strike, King had come to the realization that most Americans had less concern for social justice and equality than he had imagined earlier. Still, his monumental efforts had delivered him and his followers close to the pinnacle of the mountain. Indeed, he died knowing "that the practical meaning of Christian faith is that freedom lies in action, love in giving and living in laying down one's life for others, in the actual place and time in which the person finds oneself."[53]

Postscript

More detailed critiques of the service ethic appear in subsequent chapters of this text. However, it is appropriate at this point of summary analysis to reflect briefly upon two main criticisms of the ethic: (1) that a paternalistic emphasis seems to pervade the words and deeds of its proponents; and (2) that the notion of power over others appears to be a motivating force in some of their thoughts and actions.

A paternalistic act is one in which "the protection or promotion of a subject's welfare is the primary reason for attempted or successful coercive interference with an action or state of a person."[54] The objectives of paternalism are to prevent harm and/or promote personal or social welfare. The principal ethical concern in paternalism is to act in such a way that the persons one is serving are still respected. Have the exponents of the service ethic dealt with in this chapter acted accordingly?

The chief reason why paternalism offends is that it interferes with the individual's freedom; and since democratic societies recognize freedom as a basic right, it should not be restricted without just cause. But if it can be shown that some forms of paternalism lead to necessary states of well-being, then an interference with *negative freedom* (freedom from restraint) may be justified if the probability of *positive freedom* (ability to perform an act) will subsequently be expanded. There is a presumption in favor of negative freedom insofar as interference with it should not be arbitrary and capricious, but is expected to be based on justifiable grounds. However, John Stuart Mill and other modern day observers have recognized that freedom is not an absolute right, that there are some situations where individual freedom must be restricted: Whenever it conflicts with the rights of others, and in order to promote equality (as in cases of enforced busing, desegregation, and the like).[55] Have the advocates of the service ethic met that criterion in warranted fashion?

As for the question of whether they seek power over others, that need not be explained in terms of any Nietzschian view of "will to power" in a "superman" sense. Instead, one might consider Alfred Adler's notion of "social interest," which encompasses cooperation, communal feeling, interpersonality, and empathy for others. For Adler,

> the degree of a person's social interest determines his ability and willingness to function socially; the lack of social interest is at the root of deficiencies, failures, and pathology. Thus, Adler found that social interest was a gauge for defining normalcy, both for the individual and for the group.[56]

More complete analysis of such theoretical constructs and alternatives will be explored in the perspectives chapters that follow.

6

Education,
the Success Ethic,
and the American Dream

Formal education had an ambivalent role in the success ethic. Though the McGuffey Readers generally exemplified the character ethic, the character and personality ethics were skeptical of higher education and the more classical features of secondary education; instead, a "practical education" was urged. Yet the ideology of public education extolled the American Dream and advocated promoting talent and fostering social mobility.

The mind power ethic, though it carried on the success tradition and its attitude toward opportunity, ignored the value of self-education. In contrast, the personality ethic advocated the use of self-help manuals, but held that higher education was unnecessary for advancement; in fact, a classical or liberal arts education may be more harm than good. One could always educate oneself through public libraries and correspondence courses, since formal education usually ignored the most important part of one's education: human relations. Dale Carnegie downplayed formal education and technical ability alone; rather, he sought technical knowledge combined with the ability "to arouse enthusiasm among men."[1]

The character ethic expressed serious doubts about the connection between formal education and success, and was skeptical of the efficacy of classical studies, especially in higher education. Andrew Carnegie cited abundant opportunities for young men with certain desirable character traits and skills. They have a head start on college graduates who are "learning a little about the barbarous and petty squabbles of a far-distant past, or trying to master languages which are dead. . . ."[2]

In this chapter, our interest is not to recount any particular segment of the history of American education but to search for the success ethic and the American Dream in various aspects of formal and informal education. Also, our purpose is to describe the types of educational activities and their significance that various success ethic proponents advocated.

The Utility Function

Supporters of the new sciences and proponents of the classics struggled constantly to dominate American higher education in the late nineteenth century. The classicists aligned themselves with aristocratic tradition and resisted any attempts to dilute their required classical curriculum. Sporadic breaks in the strict classical pattern could be found in various parts of the country during the early nineteenth century as the new sciences gained footholds of popularity among the general public. Their popularity continued to grow, and by 1850 the scientific school was a fact of college life. By 1870, twenty-five colleges had opened scientific departments.

Classicists not only resisted the enlarged curriculum that the sciences were forging but also opposed the introduction of romance languages and other new disciplines in the humanities. The older classical notions began losing their position of dominance. The popularity of Latin slipped even further when the decision was made to model graduate education after the research model found in the German universities.

The utility ideal, although present to a minor degree before the Civil War, emerged during the land grant movement in the 1860s as sufficiently strong to challenge competing ideals. The Morrill Act of 1862 made available grants of land to each state for teaching agriculture and mechanical arts. Utility-minded educators became part of the system rather than, as formerly, having to make their views heard from outside. They were found largely in the applied sciences and social sciences as well as in the administration.

The spirit of vocationalism, coupled with the incorporation of new professional programs within the university structure, assured the ideal of utility a secure and significant place in higher education. Besides the land-grant movement, a great deal of technical knowledge was needed in a rapidly developing industrial economy. Industrialism also meant a greater division of labor and a need for specialized abilities. Vocational preparation, which was once handled largely through apprenticeship programs, became incorporated into higher education. The older colleges had prepared men for the professions of law, medicine, and theology; teacher preparation was relegated to the normal schools and teacher institutes. But with the installation of many new vocational curricula, such as home economics, business administration, engineering, and agriculture, a blurring of the former sharp distinctions between vocations and professions occurred. The label "profession" had formerly been reserved for those occupations requiring preparation within higher education.[3] The scope and responsibility of the university was greatly broadened as the apprenticeship route was supplanted for a number of careers. By admitting new vocations, a leveling tendency occurred among occupations requiring advanced study, while new vocations continued to rise in status. Nevertheless, though all careers were equal in principle according to Jacksonian rhetoric, the older professions still retained some of their distinctive status.

Besides preparing specialists and disseminating technical knowledge to industry, the utility ideal expressed itself in divergent ways. Some educators attacked the monkishness of scholars and the artificial and pedantic problems on which they allegedly focused. The educator, they argued, should maintain close contact with the life of the larger society, which was more "real" than the life of the university. They called for practical men, not pedants, men who could grapple with the problems of life. The university's functions would be to prepare practical men with needed technical competence, and to disseminate technical knowledge to the home, farm, and factory. Some advocated that the university assume whatever functions were requested by the citizenry. Politicians and interest groups frequently pressured educators to lower the notion of "practicality," so that preparation for a motley array of new trades would become part of the university. Success ethic proponents were generally late in recognizing these changes in higher education; in time, proponents reluctantly accepted the need for utility programs whenever these practical skills could not be obtained in the marketplace or through self-education.

Educators, administrators, and the public, however, usually failed to agree upon the meaning of utility and practicality in terms of policies and practices. Some wanted the universities to instill various civic virtues or develop leaders who would clean up politics. Others wanted scholars to develop knowledge to promote social reform. Some administrators interpreted utility in terms of crass materialism, while others conceived it in ethical terms as a crusade for public service. Rather than turning to the new American philosophy of pragmatism, educators usually thought in terms of "social efficiency." This notion was able to mesh the scientific with the practical in order to organize the university for community service.[4] Yet the ideal functioned in the hands of administrators more as a slogan and rallying cry for instituting new programs and adopting new policies than as an explanatory theory with the power to order a whole range of phenomena.

Informal Education and Success

Sources of informal education related to the success ethic include public libraries, museums, apprenticeships, the lyceum, and Chautauqua. Libraries in the nineteenth century were sometimes formed by subscribers joining together for their own use and others as well. The library was a place where young apprentices and mechanics could improve themselves vocationally and morally. The most prevalent libraries in the 1840s and 1850s were the district school libraries and the Sunday school libraries. It was estimated in 1859 that there were 50,890 libraries in the United States, holding 12,720,686 volumes, with 20,000 Sunday school libraries containing six million volumes, and 18,000 district school libraries holding two million volumes.[5] Although the district school library was seen as a public library, increasingly the term "public" was applied to those libraries that were publicly supported and controlled and open to all citizens on an equal basis. The principal trend was to popularize holdings that would be sensitive to patrons' interests; yet there were also efforts to develop research libraries that would compare favorably with the best in Europe.

From Franklin to Truman, public libraries were important in self-development. Andrew Carnegie's benefaction of more than $65 million to communities for library buildings strengthened local interest by making grants contingent upon public support. Carnegie chose libraries as a philanthropic domain for a number of reasons: he had profited as a boy by studying in a mechanics' library in Pittsburgh; the gift of a library building would require continued community participation through library maintenance; and libraries could assist those who were prepared to help themselves.[6]

Still, not all local citizens frequented the public library as did a Carnegie or a Truman. To make materials more accessible, branch libraries were established in the late nineteenth century, and traveling libraries or "bookmobiles" began to take books to readers in rural or outlying areas in the early twentieth century. More recent services include interlibrary loans, lecture series, public book reviews, juvenile collections, story hours for children, film lending, reading clubs, and microcomputers for patron use.

Museums were another source of informal education. One of the earliest museums began in 1773, when the Library Society of Charleston decided to collect materials for a full natural history of South Carolina. Subsequently, a number of private museums were established. In 1841, showman P. T. Barnum acquired both the American Museum that was languishing and Peale's Museum, which was in receivership. Barnum continued the permanent collection of machines, specimens, and paintings, but added oddities and the exotic: educated dogs, industrious fleas, jugglers, ventriloquists, rope dancers, and the like. Barnum staged events, stirred controversies, and planted news stories to galvanize people to visit his array of curiosities.

The wealthy became patrons of museums in the latter half of the nineteenth century, and museums such as the Boston Society of Natural History Museum and the American Museum of Natural History were founded for educational purposes. Many museums of the day, however, conceived their role primarily as one of preservation and custodianship rather than education. Education has only recently assumed an equal position with traditional museum functions. Public Law 93–380 stipulated that museums be resources for schools; their cost is frequently borne by educational institutions benefiting from these educative programs. Museum education consists of the study of objects from the past, the use of museum objects for enriching contemporary life, and the transmission of cultural values for the future.

The variety and types of museums in the United States has continued to grow, and can be classified into thirteen types: museums; children's and junior museums; college and university museums; company museums; exhibit areas in communities; general knowledge museums; history museums; libraries with collections other than books; national and state agencies, councils and commissions with their own museums; nature centers and zoos; park museums and visitor centers; science museums; and specialized subject museums.[7]

Two influential nineteenth-century developments that shaped informal education and disseminated knowledge were the lyceum and the Chautauqua movement. The first local unit of the lyceum was established in 1826 by James Holbrook, who formulated a plan that called for organizing local associations for mutual instruction in science and utilitarian subjects. He believed that these associations would multiply quickly and enlighten the American people. Devoting much time to the project, he promoted his ideas through lectures, and magazine and newspaper articles.

Early lyceums collected a fee of one dollar for the purchase of books and scientific equipment, and advertised themselves as "associations for mutual instruction and information in arts and sciences." Stimulated by Holbrook's scientific interests, members collected plants and geological specimens, and in later years, discussion topics included many scientific areas. Eager members invited prominent figures to lecture, and Horace Mann, Daniel Webster, and Ralph Waldo Emerson were among those who accepted the opportunity to espouse their ideas or crusade for a cause. Emerson was probably the most popular lyceum speaker of all, and could be heard by local citizens for a fifty-dollar fee in lectures in which he presented material later published in his *Essays*.

The lyceum movement enthusiastically promoted free public schools. Lyceum groups were concerned with the dissemination of information on the arts, sciences, history, and public affairs. They spread in many states and became a powerful force in adult education, social reform, and political discussion. The movement waned after the Civil War, but much of its work was assumed by the Chautauqua movement.

The Chautauqua movement, which was somewhat similar to the lyceum movement, derived its name from the institution in Chautauqua, New York, where, in 1873, John Yeyl Vincent and Lewis Miller proposed that secular as well as religious instruction be included in the summer Sunday-school institute. The institute was established in 1874, and developed an eight-week summer program in the arts, sciences, and humanities. Thousands attended each year, home study groups were offered for those unable to attend, and lecturers were sent out to supplement the material from the publishing house. The broadened program included correspondence courses, concerts, special lectures, and various types of entertainment. The traveling Chautauqua took these programs into small communities, especially in the Midwest. Other communities were inspired to form local Chautauquas, and as many as three hundred were organized, but none was as successful as the original. In 1878, reading circles were inaugurated featuring a four-year guided reading program that attracted 8,000 members and expanded greatly to almost 200,000 in the early 1890s and over 300,000 by 1918. The Chautauqua's atmosphere, which frequently used tents for meetings, was a mixture of a revival meeting and a county fair. The movement was organized commercially in 1912 by providing lecturers and entertainers on a contract basis; it was highly successful, and persisted until 1924. Following World War I, the popularity of the Chautauqua movement declined, which was partly attributable to the spread of the radio in America.[8]

Another type of informal education is apprenticeship, which is a system of learning a craft or trade from one engaged in it and paying for the instruction by a number of years of work. In early colonial times, what the young needed to know about farming was transmitted within the family. It was common for children as young as eight to carry heavy farming burdens, and some were apprenticed to other households or shops. The model for apprenticeship was taken from England and modified in light of colonial needs. Apprenticeships could be as long as seven years, but most were shorter. Some masters would share their practical knowledge, others believed that hard work itself was the best teacher, and still others sent the apprentice to school or relied on apprentices' libraries. Girls were occasionally apprenticed to learn bonnet-making or to become more skilled spinners or weavers. The values and attitudes expected in apprenticeship and later in a growing industrial society were found in Poor Richard — hard work, inner discipline, punctuality, orderliness, sobriety, frugality, and prudence. These were reinforced by detailed factory rules that rewarded observance and punished infractions with fines and dismissals. But some reformers saw industrial discipline as a rationalization for exploitation; consequently, they sought to effect alternative working arrangements through the intervention of unions or benevolent societies.

Professions as well as trades adopted apprenticeship programs. An aspiring youngster around the age of eighteen who had completed several years of schooling could apprentice himself to a practicing physician (called a "preceptor") by pledging to perform all reasonable requests and pay a fee of about $100 per year; in turn, the preceptor would provide instruction and whatever books and equipment were needed. The three-year term consisted of two phases: the first involved the study of medical and scientific textbooks, dissections, and duties in the preceptor's office; the second phase consisted of accompanying the physician on calls and assisting in medical procedures.

Physicians, however, sought to regulate entry into practice through medical schools, and by the 1840s a larger number of physicians were trained through three-year medical school programs than through apprenticeship. By 1876, there were seventy-eight medical schools, but only forty-six law schools. In contrast to medical education, a majority of those who aspired at that time to the bar still chose the apprentice-ship route.[9]

Apprenticeship training altered dramatically with the mechaniza-tion of industry. In the textile industry, no apprenticeship was needed after the 1840s, because a worker could learn to operate the machines in a matter of days. Apprenticeships in shoemaking had virtually disap-peared by the 1850s because of mechanization. After 1870, traditional craft skills were no longer needed in watchmaking, glassmaking, distilling, cigarette making, flour milling, and automobile manufacturing as a result of coal and electric power, technological innovation, and the rationalization of management and production.

Wisconsin in the early 1900s established a system of apprentice-ship training that proved sufficiently successful that Congress passed the National Apprenticeship Act of 1937, which formulated and promoted standards of apprenticeship training. Similar legislation has been enacted by most of the states.

A major reason for the vocational movement was the position of the United States in world markets in relation to such industrialized countries as Germany. The National Association of Manufacturers (NAM), in a 1905 report, claimed that technical and trade education was a national necessity, and that the nation should train its youth in the arts of production and distribution.

The rise of the vocational education movement nationally was also a feature of the Populist/Progressive era. Workers were concerned about making education more useful to their jobs, and business and industry desired better trained workers.

Differing views arose about vocational education. The NAM advo-cated a type of trade school found in Germany, whereas the American Federation of Labor (AFL) held that public schools should develop trade-skill training. The AFL feared that students might be segregated in second-class schools, as in Europe.

In 1918, the Cardinal Principles endorsed vocational education, a differentiated curriculum, and a comprehensive high school rather than a separate trade school. John Dewey opposed separating vocational education from citizenship preparation, because he considered it fatal to democracy to permit the formation of fixed classes and saw the trade school approach contributing to it. Although separate trade schools were not generally established, Dewey's ideas of integrating practical and theoretical studies were not usually followed. Instead, differenti-ated curricula, testing, ability grouping, and vocational guidance spread. The public rejected both Dewey's position and the social efficiency approach by working out a compromise within the comprehensive high school.[10]

Educational historians disagree on the social significance of this early movement. Ellwood Cubberly views these changes in schools as a way to solve social and economic problems.[11] In contrast, Merle Curti argues that manual training and vocational education were attempts to control and counteract radicalism among American workers. The values of interdependence and cooperation that were taught sought to deny the inevitable conflict between capital and labor. Curti views militant teachers as allied with labor while school administrators were allied with business.[12]

The Smith-Hughes Act of 1917 provided funds that were to be matched by the states to pay salaries of teachers of agriculture, home economics, and industrial education, and to help states prepare teachers of these subjects. The Act reinforced a dual system of education by separating vocational education from academic training and providing funds for that purpose. It represented a victory for social efficiency reformers who believed that there were well-defined social classes, that it was democratic to make industrial education available to the lower classes, and that students should be sorted out into appropriate schools according to their probable destiny.

The George-Deen Act, in 1936, supplemented funds provided by the Smith-Hughes Act and liberalized regulations. Much industrial training slowed during the Depression because there were few, if any, jobs for skilled workers.

Under an amendment in 1959 to the George-Borden Act, technical education was introduced in high schools, and nursing education was established on a cooperative basis between hospitals, schools, and junior colleges. Occupational training for unemployed persons was provided under the Area Redevelopment Act in 1961, and in the same year, the Manpower Training and Development Act initiated programs to train unemployed youth and adults and to retrain adults. The Vocational Education Act of 1963 provided grants to states to maintain, improve, and develop vocational-technical education programs. The funds were earmarked for occupations in demand. Funds were also provided for constructing area schools for vocational education, as well as provisions for vocational office education, occupational training for potential school dropouts, and work-study programs. Amendments to the Act enlarged the scope of programs under the George-Barden and Smith-Hughes acts that focused on employment in vocational agriculture, home economics, and industrial education.

McGuffey and Character Education

A case can be made that the many virtues extolled in the character ethic were largely embodied in the McGuffey Readers and the later character education movement. William Holmes McGuffey (1800–1873) had little formal schooling but worked diligently to educate himself. He began teaching in a rural school at age thirteen and occasionally supplemented his independent studies by spending periods under private tutors. After graduating in 1826 from Washington College (now Washington and Jefferson), he took a teaching position at Miami University, in Ohio. Three years later, he was ordained in the Presbyterian Church and, although he did not have his own congregation, he was a popular guest preacher. He became president of Cincinnati College in 1836, and then president of Ohio University in 1839. He was instrumental in founding the common school system in Ohio.

McGuffey collected and studied a large number of school readers for both private and common schools. His series was developed for the common schools only, and comprised a primer, a speller to replace *Webster's Elementary Speller,* and four readers. The first reader was published in 1836, and each reader, during the first decade after publication, was revised every three or four years; major revisions were made in 1853, 1857, and 1879. After that, slight changes were made in 1901 and 1920, and the material was recopyrighted.[13]

McGuffey provided his own stories and used selections from English and American literature. They were not only the most popular readers of their day, but retained their popularity throughout the rest of the century. It is estimated that one-half of the children attending school during this period used them, and the eventual sales reached an estimated 122 million.

McGuffey laced his readers with his strong Calvinistic Presbyterian theology. Judging from the stories in the *Eclectic Second Reader,* the cosmology presented is one constituted by a God in the sky, holy angels, heaven, and an afterlife in heaven. The attributes of God revealed in the stories are His goodness, kindness, mercifulness, benevolence, omnipresence ("watches over us"; "never sleeps"), creator of all things, punishes the wicked, and gave His son, the Lord Jesus, who died for us on the cross. The desirable human attributes are to be merciful, meek, serve Good, praise and bless God, and obey His commands. A concern about God's nature and His relationship with persons and the world permeates these readers. Neither the world nor our lives can be understood without God.

The McGuffey readers are highly moralistic, and insist upon such virtues as following the Golden Rule, truthfulness, industriousness, kindness, friendship, love of learning, humility, honesty, moral courage, orderliness, keeping promises, kindness to the poor, kindness to animals, self-control, and others. Traits that should be avoided are idleness, slothfulness, selfishness, thievery, gluttony, envy, drunkenness, and profanity.

By the 1879 edition, none of the emphasis on piety and salvation remain, the numerous stories from the Bible are deleted (except for the Sermon on the Mount and the Protestant version of the Lord's Prayer), and in their stead are secular character traits of thrift, sobriety, punctuality, submission to authority, and the like.[14] But some observers consider the theological aspects of the early readers as part of middle-class culture. Richard Mosier holds that the "great achievement of the McGuffey readers is the complete integration of Christian and middle-class ideals. . . ."[15]

Let us take some examples of industriousness, which is extolled in the *Eclectic Second Reader*[16] and is an indispensable trait of character-ethic proponents. Industriousness is praised again and again in the reader. The good boy whose parents are poor arises early in the morning and does as much as possible to help his parents. He walks quickly to school and applies himself to his lessons and, when coming home, avoids boys who fight, steal, swear, and lie. At home, he takes care of the little children, weeds the garden, and performs various other tasks. Nor is he envious of boys and girls who have fine clothes and pretty horses. Rather, he insists that "I am glad that I can work. I hope that I shall soon be able to earn all my clothes, and my food too."[17]

And what happens to the boy who is idle and truant? "The fear of punishment is in his breast, for he has neglected every duty." His parents are filled with grief and shame.[18] Another story tells about Mary, who was a great favorite of her father, and who showed little interest when her father would read to her; she claimed that she would never read unless she was forced. But she was distressed to see her father displeased with her and therefore the next day began to read all the books that her father had given her.[19] A more serious case was George Jones, who focused on momentary pleasure, rarely prepared his lessons, but somehow "passed a very poor examination" and was admitted to college. He found that he was incapable of responding when asked to recite, and he could not keep up with his studies. He was suspended from college and became "a poor wanderer, without money and without friends. Such are the wages of idleness."[20]

Other stories reinforced the need to eschew a host of additional undesirable traits (previously mentioned). Traits advocated in the readers and extolled in the character ethic, in addition to industriousness, are truthfulness, humility, neatness, orderliness, promise-keeping, punctuality, moral courage, and stewardship. As Mosier observed: "All the virtues of success were taught in the McGuffey Readers . . . and the middle-class virtues stressed in the McGuffey readers were those stressed by many authors of success literature."[21]

Some years after sales of the McGuffey readers waned, the character ethic movement began. A strong interest in moral education, abetted by well-funded private and semi-public agencies, arose after World War I and persisted for two decades. By the early 1920s, moral education had become mandatory in most states, and few systems were without such programs. *Character education* became the approved term to designate the movement by the late 1920s. W. W. Charters argued that a trait analysis was necessary to avoid vague and abstract approaches to the problem. He defined a trait in the field of character as a type of reaction. "The trait of courage," he insisted, "indicates the fact that the individual who possesses the quality is likely to react according to type in a variety of situations." An ideal is "a trait which has become the object of desire."[22]

Not all theories of character were based on the trait theory; other theories of the day focused on habits, patterns, factors, or the self.[23] Yet the character trait theory was dominant, and many programs were based upon it. As examples, the Hutchins Code, which appeared in 1916, won a $5,000 prize through the Character Education Institution, and the Code was influential in character education programs developed later. The Code is composed of eleven "laws," such as the Law of Self-Control, the Law of Good Health, the Law of Kindness, the Law of Duty, and the Law of Loyalty. By 1924, the Boston public schools were utilizing the Hutchins Code (plus an additional law — the Law of Obedience to Duly Constituted Authority). Fifteen minutes daily were used for presenting and discussing each trait; two weeks were devoted to each trait. That same year, the Knighthood of Youth Plan was introduced into twelve schools in New York City. The plan consisted of a study of knights, both ancient and modern, and their desirable character traits. Other similar approaches were the Pittsburgh Plan, which emphasized one major trait, such as loyalty, ambition, or perseverance, for each of the school years. Each of the twelve traits was presented in a separate booklet that utilized stories, illustrations, and questions.[24] In the Utah Plan, the objectives for grades 4 to 6 were to develop honesty, obedience, gratitude, health, thrift, courtesy, consideration of rights of others, courage and fair play, self-control, clean living, good workmanship, and others. These traits were to be developed through practice, slogans, stories, and discussions of consequences. In mathematics, the objectives were to develop self-reliance, resourcefulness, persistency, honesty, truthfulness, and integrity.[25] Thus, it can be seen that, whether intentionally or not, the character education movement supported the development of the character ethic in American society.

But the trait theory, upon which much of the movement rested, came under criticism. A trait is a name given to a combination of specific behaviors that may vary considerably, especially between children and adults. Moreover, traits deal with symptoms, and obscure the real causes of desirable and undesirable behavior. Third, an emphasis on traits focuses on the self rather than on acts and consequences. Furthermore, moderation in traits is not part of the theory. Fifth, some traits may conflict, but the theory does not explain how to adjudicate the conflict. Finally, the trait approach tends toward a conformist society, for great ethical leaders have been iconoclasts.[26]

The Character Education Inquiry in the late 1920s, a study that set a precedent for further inquiry in this area, administered 170,000 tests to over 8,000 public school pupils between the ages of eleven and sixteen.[27] The tests confronted children with the opportunity to cheat, or with a conflict between their own good and that of others. They were, for example, given an opportunity to take money while they thought they were being unobserved; to violate the time limit on a speed test; to cheat while grading their own papers; and to place dots in small circles while blindfolded without cheating.

About seven percent did not cheat at all, and about four percent cheated at every opportunity; the vast majority acted honestly in some situations and dishonestly in others, and there was a consistency in these patterns when the tests were repeated. This led the investigators to the rather startling conclusion that behavior is highly specific, depending upon the specific case; there is no such thing as an honest and dishonest child, but only honest and dishonest acts. Thus, little evidence was found of unified character traits or generality in moral behavior. The concept of character based upon specific acts fits the stimulus-response theories of learning. Some other investigators have refined the data and corroborated the findings. Gross found that children who cheat in class in one type of situation do not do so in another.[28] And Stendler found that children who regard cheating as wrong in one situation are able to rationalize it in another.[29] But other evidence indicates that these findings apply more to children than adults, because of the lengthy period needed to socialize children. A study that employed the same methodology, but with adults rather than children in situations that offered the opportunity for apparently unseen cheating, found consistency in both honest and dishonest subjects, and a general trait of honesty was evidenced.[30]

Character education still exists today; its apostles have multiplied since the 1980s, and are represented by William Bennett, U. S. Commissioner of Education in the Reagan administration, and Edward A. Wynne. Bennett would have educators not only state the difference between right and wrong but exemplify right conduct. He recommends a literary approach to character education. For instance, if we want students to respect the law, they should understand why Socrates submitted to the decree of Athens. And if we want to teach honesty, we could teach about Joan of Arc, Horatius at the bridge, and the like.

Wynne would teach common moral values as belonging to a great tradition, a tradition concerned with good habits of conduct rather than moral concepts and moral rationales. The tradition focuses on such issues as telling the truth in the face of temptation, being polite, and obeying legitimate authority. He recommends using McGuffey Readers, and approves of indoctrination. Both Bennett and Wynne strongly object to such other developments in values education as values clarification, Piaget's structuralism, Kohberg's cognitive moral development theory, and Dewey's pragmatic problem-solving approach. Thus, contemporary character education differs from other forms of values education on psychological, philosophical, ethical, and methodological grounds. The appeal of character education is greater today than in the 1970s, especially among the middle class, in a society of escalating violence, dysfunctional families, and heightened social disorganization, because it promises to inculcate revered character traits in the young.

Educational and Career Opportunities for Women

In contrast to men, success for women was usually defined as having a sound marriage, being a capable mother, and maintaining a good home. Whatever career opportunities were available outside the home — and frequently they were opposed by tradition and prejudice — were found primarily in the realm of the service ethic.

The chief duty of the wife in colonial America was obedience to her husband. She was regarded as inferior to her husband in virtually every respect; moreover, she was viewed with an undercurrent of fear and suspicion because she was not considered entirely trustworthy.

Although the Puritans proclaimed female mental inferiority and insisted on the wife's duty to obey her husband (except when he violated divine law), parents required both girls and boys to learn to read the Bible to seek salvation. Parents made provisions in their wills for teaching their daughters to read and sew and their sons to read and write.

Girls could not attend the Latin grammar schools but were admitted to private dame schools for child-tending and instruction. Dame schools, which were forerunners of public primary schools, taught girls spelling, the alphabet, simple religious material, and knitting and sewing. This program was designed to prepare girls for their religious and family duties. More affluent families could provide their daughters opportunities to attend private female seminaries.

By the late eighteenth century, coeducation had become common for young children but not older children. Opposition to girls' grammar schools was strong, as opponents asserted that female minds were inferior, and that such education would undermine the social order.[31]

The Revolution, followed by rapid changes in nineteenth-century life, offered new possibilities for women. First, the status of the wife changed. A rapidly expanding industrial nation offered many opportunities and considerable risks in a world of Darwinian struggle for survival of the heartiest. The breadwinner faced toil and economic dangers, and increasingly saw the family as a refuge in a heartless world. The erstwhile reciprocity between family and community during colonial times changed to an adversarial relation in the nineteenth century. Despite the sense of openness and egalitarianism of the outside world, and the opportunity to become a "self-made man," the threat to traditional values was real. Thus, society at large and the home became two different spheres with divergent values. Home and wife were highly sentimentalized: home as a sanctuary for protection and renewal; the wife as a preserver of the cherished home and family, a higher moral being than her husband, who had to make many compromises in the marketplace. She was expected to nurture the children and prepare them for the world, to create a cheerful and tranquil home, and to engage in selfless service.[32] A wife usually was not permitted to work outside the home, but was expected instead to be obedient to her husband, a comforter who administered to family needs and morally uplifted the household. Although this ideal increasingly came under attack by feminist groups by the turn of the century, women entered a transitional period of struggle before new role models were finally forged.

Reformers sought to refute the stereotypes about the mental inferiority of women, and also asserted that females were persons with the same rights as males. In order to assume their appropriate roles, women required a broader education than the traditional one. Judith Sargent Murray, a staunch advocate for women's equality, insisted that women did not lack mental ability but only the opportunity to acquire knowledge. Women's education, she argued, should not merely enhance chances for marriage but provide a decent income for those who remained single or were widowed. Benjamin Rush, a signer of the Declaration of Independence, wanted to "Let the ladies of a country be educated properly and they will not only [indirectly] make and administer laws, but form its manners and character." He wanted women to study practical subjects so they could "be the stewards and guardians of their husband's property." To this end, they should study history, travels, poetry, moral essays, and the Christian religion.[33]

Emma Willard, Catherine Beecher, and Mary Lyon created female seminaries that stressed intellectual achievement and moral character. They expected women to fulfill their feminine destiny but not move outside their own sphere. Nor did they question the Christian ideal of womanhood, summarized in the precepts of piety, purity, obedience, and domesticity. Though they defended women's rights to education, they avoided the slavery issue and often opposed women's suffrage.

The number of female teachers grew substantially, until by the late nineteenth century, women predominated at the elementary level. Yet women were only slowly accepted as teachers, because in the early nineteenth century women's ability to teach, especially their ability to control older boys, was questioned. Some women used teaching as a steppingstone to other employment or activity. Susan B. Anthony and Abby Kelley (Foster) became lecturers for abolition and temperance, and Antoinette Brown used her salary to pay for an education at Oberlin that led to her ordination in 1853 as a Congregationalist minister.[34]

Many women were expected to return home after college and assume household responsibilities until marriage. Middle- and upper-class families disapproved of work outside the home and, in some cases, objected to unpaid volunteer work. Even to take a job was usually temporary until marriage. Young women had to make a choice between marriage and career, and those that chose the latter had various motives: economic independence, uneasiness with marriage, lack of desirable suitors, desire for nontraditional life patterns, aspirations for professional leadership or social reform. Although a majority of college women married, they married later than less educated women and had fewer children.

Women encountered much resistance in such professions as the ministry, medicine, law, and college teaching. Women rarely became members of the ordained clergy, and only in a few denominations — Congregationalist, Methodist, and Quaker — did some become ministers.

Pursuing a law career was a possible means to improve a woman's status in society; yet women discovered that after graduation from law school, passing the bar exams and establishing a practice did not always follow. Even by 1920, women constituted only 1.4 percent of lawyers in the U.S., though law schools began to open to women in the late nineteenth century. Most women at this time who practiced law joined their fathers' or husbands' law firms.

Medicine perpetuated the image of the male physician. The number of women doctors, however, increased from fewer than 2,500 in 1880 to about nine thousand in 1910. But as medicine advanced scientifically, and as women patients were no longer the special clientele of female physicians (as they had been in the nineteenth century), opposition from the male establishment intensified.

While women's colleges usually promoted liberal arts study, attempts by women to continue studies for the Ph.D. degree met widespread opposition. By the end of the nineteenth century, 228 women and 2,372 men had received doctorates. Faculty were unaccustomed to consider women potential scholars. Some women, in meeting resistance, pursued graduate education in European universities. But even when accepted into American graduate programs, female students found that professors did not usually assume that women had the same professional goals as men. The expectation that women would not pursue an academic career because of marriage restricted opportunities.[35] But opportunities for women have expanded as a result of their participation in World Wars I and II, passage of the Nineteenth Amendment, the women's movement, and other influences, so that, even though a number of obstacles remain, career opportunities for women are greater today than ever before.

The Media and Images of Success

What role do the media, especially film, have in creating popular images of success? Different theories of mass communication seek to explain how media affect society and shape our lives. Harold Innis suggested that preliterate cultures have to be small because people must organize their culture within the short range of the voice. The introduction of writing would change this arrangement, because the culture could then disperse and remain in contact through writing. Reason replaces traditional sacred authority in a culture that includes writing, because people can examine records and develop different standards of judgment. As writing materials became more durable, cheaper, and more portable, a literate culture was able to spread more rapidly. Papyrus, a considerable improvement over clay tablets, was replaced by parchment and then by paper, which not only allowed written documents to become more commonplace but also provided one of the conditions for the invention of printing.[36] Innis claims that the nature of the prevailing media technology in a given society greatly influences how its members think and behave. Books and other print media, for example, are said to promote cause-effect thinking where print media dominate, because the technology forces a linear form of presentation either across, or up and down a page.[37]

Marshall McLuhan has provided a contemporary reformulation of Innis's thesis. McLuhan depicted the media as extensions of the human body. The media enable people to extend the power of their senses, just as the movies permit the visualization of things distant in both time and space. Preliterate cultures focused on hearing, since it was the only way that they related to others' thoughts. But in literate cultures, people depend more on the eyes; it is as though literacy enlarges the eyes and shrinks the ears. A nonliterate person's senses are kept busy collecting impressions from various sources in no particular order, but a literate person experiences culture through words arranged in a logical order. With electronic media, a society enters a "postliterate" era in which television counters some of the effects of literacy by having us use our ears as much as our eyes. People in different parts of the world are being linked through electronic connections, and most of the literate world is becoming a "global village."[38]

McLuhan asserted that "the medium is the message." Most social scientists, however, would reject his claim that the content of media messages has no influence on the audience. Social scientists generally dispute the idea that any single factor can be the sole cause of social behavior. Several other theories of mass communication are more widely accepted.

The individual-differences perspective holds that perception differs systematically from one person to another according to the nature of individual personality structure. Different types of people in an audience select and interpret mass communication content in divergent ways.[39] Individuals selectively attend to messages, depending upon whether they are related to their interests, consistent with their attitudes and beliefs, and supportive of their values.

In contrast, the social categories perspective reduces the range and variety of differences by identifying social categories, especially in urban-industrial societies, in which behavior in confronting a given set of stimuli is reasonably uniform. Such characteristics as age, sex, and educational attainment provide guidelines to the type of communication content a given individual will or will not select from available media.[40] This can be seen in magazine readership *(Reader's Digest, Cosmopolitan, Field and Stream, Dissent)* and movie audiences' interests (westerns, romances, foreign films). These similar modes of orientation and behavior based on social categories relate people to the mass media in a fairly uniform manner.

But it has also been found that informal social relationships play a significant role in modifying how individuals act upon mass media messages. It was discovered that many persons' firsthand exposure to the mass media was quite limited, and that such persons learned about election campaigns from other people who had obtained information firsthand. Thus, according to the social relations perspective, information moves from the media to relatively well-informed individuals and then moves through interpersonal channels to those with less exposure to the media.[41] Those in contact with the media are called "opinion leaders" because of their important role in shaping the intentions of voters who received the information.

While it may be thought that critics (opinion leaders?) may shape mass tastes, a look at best seller lists, as compared to books recommended by critics, will dispel such notions. Critics, however, may shape views as to what book or movie will have lasting value.

Similarly, the social categories perspective assumes that low-taste content appeals primarily to the relatively uneducated. While more educated people say they prefer high-taste content, it has been found that there is little difference between the two groups in their exposure to low-taste media content.[42] The relatively uneducated spend more time than the more educated exposed to the mass media.[43] Since the relatively uneducated have less income than the more educated, they likely have less choice in their leisure-time activities.

Success in American movies, observes Michael Wood, "is almost invariably linked with an unscrupulous disregard for decency and fair play, and successful people are projected as weird, fascinating monsters."[44] They finish first but are not nice guys. Akim Tamiroff, playing a mobster in *Dangerous to Know* (1938), asserts: "I'm sitting on top of the world and I am not happy." And if you are a nice guy, it provides a rationale why you are not at the top.

The amoral charm of protagonist Sammy Glick in Budd Schulberg's novel *What Makes Sammy Run?* allows us to fill in a moral perspective; it serves as a source book for success legends. Both Sammy and Eve, in *All About Eve* (1950), assert a voracious hunger for success, but they have no self-identity apart from consuming ambition. There is an implicit warning that success will not make you happy, but if you recognize that fact and still want to strive for it, then anything goes. Success icons are the fastest gun in the West, the best pool player or poker player, or the heavyweight champion.

Just as sport is a metaphor for success in America, such movies as *The Hustler* (1961) and the *Cincinnati Kid* (1965) explore the theme through pool and poker. Both movies proclaim, but without conviction, that the cost of success is too high.[45] *The Hustler,* structured around two pool games between the master, Minnesota Fats, and the ambitious hustler, Eddie Felson, expands the notion of "winning" from sports to larger areas of life. The film draws upon the American mythology of success and also makes references to *Body and Soul* (1947), a boxing film about success and failure.[46] *Rocky* (1976), another prominent sports film, depicts a broken-down but generous and altruistic pug whose big moment arrives when he has a shot at the heavyweight title. *Rocky* made the working class briefly fashionable and evoked nostalgia for the simpler past.[47]

Quart and Auster observe that "American films moved from the relatively self-confident affirmation of the American Dream in the late forties (Hollywood at its zenith) through the films of the sixties and seventies and the politically retrograde and nostalgic Reagan eighties, when, despite a continued dependence on big budgets, stars, and genre formulas, films grew increasingly more anxious, alienated, and nihilistic."[48] Michael Medved finds many manifestations of this trend, such as the hostility to heroes. In the heyday of Greta Garbo, Gary Cooper, Kathryn Hepburn, and Jimmy Stewart, Hollywood was accused of creating personalities larger than life. But today, he asserts, Hollywood focuses its energy on "loathsome losers" and "irresponsible misfits." As an example, of those five nominated for Best Actor in 1991, three played deranged and sadistic killers, one played a psychotic, and the fifth depicted an unemployed and adulterous husband. In addition, the movie industry seldom looks back to early icons; but when it does, it emphasizes their imperfections.[49] Films are becoming more violent and nihilistic without offering any solutions. Quart and Auster find that "American films that proffer alternative political and social visions are very rare. Far more common are films that see the world as dark and murderous — without political or social alternatives — and provide no concluding image of hope and reconciliation."[50]

Although Medved claims that opinion polls show that the public wants more wholesome fare, it would seem that producers are operating with the social categories perspective. Because of the commercial nature of Hollywood, studios seek to guarantee the widest possible acceptance by the largest audience and to pinpoint the type of audience to which a film is likely to appeal. To do so, they must create films with familiar themes, clearly identifiable characters, and understandable resolutions, though they may be given license to provide plot twists and sufficient new elements to attract a large audience. "The mass audience," according to Jowett and Linton, "will simply not go to see a movie that it has heard is 'difficult' or that deals with unpopular themes."[51]

Movie images of schools as hostile environments began decades before the pervasiveness of violence and nihilism in films. Oliker finds a turning point in the 1940s, after the 1930s had featured tough male star James Cagney cleaning up a reform school in *The Mayor of Hell* (1933), and Humphrey Bogart doing the same in *Crime School* (1938). The decade ended with Robert Donat's Oscar-winning performance in *Goodbye Mr. Chips*. The 1940s featured film noir, which constructed worlds where paranoia was the dominant feeling and nobody could be trusted. Bela Lugosi played a psychology professor who leads a band of killers in *Bowery at Midnight* (1942), and Loretta Young depicted a female teacher involved in murder in *The Accused* (1949).

In the 1950s, teachers were no longer portrayed as dangerous figures, but as impotent instructors caught in a dangerous environment, as in *The Blackboard Jungle* (1955) and *The Unguarded Moment* (1956). The early 1960s continued the themes of the 1950s, but by the late 1960s the teacher had become the enemy, in *If* (1968) and *The Strawberry Statement* (1970). Teachers in the 1970s were featured in hard-boiled detective stories, as in Clint Eastwood's portrayal of an art history professor, in *The Eiger Sanction* (1975), who financed his art collection by killing for hire. Thus, by the 1970s, the teacher was depicted as a male capable of ruthless behavior.[52]

Farber and Holm, in a study of sixty-eight American movies of the 1980s in high school settings, found that the majority of the movies focus exclusively on a few students and show little interest in educators or the learning process. Yet in a small number of movies an educator-hero is depicted: a male renegade or outsider who finds a way to gain the trust and respect of students, despite obstacles and despair, and thereby triumphs in the end. These films include Jaime Escalante's work with inner-city Hispanic students in *Stand and Deliver,* Joe Clark's reform of an urban high school in *Lean on Me,* and burnt-out Alex Jurrel, who makes a comeback in *Teachers.* The educator-hero film, however, largely neglects institutional realities of inequalities in socioeconomic background and limited opportunities for advancement. The films build on wish-fulfillment of love and care between students and teachers, a wish for achievement, and a wish to transform unhappy and unsuccessful students. But no illumination is provided as to needed measures for changing the system itself and utilizing wider spheres of interest and power.[53]

In conclusion, though Hollywood no longer plays the dominant cultural role that it did in the 1940s, it still has the potential to create cultural myths. With the advent of videocassettes and cable television, which both compete with and provide a market for the film industry, Hollywood may be forced to provide a more varied and imaginative product. Hollywood films still deserve scrutiny as barometers of America's changing dreams and desires.

Postscript

Except for the service ethic, the various forms of the success ethic tend to minimize the impact of formal education. These latter success ethic proponents seem more motivated by practicality and utility. They are likely to seek out public libraries, correspondence courses, apprenticeships, and the like as sources of knowledge and training. Experience, on the other hand, is important to them; yet that experience seldom appears to place a high premium on serious reflection or, in Deweyan terms, the continuous reorganization, reconstruction, and transformation of experience.[54]

However, it must be kept in mind that the history of education is the history of formal education for an elite — a social and hereditary, but not necessarily an intellectual, elite. Ironically, the varieties of experience opened up by informal education might serve to broaden the narrower confines of classroom walls. If that be the case, Deweyan possibilities exist for making that kind of experience and education at one with growth and development.

7

Psychological Perspectives

The next three chapters provide critical perspectives on the various success ethics from the vantage points of some major psychological, philosophical, and social thinkers who introduce trenchant and often persuasive arguments against unreflective adoption of the idea of success in American life. Despite overwhelming dominance of the success ethics as models for everyday existence, significant opposition to them is reflected by the authors cited in these chapters.

In his *The Company of Critics* (1988), Michael Walzer makes the case that "connected critics" are needed to bridge traditional gaps between academic scholarship and public discourse. Such "engaged intellectuals" appear in the chapters to follow. They strongly contend that historical and contemporary analysis shows that the success ethics under discussion can erode personal hope and social action as Americans seek to achieve the American Dream. Walzer sketches out certain key roles that public intellectuals play:

> [He or she] exposes the false appearances of his own society; he gives expression to his people's deepest sense of how they ought to live; and he insists that there are other forms of falseness and other, equally legitimate hopes and aspirations.[1]

Chapter 7 offers a comparative and critical overview of how some important psychological schools of thought treat the subject of human needs, motivations, and aspirations and how that crucial concern becomes entwined in any substantive analysis of competing success ethics. Accordingly, the chapter considers the following prominent thinkers and their relevant theories: Sigmund Freud and the notion of "enlightened self-interest"; Alfred Adler on "social interest"; Carl Jung's studies on the progression from fantasy to reality; Erich Fromm's schema of social character orientations; Karen Horney's characterization of anxiety and neurosis in the modern age; Carl Rogers' concern for genuineness and authenticity; Albert Ellis' elaboration of faulty belief systems; and David McClelland's psychological synthesis of achievement motivation in achieving societies.

Akin to secular forms of religious expression, psychological perspectives often exhort people to make a kind of stoic reconciliation and transcendence of their earthly dilemmas, i. e., to overcome their psychic problems through a largely internalized exertion of rational insight, will power, and behavioral change. As such, many psychological perspectives tend to subordinate the need to alter external cultural and social constraints which impede individual change.

Freud: Enlightened Self-Interest

An enormous influence on personal and cultural judgments since he strode upon the intellectual scene in late-nineteenth-century Austria, Sigmund Freud's psychoanalytic theory harbors vast implications for the various success ethics as well. In this section we will explicate some of his major theoretical constructs and then show how they might shed additional light on several notions of success.

Freud characterizes the Id as representative of animal-like instinctual impulses (largely of an unconscious sexual nature), the very core of human being, and the repository for primary thought processes. In essence, the Id signifies what we would primordially desire to do if there were in fact no restrictions on our desires. These desires are most clearly demonstrable in dreams, fantasies, and similar unconscious thought phenomena. Freud further hypothesizes that the Id plays a predominant role in infancy and early childhood development, a period he considers most critical in the overall growth of the individual.

To counter-balance the Id, Freud introduces the term Ego, to signify that more self-regulating product of secondary (more conscious and rational) thought process that serves to bring the Id under some tenuous executory control. However, ego functions are refined only slowly and gradually, as the child grows and matures.

Most important for moral development, in Freud's psychology, is the role of the Superego, i.e., the inhibiting, restraining, prohibiting standards imposed on the child by outside social forces, initially and primarily by one's parents and later by teachers and other adult authority figures. From such social sources, the child, if she is to be "normal" and "adjusted," develops an ego-ideal and conscience. Indeed, for Freud, guilt operating via the conscience is a form of "social glue," which cements, as it were, the cultural bonds of any society. Without guilt and conscience, life would degenerate into a "tooth-and-nail" existence and attendant societal chaos. Of course, according to Freud's psychic balancing scheme, excessive guilt disables individual action and may well lead to "neurotic," even "psychotic," behavior.

On the whole, however, Freud points to an optimal realization of self-control though an almost stoical exertion of rationality. He invokes such individual self-control because he contends that a substantial measure of repression is necessary to balance one's psychic apparatus, especially Id impulses, with the demands of culture. Freud thus employs the concept of repression to regulate the seemingly irreconcilable conflict between personal autonomy and cultural restraint.

Freud uses the term repression to express that most general, largely unconscious, defense mechanism which enables us to keep out of consciousness those thoughts, wishes, and desires too dangerous to one's conscious mental processes. A form of repression, sublimation refers to that specific defense mechanism which transforms id-like excitations into more socially acceptable patterns of behavior. Indeed, for Freud, sublimation serves to build culture in the form of art, religion, literature, etc. Accordingly, he calls upon human beings to sublimate what he assumes to be primary aggressive sex instincts with what is deemed necessary to constitute civilization.

Thus, the demands of civilized life require us to struggle with repression, i. e., to practice a kind of frustrating, "heroic" individualism. To do otherwise would imperil cultural cohesion, which would, in turn, endanger individuals in society. This scenario summarizes Freud's version of "enlightened self-interest."

Freud also promulgated a psycho-sexual stage theory of development which focused on different erogenous zones and whether one resolved psychological problems or became fixated at each stage. In the oral stage, roughly the first year of life, one's pleasures are derived largely from the mouth (e.g., biting, chewing, sucking, and eating), and undesirable character traits might well emerge from this stage if one is satisfied either too much or too little. Examples of the latter include avarice, argumentativeness, gullibility, and sarcasm, to name a few. In the anal stage, approximately the second and third years of life, toilet training becomes a decisive life marker; if this phase is not handled well, expulsive traits may dominate one's later personality in such forms as obsessive neatness and cleanliness, excessive messiness, hoarding behavior, frugality, cruelty, and the like. Freud next uses the classical myths of Oedipus and Electra to describe the phallic stage, one in which he claims that young boys fear castration and thus internalize and identify with the father figure. For Freud, fear of castration permits moral growth in young males. On his terms, it becomes a psychological impossibility for girls to achieve a strong sense of Superego development since they are, as it were, already "castrated" and cannot experience the same fears and threat of loss. As a consequence, according to Freud, they develop "penis envy," a very controversial notion still under severe attack by both feminist and non-feminist psychologists.[2] Freud's final stage of maturity culminates in the genital stage, where one begins to learn, in adolescence, how to balance the two major issues of adult life: work and love *(arbeiten und lieben).*[3]

Early psychoanalytic theory equates money with filth, thereby illuminating the success ethic in a distinctive fashion. As has been seen above, personality patterns during the anal period later influence one's perception of money. The child finds instinctual libidinal pleasure in eliminating feces. Toilet training becomes a psychological battleground over whether the child will control the sphincter muscles or will submit to parental demands from fear of punishment or loss of love. The key to the adult's attitudes toward money is in deciding whether to hold back or let go. The miser's holding back is symbolic of the child's refusal to eliminate feces. In contrast, the spendthrift learned that submitting to parental authority in eliminating feces leads to love and approval.[4]

Some Marxist interpretations of Freud's theory of neurosis have characterized the hoarding personality as providing the image and "reason for the disciplining and submission of human sensuality under the [capitalist] exchange principle." In this view, "the hoarder is the incarnation of endless 'instinctual deferral' and 'instinctual renunciation' in favor of an accumulation of abstract wealth." In terms of the various success ethics under discussion, proponents of the character ethic would need to be especially wary should such a Marxist/Freudian analysis prove to be correct. For the essential ingredients of success through character include such anal traits as perseverance, industry, frugality, sobriety, punctuality, reliability, thoroughness, and initiative.[5]

Advocates of the other success ethics would fare little better in the Freudian world view. In general, maintaining psychic structure becomes a tenuous balancing act, forcing one to sift through myriad forces of aggression, instinctual gratification, sublimation, and repression, with one's enlightened self-interest, a veritable cauldron of conscious and unconscious processes. Thus, the personality ethic might suffer from an unduly outward striving for success, i.e., living for external appearances and more direct, if effervescent, satisfactions. Meanwhile, mind power proponents might be accused of mere wishful thinking (*vide* the power of positive thinking), particularly if the external world around them is really more insufferable than their belief systems would permit them to admit. Even humble disciples of the service ethic would not be credited with altruism and selflessness; for they might well be simply sublimating their instinctual desires in doing good deeds, seeking an appropriate arena for an overdeveloped Superego, or failing to release fully their libidinal energy. Alas, in the Freudian scheme of things, it is difficult to be a winner.

Alfred Adler: Social Interest

One of Freud's original disciples, Alfred Adler broke away from his teacher to form his own school of thought ("Individual Psychology"), on the grounds that Freud's theory of sexuality was too reductionistic and that psychoanalytic dependence on aggressive drives posited an overly deterministic, largely intrapsychic and biological, view of human nature. In essence, Adler proposed to avoid any such reductionism and determinism by formulating a dialectical account of social dynamics and social relationships. Though Adler also emphasized the importance of the early years of development, he was much more concerned with social influences, which impinge upon thought and action. Indeed, his overarching theory of "social interest" placed the whole range of viewing human behavior in an entirely different perspective.

Adler claims that all humans enter the world in a position of "inferiority," i.e., we are all relatively helpless and dependent in infancy. From that original station in life, we gradually "strive toward overcoming" a feeling of powerlessness.[6] Adler modified Nietzsche's term "will to power" to describe how humans could "perfect" their existence, and not to depict any yearnings for power and authority over other persons. In fact, on Adler's terms, any such egocentric striving would be viewed as "neurotic" and counter-productive to his own value system, which stressed cooperation as a prime motivating force, perhaps the most necessary invention, in human evolution.[7]

For Adler, social interest encompasses communal feeling, interpersonality, and empathy for others. He sees the history of humankind as a continual movement toward more socially "superior," cooperative, and democratic directions necessitating equality in all aspects of life.[8] Adler and his disciples invoke the standard of social interest to judge the extent to which culture and individual personality have matured.

Given that set of assumptions, Adler would doubtless extol the intentions and work of those advocates of the service ethic who act in behalf of humanitarian and communitarian interests. Indeed, he would consider their credo as a criterion for normalcy rather than deviance. Adler would also concur with their progressive ideology and their faith in human potentiality. However, some Freudians might counter that Adler and various proponents of the service ethic seem too naively optimistic about human progress through cooperative means.

Because Adlerian psychologists encourage the development of life plans and goal-directed behavior, they would tend to support the dedication, stamina, and grit of those who practice the character ethic. They would also applaud that ethic's propensity to do work for the good of others as a manifestation of social interest. At the same time, they would deemphasize any immoderate interest in materialism and rugged individualism.

As for the mind-power ethic, Adlerians would caution against mentalistic activities devoted solely to moneymaking ability. However, they might well praise that ethic's warnings against excessive diffidence, worry, and discouragement in the face of life's problems. Yet Adler did not want his followers to engage in unrealistic, wishful thinking (as often seems to be the case in the mind-power ethic). Rather, they should show courage in facing the difficulties and challenges of life.

Adler would perhaps save his most scolding criticism for proponents of the personality ethic, especially those who seek success through manipulating others and showing superiority over them. Their egocentric striving for success would also exhibit a lack of social interest and a cavalier unconcern for communal feeling and fraternity.

Carl Jung: Fantasy and Reality

Another of Freud's original disciples and apostates, Carl Jung viewed personality development as a lifelong process resulting in self-actualization for comparatively few individuals by the time they have reached middle age or beyond. His intense interest in archaeology, anthropology, and religion led him to study primitive artifacts from various cultures that seemed to have traits in common, e.g., the adoration of the virgin, or Mother, figure, as well as universal curiosities attached to the circle (Mandala).

From such exploration, Jung concluded that human forces derive primordially from a collective base and that all men and women share certain core components from that human condition. At root, this primitive collective sharing rests in the unconscious. The ultimate task of life is to differentiate those components of the unconscious that will make for a balanced psychic life, to eventually enable the conscious personality to become self-regulating and unified in all its parts. In psychodynamic terms, Jung's neo-analytic mission is to permit the relatively impersonal collective unconscious to be refined to the point that it is appropriated by one's personal ego.

According to Jung, the maturation process becomes one of restructuring and integrating childhood fantasy life to make it complementary with "real" life, through an ongoing broadening of consciousness in adolescence and adulthood. The child must eventually separate herself from the "land of childhood" (fantasy) by employing reason, melding it to her earlier "historical soul" (archetypes) and largely instinctual existence. Throughout life, the compensating features of instinct and reason, fantasy and reality, must be assimilated constantly if one is to live a whole, unified life. The instinctual resources of childhood ideally provide a perennial flow of life force; without them, mature human beings would take on a dried-up, sterile, overly rationalized visage. Indeed, it is fantasy which breeds creativity and sensitive reflection.[9]

Throughout his own life, Jung employed the circle symbol to represent the totality of psychic life in its basic functional components: thinking, feeling, intuition, and sensation. Thinking and feeling are evaluative in that they make use, respectively, of cognitive and affective judgment from the standpoint of "true-false" and "agreeable-disagreeable" discernments. Intuition and sensation are termed "irrational" by Jung because they involve perceptual phenomena which are irreducible to cognitive interpretation. In Jung's view, each and every person predominates in certain of those functions. In fact, it is such predominance in typology which marks the general orientation of one's personality.[10]

The development of psychological attitudes is related to several concepts with which Jung's name is even more widely popular: "extroversion" and "introversion." For Jung, these distinctive psychic orientations condition one's entire behavioral tone in all its manifestations. An extrovert "thinks, feels, and acts in reference to . . . [external] objects." That is, she is primarily influenced by consensual, collectively validated, social norms and codes of conduct. On the other hand, introverts relate more negatively to external objects, instead relying on their own subjective internal experience. In accord with his interest in reconciling opposites in order to form a more total personality, Jung claims that the unconscious of each type carries on the psychic work left undone by one's consciousness. In other words, the unconscious of the extrovert is introverted, and vice-versa.[11]

Lurking beneath the surface of Jung's attempt at dialectical synthesis, however, is the crag-like possibility that humankind is fighting an uphill battle against dualisms throughout development. This cruel, harsh reality is perhaps best demonstrated in his notion of the "shadow." That archetypal figure expresses the symbolic "other aspect," or "darkness," which is inseparable from totality. For Jung, the point of evil is to elucidate that which is goodness and light, to permit us more perceptive penetration into moral enlightenment. Nevertheless, the shadow concept poses greater imponderables to the extent that, if Jung is correct, evil may indeed be an irreducible fact of human existence, and not to be overcome lightly.[12]

Thus, on Jung's terms, the critical challenge of life is how to emerge as an individual while maintaining harmony with the whole of life surrounding one's existence. Human beings should be treated as unfolding individuals, slowly and relentlessly differentiating themselves from the mass of humanity. They should also be allowed to synthesize life in order for it to take on more holistic meaning. Accordingly, strong elements of stoicism, integration, and transcendence underlie Jung's psychology. In the long run, Jung looks toward an obligation to the human species, not merely enlightened self-interest, as an ultimate benchmark for moral and spiritual renewal. And because this task of life is so great, relatively few persons approach full levels of individuation and self-actualization, i.e., the creation of a whole personality wherein one's self becomes almost completely defensible and indestructible.[13]

Jung's theories bear particular relevance to several of the success ethics. His extroverted type closely resembles the archetypal advocate of the personality ethic in its concern for outward striving and external appearances. Also, such personalities appear to be more sensate in their psychological attitudes. Moreover, they seem less able to attain Jung's vision of individuation and self-actualization in any fully sustained way because they appear to imbibe life's surfaces rather than either its ultimate purposes or its divergent existential meaning.

Proponents of the character ethic would fulfill part of Jung's circle of psychic balance in their sense of duty and obligation to the world beyond themselves. Integrity, self-reliance, honest work, and dependability are traits which would be honored by both Jung and character ethic advocates. However, Jung might well admonish the latter to enliven their daily rounds with affective, creative impulses that would ensure a life that was not barren of instinctual desires. That is, they should balance their reason and morality with appropriate doses of fantasy and imagination. Finally, the prototype of the character ethic curiously mimics the ways and means of Jung's introverted type in its emphasis on character traits that stress internal motivations for behavior, e.g., honor, industry, initiative, and the like.

From Jung's perspective, the mind-power ethic would fail to come to grips with harsher realities. Its emphasis on positive thinking implies that mere happy thoughts can overcome almost any external barrier or constraint. Jung would want individuals to confront and attempt to reconcile both the darkness and light in the world around them. Nor does the mind power ethic address his existential concerns for more fully developed personhood through individuation and self-actualization. Recipes for "successful living" through auto-suggestion and visualization scarcely approach what Jung has in mind.

At the same time, service ethic advocates will need to take care that their collectivist and humanitarian drives do not suppress the idiosyncratic individuality that Jung cherishes. In light of his treatment of the shadow figure, they might also require some tempering of their confidence in human perfectibility, mass social movements, and societal progress as an inevitability. Above all, from Jung's vantage point, they must make sure that social reforms do not involve undue political manipulation of individual freedom and autonomy.

Finally, it is interesting to note how Jung's notion of archetypes can be used to characterize various portraitures of the success ethics. Archetypes are symbolic representations of those instinctual clusters of transcendent ideas that have been formed unconsciously over the centuries. They compose part of one's personal as well as collective unconscious, and allow us to draw "self-portraits," as it were, of our instincts so that we can imagine and elucidate the idea of certain mental constructs, e.g., "mother," "father," "God," "demon," and the like. (Jung cautions that it is unwise to overgeneralize from any archetypal image; to do so would be to pigeonhole and stereotype complex human beings in unwarranted fashion.)

For example, the "trickster" or "huckster" archetype conveys the mythical picture of the manipulative peddler, one who hawks his wares and manipulates unwary customers in the manner of some extreme devotees of the personality ethic. Similarly, the "power" archetype might suggest that ethic's image of energy, force, and strength in business affairs and interpersonal living. On the other hand, the archetype of the "wise old man" might remind us of some proponents of the service ethic who seek to lead through reason, virtue, and conscience.

Erich Fromm: Character Orientations

A leading interpreter and synthesizer of Freud and Marx from 1940 to 1980, Erich Fromm's cultural school of psychoanalysis is especially relevant to any critique of the success ethics that seeks to incorporate broad-ranging findings and speculations from the interdisciplinary social sciences. Though Fromm's intellectual interests, like those of Jung, are sweeping in their scope, the principal focus of this section is devoted to his identification and description of certain social character types that appear to be particularly germane to the present analysis.

Fromm locates the following character orientations in contemporary society: receptive, exploitative, hoarding, marketing, and productive. He considers only the latter to be a mature, healthy orientation; the others he views as deficient and destructive to human well-being. In a striking manner, each poses definite implications for the individual success ethics.

The *receptive* character type perceives "the source of all good" in external objects, events, and activities, i.e., "he believes that the only way to get what he wants . . . is to receive it from that outside source." People habituated to this orientation place a heavy premium on "being loved," as in the case of Willy Loman and the personality ethic. Receptive characters are dependent on others for most all kinds of support, from knowledge to personal fulfillment. Again, the ghost of Willy Loman looms as a prime exemplar. And, like him, receptive types like to appear "optimistic" and "friendly"; however, "they become anxious and distraught when their 'source of supply' is threatened" (e.g., when Loman loses his job in the hosiery trade).[14]

The *exploitative* orientation is also externally motivated, but this character type seeks to take things from other people "by force or cunning." Akin to certain examples in the personality ethic, they "use and exploit anybody and anything from whom or from which they can squeeze something," as in the various and sundry business transactions of Nabisco's F. Ross Johnson. In a word, other people are meant to be used, manipulated, and placed under one's control by charm or coercion. In their focus on obtaining pleasure from outside sources, both the receptive and exploitative types are remindful of Freud's orally-oriented personality.[15]

The *hoarding* character type bases her security and survival on saving. Similar to Freud's anally fixated person, she builds "a protective wall . . . to let as little as possible out of it." Her miserly sterility extends to feelings and thoughts as well as money and material possessions. Other cardinal characteristics include "pedantic orderliness," "compulsive cleanliness," and "obsessive punctuality." In these attributes, hoarding types are reminiscent of prime examples from the character ethic, especially in the form of frugality, punctuality, thoroughness, and similar Boy Scout badges of honor.[16]

Fromm's *marketing* orientation, which he holds to be the most distinctive to contemporary culture, refers to that social character type that relies upon exchange, rather than use, value in the marketplace of everyday affairs. Marketing types "are dependent for their material success on a personal acceptance by those who need their services or who employ them." Thus, such types have much in common with many purveyors of the personality ethic. Indeed, personality becomes more important than skill or ability in working one's way up the ladder of success. Given that comparison, marketing types could not sustain themselves on the aptitudinal and achievement motivations fostered by the character ethic. Instead, in language similar to that of Packard and Whyte, Fromm characterizes the marketing type as one who is willing to "package" and "sell" herself to make the deal.

For Fromm, the standard for healthy maturity can be found in the *productive* personality. He defines productiveness as one's "realization of the potentialities characteristic of him," i.e., the ability to use one's capacities to actualize one's self, not to dominate or repress others. According to Fromm, if one approximates an Aristotelian golden mean and conditions herself in accord with reason and virtue, one should create a productive life for oneself and others. Those advocates of the service ethic who meld self-actualized fulfillment with their communitarian interests would largely model such a definition of productiveness. The character ethic would also include a certain flavor of Fromm's internalized productive orientation, though its primarily individualistic focus is not nearly as socially motivated as is Fromm's notion. The other success ethics would fall short of his criteria on a number of counts. For example, the personality ethic, as has been seen, would be much closer to incorporating significant elements of the marketing, exploitative, and receptive orientations. Meanwhile the mind power ethic would hardly employ reason and virtue in any self-critical way; nor does it imply the necessity for social critique, which would be crucial in Fromm's analysis.[17]

Karen Horney: Anxiety and Neurosis

A pioneer in feminine psychology whose theories incorporate and transcend Freudianism, Karen Horney's major work appeared in the middle decades of the twentieth century. Her principal concept of basic anxiety underlies much of her theorizing, and her overarching concern for "the neurotic personality of our time" has special significance for the success ethics. Like Fromm, Horney makes use of broader cultural constructs as well as merely psychological phenomena.

Horney defines basic anxiety as "the feeling . . . of being isolated and helpless in a potentially hostile world."[18] Such insecurity may be caused by various adverse environmental factors, out of which one seeks to develop psychic strategies in an attempt to cope and survive. Oftentimes these strategies create psychic damage to the extent that neurotic needs are produced to solve one's problems. Some of Horney's examples of neurotic needs seem especially germane to any inquiry into the success ethics.

Closely paralleling the drives of certain disciples of the personality ethic, some individuals display an inordinate need for affection and approval. They exist to please others, and persistently want to be friendly with everyone. Much like Fromm's receptive character types, their needs are rooted externally and are based "in the neurotic's profound conviction that he cannot live on his own resources, that all he needs has to be given to him, that all the responsibility for his life rests on others and not on himself." Like Willy Loman, he or she fears rejection at all costs.[19]

Fearing isolation and aloneness, other persons express neurotic needs by overvaluing love and placing too much reliance on a life partner. These individuals manifest extreme emotional dependency and encounter difficulties in life as a consequence. Almost parasitically, they work on, and lose themselves in, other people to the point that they may be unable to give love in return. Again, some proponents of the personality ethic have had to deal with this same malady.[20]

Reminiscent of Fromm's characterization of the hoarding personality, another form of neurosis is expressed in the excessive yearning to restrict life's parameters to narrow zones of comfort. "Such a person is undemanding, content with little, prefers to remain inconspicuous, and values modesty above all else."[21] Certain exponents of the character ethic, in their zeal to order their lives around explicit internalized goals of success, may be especially prone to this kind of neurotic need.

The neurotic need for power is a more all-embracing concept that applies to several success ethics. Partially echoing Adler's analysis, Horney postulates that this neurosis stems from "anxiety, hatred and feelings of inferiority." Expressed in a headlong drive for superiority over others, either physically or intellectually, such motivation offers only a thin veneer of "protection against helplessness and against insignificance." In its emphasis on the force of will to attain all ends, this neurotic need reminds one of those mind power advocates who practice similar mentalistic attitudes in an attempt to achieve their objectives. At the same time, its modus operandi resembles that of some devotees of the personality ethic who use their wit, charm, and physical appearance to accomplish powerful goals in subtle, and sometimes obvious, ways.[22]

Related to the craving for power is the personality that is exploitative in its aims. Reiterating Fromm's notion of the exploitative character in slightly varied form, Horney notes that such persons seek to "experience the triumph of getting the better of others." Their character tone seems similar to those features of the personality ethic that stress the utility of human manipulation.[23]

The quest for power is often supplemented by the neurotic need for prestige and admiration. For such individuals, the need to be recognized and appreciated by the external public is more important than any concern for growth in inner resources. Once again, Horney has pinpointed a neurotic tendency peculiarly relevant to the personality ethic.[24]

Implicit connections to the character ethic form the backdrop to an analysis of the remainder of Horney's characterization of neurotic needs: unhealthy competitiveness and overblown achievement orientation; excessive yearning for independence and self-sufficiency; and the irrational urge to be perfect and unblemished. Each of these aims goads the individual "to be unique and exceptional"; as such, they prepare her for psychological imbalance in an imperfect world. Like some exemplars of the character ethic, those individuals so influenced internalize an idealized view of the universe, which disables their capacity to live flexibly and sort out ambiguities.[25]

Carl Rogers: Beyond Masks and Facades

The major force in client-centered, humanistic psychotherapy from the 1950s to the 1980s, Carl R. Rogers's self theory bears particular relevance for those critiques of the various success ethics that summon men and women to genuineness and authenticity. For the elemental goal of Rogers's psychology is to allow individuals to become their "real selves" in a fractured world of constraints, illusions, masks, and facades.

Rogers assumes a basic self-actualizing potentiality in all human beings. Accordingly, he emphasizes the importance of positive self-regard and the need to fulfill one's "real" self in an honestly congruent manner. This existential task requires one to listen to one's own voice, to be readily open to experience, and to refuse to guide one's life by external social standards. Rogers asks us to transcend such artificial roles and functions if we are to become true to the meaning of our own existence, i.e., to be "fully-functioning" persons.[26]

Thus, Rogers's psychology necessitates a good deal of reflection, empathy, and self-awareness from both clients and therapists. Each must be willing to confront crises and change habits of behavior when psychic health depends upon such change. Each must strip away the inauthentic facades of life that lead to a false, sterile, or hypocritical existence.[27]

In terms of the distinct success ethics, it would appear obvious that rigid adherents to the character ethic would encounter difficulty with the fluidity, flexibility, and openness of Rogers's psychological system and processes. Likewise, those extremely inner-directed persons in Riesman's "lonely crowd" would doubtless find Rogers's theories to be problematical.

Nor would most prototypes of the personality ethic fare any better. In their "buyer-beware" universe of charm, cunning, physical appearances, and human manipulation, they would also have little in common with Rogerian principles. They would continue to sell themselves, cheesily protected by the masks and facades of a market culture.

As for mind power advocates, the non-directive Rogers would remain in a listening posture, hoping, sometimes beyond hope, that they might face up to the actual predicaments confronting them, rather than simply chanting mantras of success (however sincerely they did so). In time, he might help them pierce their own illusions if he could re-channel their sturdy will power in other directions.

Finally, practitioners of the service ethic would need to be reminded, however gently, that their social crusades and reform movements should be congruent with their own consciences. They should monitor social progress in such a way that they can adapt to change in both their personal and cultural lives. Yet they should not allow social standards and expectations to dictate the form that change takes.

Albert Ellis: Faulty Belief Systems

Albert Ellis, founder of Rational-Emotive Therapy (RET), established The Institute for Rational Living in 1959 and The Institute for Advanced Study in Rational Psychotherapy in 1968, both headquartered in New York City. Since then, his therapeutic movement has vigorously maintained training programs, clinics, schools, adult education courses, and outreach publications across the nation and abroad. Ellis's hard-nosed approach to psychotherapy would have much to say about the irrationalities and faulty thinking processes so prevalent in each of the success ethics.

In succinct fashion, Ellis explains the fundamental elements of RET:

> . . . When a highly charged emotional Consequence (C) follows a significant Activating Event (A), A may seem to but actually does not cause C. Instead, emotional Consequences are largely created by B — the individual's Belief System. When, therefore, an undesirable Consequence occurs, such as severe anxiety, this can usually be quickly traced to the person's irrational Beliefs, and when these Beliefs are effectively Disputed (at point D), by challenging them rationally, the disturbed Consequences disappear and eventually cease to reoccur.[28]

Historically, Ellis traces the essential roots of RET to such ancient Stoic philosophers as Marcus Aurelius and Epictetus. The latter once noted that "men are disturbed not by things, but by the view which they take of them."[29] Alfred Adler is a more recent precursor of RET; in fact, Ellis acknowledges his influence extensively to the effect "that *a person's behavior springs from his ideas.*"[30]

According to Ellis, though human beings are obviously capable of rationality, they tend to be "uniquely irrational and crooked" in their thinking. Cultural prohibitions ("oughts" and "shoulds") drummed into our thoughts establish a faulty belief system that eventuates in wishful thinking and self-inflicted psychic damage. In a word, Ellis believes that emotional disturbance stems from "magical, superstitious, empirically unvalidatable thinking."[31]

In order to stamp out injurious self-indoctrination, Ellis's therapeutic regimen employs confrontational techniques to force the client to face up to his irrational beliefs, so that "they can be clearly observed, parsed, challenged, questioned, and changed." Thus, his therapy runs directly counter to some main assumptions of the mind power ethic. In Ellis's own words:

> Many people think that rational therapy is closely related to Emile Coué's autosuggestion or Norman Vincent Peale's positive thinking, but it is actually just the reverse of these techniques in many ways. . . . Accentuating the positive is itself a false system of belief, since there is no scientific truth to the statements that "Day by day in every way I'm getting better and better" — which was Coué's creed — or that "Because God loves you, you need have no fear of anybody or anything," which appears to be Norman Vincent Peale's latterday version of autosuggestion.[32]

Although he has been greatly influenced by Adler, Ellis claims that Adlerians tend to "overemphasize" social interest as a therapeutic objective. Consequently, he would also admonish advocates of the service ethic who steer too far away from more realistic portrayals of Freud's notion of "enlightened self-interest." Ellis would likewise warn them to forego making people feel guilty if they are not fully able to love all humankind. On his terms, such an absolute goal would be an irrational thought.[33]

Similarly, Ellis would confront the ideas of those personality ethic proponents who feel that they must love someone or be loved themselves. He would consider such thinking to be obsessively narrow and totally unreasonable. Nor would he expect them to be compulsively fixated on their physical appearance. Lastly, he would teach them to seek control of their own thought systems, rather than attempt to exert irrational power over others.

Ellis's therapeutic counsel to disciples of the character ethic would be equally pointed: They should desist from any rigid setting of boundaries in their lives, but live realistically within the bounds of reason. That is, they need to look at their goals in manageable ways and, more generally, "ignore many of the unnecessary restrictions of our culture."[34]

David McClelland: Achievement Motivation

Currently professor of psychology at Boston University, David C. McClelland has devoted himself to research into multi-faceted features of human motivation and the identification of competencies related to effective performance. He has held professorships at Wesleyan and Harvard, and written books on such topics as achievement motivation, power, and liberal education.

Originally influenced by Freud, and by Henry A. Murray's theory of personology and his projective Thematic Apperception Test (TAT), McClelland departed from his Harvard colleague's research because he "had no inclination to explore the murky regions of the mind unless doing so would produce some kind of rational, quantifiable, productive payoff."[35] McClelland's pragmatic excursions into such all-embracing fields as psychology, sociology, economics, education, and even art and literary criticism would later evoke similar scholarly attacks from his own critics. Recently, other interpreters have claimed that McClelland has not received the wider acclaim he deserves within psychological circles and the applied industry of motivational training.

In *The Achieving Society* (1961), McClelland devised a scientific method for assessing whether a high level of n Achievement produced more economically advanced, i.e., "achieving," societies. He coded and scored each nation's prominent children's stories based on their fantasy content and underlying themes of achievement, for the time periods around 1925 and 1950. Such associative themes as achievement, obligations, boasting, politeness, pride, and cleverness were embedded within the stories. Given his mode of evaluation, McClelland's conclusions were not totally surprising: Societies grow economically under cycles of high n Achievement, and they decline during episodes of high n Power and n Affiliation levels.[36]

McClelland imbued his notion of achievement motivation with countless references to the rise of capitalism entailed in Max Weber's classic treatment of the self-reliant Protestant Ethic. In terms of child-rearing practices, McClelland's findings favored those Protestant households that produced high-achieving sons through the setting of "moderately high" standards of excellence and appropriate positive reinforcement for their good performance. Likewise, he applauded Protestant parents for their "optimism" and "activism," as opposed, for example, to the more "traditionalistic" teachings of American Catholics.[37]

Though Freud and Murray were pessimistic about psychological change after the critical first few years of human development, McClelland hypothesized that motivational techniques could spur people to alter their behavior in adolescence and adulthood. In the inviting cultural milieu of the 1950s, his book *The Achievement Motive* was largely welcomed by both academic and popular audiences:

> . . . Achievement looked like the good need and Power and Affiliation like the bad needs. *N* Power connoted Hitler and Stalin or, at the very least, the petty despotism of politicians and corporate executives. *N* affiliation brought to mind David Riesman's "other-directed" conformists, the Organization Man, gray flannel suits, suburban cocktail parties, and similar bugaboos of fifties intellectuals. *N* Achievement was pure: democratic, independent, productive.[38]

By the 1960s, however, McClelland's efforts to establish wide-sweeping achievement motivation courses and networks throughout the globe would be substantially stymied by changing social and political mores. Yet his idea of an "ideal self-image" still resembles what the present-day motivation industry refers to as a "positive mental attitude." Similar to McClelland's lessons on motivation, that industry relies heavily on goal-setting behavior, the use of retreats to inculcate "membership in a new and continuing reference group," and the deployment of entrepreneurial spirit and "prestige suggestion" attached to these activities to attract and motivate trainees.[39]

Without success, the Educational Testing Service (ETS) tried, in 1973, to enlist McClelland's assistance in revamping its Scholastic Aptitude Test (SAT) to take into account "performance" or "competency." Though he spurned its invitation, ETS has, in recent years, supported the more wide-ranging National Assessment of Educational Progress and changed the SAT to the Scholastic Assessment Test.[40] Translating his argument for achievement motivation to the liberal arts, McClelland contends that the standards for excellence in raising children who are high in *n* Achievement look "a lot like the image that many liberal educators have of what they are and how they teach."[41] At the same time, he is honest enough to admit that the research literature does not yet confirm any correlation between achievement motivation and actual academic success.

Of course, McClelland's emphasis on achievement motivation is explicitly relevant to any consideration of the character ethic. His "achieving society" directly parallels the time period in nineteenth-century and early twentieth-century America when the character ethic appealed to a rising industrial nation undergoing vast economic development. The attendant Protestant Ethic traits of ambition, self-reliance, and self-discipline, which he would extol, are all noteworthy elements of the character ethic as well. In addition, his call for resource-fulness and "positive mental attitudes" in business, industry, and education is remindful of some cardinal appeals of the mind-power ethic.

On the other hand, McClelland's views should give serious cause for concern and caution to proponents of the personality ethic. Over-investment in power and affiliation would seem to yield adverse consequences for growth in achievement and personal success. As for the service ethic, McClelland would be relatively silent, though he does acknowledge some room for altruism in modern entrepreneurial practices, as opposed to a largely unrestricted sense of greed and selfishness.[42]

Postscript

In a curious manner, the psychological perspectives proffered in this chapter afford both suggestive critiques of the success ethics and peculiar paradoxes for any complete realization of the liberation of human beings. Many of those perspectives turn largely on the *internal* function of *individual* character. As such, they count on strenuous effort and a stern denial of external repression (as in mind power) as suitable conveyers of freedom and autonomy. Thus, these predominantly psychological views of the world tend to interpret social problems through a more or less stoic lens of analysis, seldom reconciling their prescriptive advice with the sometimes enormous societal constraints that individuals confront in everyday life. To that extent, they mimic the very success ethics they aim to criticize. Kenneth Benne adroitly articulates this deep irony in direct terms: "Counseling and therapy have traditionally sought to facilitate change in persons with little or no assumption of responsibility for facilitating changes in the cultural environment in which people function outside the counseling or therapeutic setting. This tends to place the entire burden of behavioral [change] upon the individual."[43]

8

Philosophical Perspectives

This chapter presents leading Western ethical systems as sources for critically evaluating the success ethics. These perspectives are drawn from Aristotle, Kant, Buber, Nietzsche, Mill, Marx, Dewey, Niebuhr, and Tillich. Despite the dominance of the success ethics, significant opposition to them is reflected by these authors. This chapter draws upon thinkers from various traditions to show how their interpretive thinking would identify weaknesses in the different success ethics. The opening section introduces paternalistic critiques of the service ethic. First, however, we need to explore briefly the nature and purpose of philosophy.

Philosophy began in ancient Greece before the time of Socrates, and relies on reason to explain the world and human nature. It posed an alternative to other approaches to explaining and coping with life, such as myth, superstition, tradition, mysticism, and dogma. Since philosophy antedates the discoveries of modem science, some philosophers sought knowledge and understanding of physical phenomena as well as knowledge about human nature and the good life.

The philosophic quest, generated by a sense of profound wonder about human life, attempts to sort, sift, and analyze phenomena and then to reorganize them into a logically consistent, embracing framework. This not only enables the philosopher to envision life in broader perspective, greater depth and meaning, it makes it possible to organize and systematize human experience. The philosopher has traditionally raised questions about the individual and the cosmos: what is mind and what is matter? Why are we here? Does the universe have a purpose, or does it seem to have purpose only because of our imaginations? Can humans ever acquire incontrovertible knowledge? How do we determine what is good and bad? How can a work of genuine artistic merit be identified?

Philosophy has been viewed in numerous ways. Plato envisioned philosophy as the search for ultimates: a quest to discover ultimate reality or the general cause of all things. Whether there is a reality higher than scientific discovery provides is a philosophical issue. But other philosophers, such as John Dewey, have seriously questioned whether philosophy can provide such knowledge.

With the advent of modern science and increased specialization into numerous new disciplines, some view philosophy's role as limited to areas not investigated by science or areas in which philosophers have special expertise. Although some philosophers still attempt to formulate major systems of thought, specialists have multiplied who operate with considerable precision in limited areas. The older view of philosophy as the search for the meaning and purpose of life is repudiated by analytic philosophers, who reject the notion of the philosopher as a sage. They envision the philosopher as an analyst of language and concepts, because all philosophical problems, they believe, arise within ordinary language and must be resolved there. Postmodernism generally rejects any foundation for knowledge-claims, and finds that numerous philosophical perspectives need to be entertained. But other modern movements, such as existentialism, consider "human existence" and "the individual" as the starting point for philosophical inquiry.

Paternalism and the Service Ethic

It was suggested in chapter 5 that the service ethic may have a problem: it may be guilty of being paternalistic. What would that mean? And if it were paternalistic, would that be a serious problem? Could paternalism be warranted and, if so, under what conditions?

What is paternalism? A paternalistic act, according to Rosemary Carter, is one in which "the protection or promotion of a subject's welfare is the primary reason for attempted or successful coercive interference with an action or state of a person."[1] Such an act is done in the person's best interest whenever the person is incapable of performing the act independently.

The following laws, rules, and school practices are usually paternalistic, depending on the context: compulsory school attendance laws;

school safety regulations; federal subsidized lunch program; school health check-ups; rules for using equipment in science laboratories, home economics, and shop courses; certification of educational personnel; and censorship of textbooks and library materials. Some of these practices are not clear cases of paternalism; they may be enforced to protect the public interest or rights of certain groups rather than the student's interest. Compulsory attendance, for instance, is usually claimed to be in the public interest (the need for an educated citizenry in a democracy) as well as the student's interest. Others, such as teacher certification and health check-ups, also involve a larger public interest. Some also protect property (rules governing the use of school equipment) as well as the student. One aspect of paternalism is to prevent needless harm or suffering; therefore, safety regulations, rules for equipment use, and censorship fall under this category.

Among adults in the larger society, paternalism may take a number of different forms. Statutes requiring automobile drivers to wear seat belts and motorcyclists to wear helmets, and the removal by the courts of a child from an abusive home environment would likely be paternalistic without full consent of all parties; whereas a surgical operation usually could be classified as paternalistic with consent. Thus, informed consent would be a distinguishing characteristic in such cases.

Informed consent occurs when an individual is capable of acting rationally and has sufficient information about a situation that a reasonable decision can be made. Through informed consent the individual would be more aware of the probable risks involved, and would be able to weigh the risks against the likely benefits. Paternalism involves intervention in another's life, and would, by definition, observe the principle of nonmaleficence, which holds that it is wrong to intentionally inflict harm on another person. Much depends, however, on the definition of "harm." Individuals could be said to be harmed whenever any of their interests are violated. Interests are those matters that individuals have a stake in, whether or not they are fully aware of them. A minor, for instance, may not be cognizant of her stake in the family's estate upon the premature death of her parents, but the courts will likely recognize the minor's interests.

But the interventionist will not only want to observe the principle of nonmaleficence but the principle of beneficence as well. The latter principle says that one should do good or effect good. Thus, if the two principles are applied, the interventionist will seek to bring about good outcomes and avoid harm.

In terms of informed consent, competence is an important variable. The competent person "has a sufficiently broad range of capacities primarily to reason and choose but also to act in ways likely to be prudent under a wide range of circumstances."[2] Areas of incompetence do not preclude the existence of general competence (e.g., one may be an incompetent housekeeper or letter writer). One may be incompetent to grant consent because of immaturity (infants and young children), diminished capacity (mental illness, retardation, disease, senility), or temporary losses of capacity (drunkenness, drug abuse, unconsciousness). Informed consent is a means of waiving the right that the intervention would violate. Usually it means that an outside agent interferes with an individual's freedom. But, as Dan Brock observes, "since persons can and sometimes do consent to what does not promote their good, as well as refuse consent to what would promote their good, consent could not be a requirement, a necessary condition, for justified action undertaken for another's good."[3]

In order to intervene paternalistically, first one must be qualified to do so: either professionally (as a cardiologist to aid a terminal heart patient) or by legal authorization (as in parent-child relations). Second, one must strive to do what is in the person's best interest. In some cases, what is in the other's best interest is clear-cut (the diabetic in shock needs to be administered insulin), and in other cases it is debatable (should an unmarried woman get an abortion?). Thus, the interventionist is not expected to be infallible but would be expected to reason soundly, gather accurate evidence about the case, and utilize the latest knowledge in arriving at a rational decision.

Many social reformers work with some notion of the public interest in mind. The public interest would require policies (or legislation) ratified by justified authority. However noble policy goals may be, in a democratic society undemocratic means cannot be used to attain such ends: means and ends should be consonant. Thus, to say that something is in the public interest is to imply that divergent interests have been reconciled in policy deliberation and execution. A democratic representative has a duty either to safeguard constituents' interests or, as an assembly member representing the populace, the interests of the people at large. Since the citizenry is composed of a highly diversified complex of interest groups with crisscrossing memberships, this is no simple matter. Thus, it seldom makes sense to talk of the majority except with reference to the results of a particular referendum or election, to describe how votes were cast. A basic test for a political system is whether it tends to provide for the interests of the governed and protect them against the abuse of power.

Policies promoted in the public interest must not only be democratically developed but should be supported by appeal to a moral principle. A moral principle could be generic (Kant's categorical imperative or Mill's utilitarianism), or apply to an area of social life (principles of equality, freedom, justice, honesty, loyalty, and the like). The public interest is largely a normative concept, by appealing to moral principles for support and by referring to valued conditions to be realized. Thus, in any pronouncement about the public interest, the observer should determine whether an appropriate moral principle is cited and that the policy adopted will likely bring about the desired values. A moral principle is sought because doing so will likely support the good of society as a whole, rather than a constellation of special interests.

The public interest can be supported by both affirmative and preventive acts. Affirmative acts would provide goods and services or promote human rights; preventive acts would be undertaken to avoid harm. Affirmative acts are designed to achieve educational goals, while preventive acts seek to remove impediments. Affirmative acts would be the provision of a comprehensive curriculum, and taxation for financial support, whereas preventive acts would include the imposition of safety restrictions on power tools, and quarantining students with serious contagious diseases.

Returning to our original question: Is the service ethic paternalistic? The answer would need to be determined on a case-by-case basis. But if in some cases it is found to be paternalistic, this is no fatal flaw. Paternalism can be justified under certain conditions. The paternalist must be qualified to intervene, and must strive to do what is in the subject's best interest. When these two conditions are met, paternalism may be justified without consent in such instances of incompetence as immaturity, diminished capacity, and temporary loss of capacity. Policies in the public interest without consent may be paternalistic and justifiable. The policies must be democratically developed, ratified by justified authority, and appeal to a moral principle. The interventionist, in whatever type of situation outlined above, will need not only to observe the principle of nonmaleficence but the principle of beneficence, in addition to a specific moral principle.

There might be cases of consent that could be judged paternalistic insofar as they involve coercive interference with the action or state of a person. Consent may be granted because of weakness of will, by which the individual is unable to gain control over her excessive drinking, smoking, drug taking, or suicidal attempts, and, though she feels compelled to continue these activities, is fearful of the consequences and requests intervention to avert dire consequences. In conclusion, paternalism without consent may be justified either in the public interest or because of incompetence, and with consent when the person still perceives the intervener as engaged in coercive interference for her own good.

Aristotle and the Golden Mean

Aristotle (384–322 B.C.) was a student of Plato, and remained for nearly twenty years at the Academy. He later tutored Alexander the Great and founded the Peripatetic school in the Lyceum at Athens. Aristotle's extant works cover almost all of the sciences known in his time. He was the founder of deductive logic, and was a systematic scientific researcher who gained a wide mastery of empirical facts. Aristotle had great influence among Arabian and Jewish philosophers after the ninth century, and was the single most important authority during the later Christian Middle Ages. He is generally thought to be one of the two or three most influential philosophers in the history of Western thought.

Aristotle holds that all arts, investigations, and practical pursuits aim at some good; therefore, the Good is that at which all things aim. Among the many ends for our action, if there is one for which we strive for its own sake, this one must be the Supreme Good.

What defines happiness, he says, is a matter of dispute. Ordinary people identify happiness with such visible goods as pleasure or wealth or honor. But he avoids an infinite regress by holding that there is something good in itself that is the cause of all other goods being good. Three types of lives are usually pursued: the Life of Enjoyment, the Life of Politics, and the Life of Contemplation. No one, however, chooses happiness as a means to something other than itself; therefore, happiness is self-sufficient and the end at which all actions aim.

But what is happiness? Aristotle states that this can be determined by ascertaining man's function. He finds this function as the active exercise of the soul's faculties in conformity with rational principle. (The "soul," for Aristotle, is not given a spiritual connotation but is a function of all living things.) The excellence or virtue of each thing, according to the meaning of areté, lies in the efficiency of its particular function. Thus, human good is activity of the soul's faculties in accord with virtue and, if there is more than one virtue, in accordance with the highest virtue. The life of active virtue is essentially pleasant, and therefore the virtuous have no need of pleasure as an ornamental appendage.[4]

Virtue is of two kinds: intellectual and moral. Intellectual virtue is largely produced and increased by instruction, and requires experience and time, whereas moral or ethical virtue is the product of habit. The moral virtues are not given to us by nature, as a natural property cannot be altered by habit. Faculties given to us by nature (e.g., our senses) are endowed first in their potential form, and later we exhibit them through exercise. Our senses were not acquired by repeatedly seeing or hearing; rather, we had the senses and began to use them. In contrast, the virtues are acquired by practicing them; otherwise, there would be no need for teachers of the arts, as one would be born as either a good or bad craftsman. Since our moral dispositions are formed from our activities, it is important to control the quality of these activities.

Aristotle advances his theory of the Golden Mean. Temperance and courage are destroyed by excess and deficiency, and preserved by observing the mean. The former can be seen in the case of one who indulges every pleasure and refrains from none, and thereby becomes a profligate, or another who shuns all pleasures and becomes insensible. In the matter of courage, one who constantly retreats in fear becomes a coward, whereas another who rushes headlong into every situation without considering consequences is rash. The Golden Mean, however, does not apply to attitudes and actions that are bad in themselves because excess or deficiency is not the problem. Here Aristotle has in mind cases of malice, shamelessness, envy, and such acts as adultery, theft, and murder.[5]

If happiness were simply a certain disposition, it might be a feature of someone who spent his whole life asleep; instead, it is a form of activity in accordance with virtue. To perform noble and virtuous deeds is desirable for its own sake. But amusements are also desirable for their own sake, although they are more often harmful than beneficial, and cause individuals to neglect their health and their estates. Thus, happiness cannot be found in amusements, because they are not usually virtuous. Since happiness should be not only in accord with virtue but with the highest virtue, then the task is to identify this virtue. For Aristotle, the highest virtue is contemplation. He argues that the intellect is the highest human feature, and that it deals with the highest things that can be known. Happiness also possesses the highest degree of self-sufficiency, and it is the only activity loved for its own sake. It produces no results beyond itself, whereas practical activities seek some gain or advantage. If the intellect is divine in comparison with man, the life of contemplation is divine in comparison with human life. Contemplation has more continuity than other action, it requires fewer natural necessities, and its pleasures are pure and lasting.[6]

If the Golden Mean is applied to three success ethics (excluding momentarily the service ethic), it will be noted that these ethics, for the most part, do not observe this principle, because of their unbridled ambition, the desire to advance rapidly, and the desire to achieve abundant material goods. People goaded by such ethics do not usually achieve a mean, because of the one-sided quest for material success and the lack of balance in other areas of life, in terms of intellectual and aesthetic pursuits, leisure, family life, and social service. The service ethic also fails to achieve the Golden Mean because of excessive and extreme devotion to a social cause to the exclusion of everything else, including even one's own health and general well-being.

For Aristotle, the four success ethics would not provide genuine and lasting happiness for their adherents, because they promote activities that are not self-sufficient or are not in accord with the highest virtue (contemplation). Thus, leading proponents of the success ethics are misleading followers by even implying that such ways of life can ultimately promote happiness. Of course, success ethics proponents could argue that Aristotle's reasoning is faulty, or that the contemplative life is only for philosophers; other people, who have different natures, will best find happiness by devoting themselves primarily to divergent pursuits. Then again, they may just claim that service or material accumulation provides longer-lasting satisfaction for them, which is happiness enough.

Kant, Buber, and the Treatment of Persons

Immanuel Kant (1724–1804), German philosopher, in 1755 advanced the nebular hypothesis forty-one years before Laplace. He became professor of logic and metaphysics in 1770 at the University of Königsberg and published *The Critique of Pure Reason* in 1781. Within a few years his philosophy was being taught in all the German universities. The results of Kant's work are incalculable; his philosophy has influenced almost every area of thought.

Some of Kant's ethics has a particular bearing on the personality ethic. Kant states that moral concepts originate in reason completely a priori; in other words, they cannot be abstracted from any empirical knowledge. Since moral laws have to hold for all rational beings, our principles should be derived from the general conception of a rational being. Since everything in nature works in accordance with laws, only a rational being can act in accordance with his ideas of laws (i.e., principles). Reason is required to derive action from laws, and, therefore, the will is nothing but practical reason. Thus, the will has the power to determine that which is good.

An objective principle for a will is called a command (of reason), and the formula for this command is an imperative. All imperatives are expressed by an "ought." That which determines the will by concepts of reason is objectively valid for every rational being. All imperatives command either hypothetically or categorically. Hypothetical imperatives relate to action that is willed as a means to a particular end, whereas the categorical imperative represents action "necessary of itself" without referring to another end. There are numerous hypothetical imperatives. One usually values the products of our technological culture for the ease and convenience that they bring into our daily lives, but they are not usually valued as ends-in-themselves. In the business world, honest practices may be observed, not necessarily because honesty is good in itself, but because it helps one keep one's customers. Even an imperative concerned with the choice of a means to one's own happiness is a precept of prudence, and remains hypothetical.

Kant's primary concern is to state a categorical imperative, or practical, law that holds in all social and moral relations. There is a single categorical imperative: "Act only on that maxim through which you can at the same time will that it should become a universal law."[7] As examples, Kant raises questions about committing suicide and promise-keeping. A man in despair from a series of misfortunes considers suicide. He needs to apply the test, "Can the maxim of my action become a universal law of nature?" Another person is driven to borrow money because of need; he knows that he will not be able to repay it, but he recognizes that the loan will not be granted without a firm promise to repay. But if one considers the promise in terms of not only personal advantage but whether it could become a universal law and be self-consistent, it would be recognized that the very purpose of promising would become impossible to fulfill.

Could there be something whose existence has an absolute value? Kant states that "man, and in general every rational being, exists as an end in himself, not merely as a means for arbitrary use by this or that will: he must in all his actions, whether they are directed to himself or other rational beings, always be viewed at the same time as an end."[8] Beings whose existence depends not on will but on nature, if they are non-rational beings, have only a relative value and are called things. Rational beings, in contrast, are called persons.

The will conforms to universal practical reason. This means that the will of every rational being makes universal law. Thus, the will as supreme law-giver cannot depend upon any interest, for this would require further law to restrict the interest of self-love; therefore, the will is autonomous.

Kant speaks of a "kingdom of ends." By a "kingdom" he means a systematic union of rational beings under common law. By treating persons never merely as means but always as ends under this systematic union, the kingdom can be called a kingdom of ends.

Another leading thinker who has been concerned with the treatment of persons is Martin Buber (1878–1965). Buber, Jewish philosopher and mystic, was born in Vienna and studied there and in Berlin. He was a professor of religion at the University of Frankfurt am Main, 1922–33, and, after 1938, was professor of philosophy at Hebrew University in Jerusalem. He made available to Christian theology a rich cultural and religious perspective, and significantly influenced subsequent theology and ethics.

For Buber, there is no independent "I" that first establishes its own existence and then moves outward to God and the world. Instead, there is no "I" in itself but only in relation. The two primary relations are "I–It" and "I–Thou." The "It" and the "Thou" do not represent different things, but two possible relations between the self and an "object."[9]

The "I–It" is the typical subject-object relationship. "I–It" symbolizes experiencing and using; it depends upon an "object," a thing. It is an unlimited experience, in which the "I" is active and does not treat the "object" or "other" as capable of entering into a relationship bound by mutuality. The "It" becomes a thing. It is true, he observes, that man can live securely in the world of the "It," but if he lives only in that world he is not a man.

The relation of "I–Thou" is a direct and intense mutual relation, in which one meets the "other" as genuinely different than oneself but as someone with whom one can enter into an active relation. One becomes an "I" by virtue of a "Thou"; in other words, self is a social and relational concept. We can study things in terms of their components in an objective manner ("I–It"), but when they are encountered with "the power of exclusiveness," the components become united in a relational event. Buber maintains that art is of the "I–Thou" relationship. One can study music in terms of bars, chords, and notes; this is the realm of the "I–It." But the same music can be encountered as an "I–Thou" relation in which the components become an inseparable unity. The "I–Thou" relation combines subjectivity and objectivity in a totality that transcends the "I–It" relation.

The relation of "I–Thou" is a relation of love. It also is the instinct for communion.[10] The educative relationship is one of inclusion; it is a "true inclusion of one another by human souls."[11] The educator's concern is the person as a whole in his present actualities and future possibilities.[12]

We can see that in Buber's philosophy the treatment of persons should take the form of an "I–Thou." This has a rough similarity with Kant's categorical imperative to treat persons always as ends and never merely as means. Undoubtedly such action would diminish dehumanization and alienation.

Kant's ethics and Buber's philosophy provide sharp criticisms of the personality ethic. The objective of the personality ethic is to get others to do what you want. Proponents of the personality ethic emphasized that an understanding of human relations pays off in profit-making situations; and though a knowledge of the product is helpful, the sales pitch is even more valuable. The personality ethic provided ample advice on how to manipulate people and develop an attractive personal and physical appearance.

Applying Kantian ethics, one could charge the proponents of the personality ethic with a failure to observe the categorical imperative, and therefore with treating persons strictly as a means. The personality ethic could not be universalized, for what would happen to society if everyone acted this way? Morality would be nonexistent if each and every person manipulated others to gain some material advantage. It would be tantamount to creating an Hobbesian universe.

The implication of Buber's philosophy is that the personality ethic emphasizes "I–It" relations. Thus, to get ahead one treats others as objects to be manipulated rather than in an "I–Thou" relation.

Nietzsche and the Shattering of Illusions

Friedrich Wilhelm Nietzsche (1844–1900), German philosopher and classical philologist, studied Greek and Latin at Bonn and Leipzig, and was appointed to a chair of classical philology at the University of Basel in 1869. He resigned the professorship in 1879 because of ill health, and spent the next ten years largely in solitude as an author living in Italy and Switzerland. He collapsed on a street in Turin in 1889, and died in 1900, after eleven years of insanity. After his death, his writings eventually became widely influential with writers and scholars. Apologists for Naziism drew upon his ideas as a justification of their doctrines, but most scholars consider this a perversion of Nietzsche's thought.

Nietzsche was not a systematic philosopher but a moralist, who passionately rejected Western bourgeois values. He claimed that a morality in which all persons are treated as equals, however unequal their merit and attributes, is a slave morality detestable to the person of knowledge and integrity.[13] One has duties to one's equals, he said, but one may treat beings of lower rank as one chooses. The masses, with their slavish mentalities, may be sacrificed in the pursuit of knowledge and higher ideals. Their sacrifice will bring about a higher civilization led by the *Ubermensch,* the higher man, or superman. Nietzsche viewed compassion and charity as the products of a herd mentality. Sympathy and pity are weaknesses, not marks of virtue. To be hard of heart, to be severe with oneself, is the mark of a virtuous man. Christianity and socialism are faiths of "little men" where excuses for weaknesses are paraded as moral principles. Furthermore, the masses should learn to fear the higher classes, who by right should control them and use them for their own purposes. The idea of one morality for all is an illusion, and is detrimental to the higher man. Nietzsche believed that his era was a transitional one, and that the best one could do was to prepare for a more fortunate age in which the higher man is a creator and has developed his will to power, using his abilities fully to overcome obstacles of self and others.

God is dead, Nietzsche asserted, because we have killed him. What people have revered as God is not godlike. He considers that the way Christians claim to express faith in God, and the acts they believe their faith entails, diminish man; yet, when people realize the consequences of what they have done, resulting in the death of God, these consequences will threaten life by diminishing its purpose and significance. Nietzsche saw his role as that of questioning, rather than rationalizing, the values of society, which was why he believed he could see more clearly the death of God.

The problem entailed by positing the death of God was to escape nihilism by developing naturalistic values that would not resort to invoking God for explanations. To affirm life, one ought not rationalize the values of society. Too much hypocrisy, delusion, and comfortableness are hidden behind these moralities. One must question accepted moralities in order to bring about a reevaluation of values. In this process, we will find how many idols of our age and of the past have a hollow sound when questions are posed by a hammer. The striking illumination that follows will be more than traditional values can withstand. Nietzsche felt that he could obtain a new openness, a free and unlimited view.

Thus, his purpose was to find a way (a way at least for him, since a general way or "the way" does not exist) of affirming life, saying "yes" to life. Nietzsche outlined the problem in *Thus Spoke Zarathustra:* "For whatever is his own is well concealed from the owner; and of all the treasures, it is our own that we dig up last. . . ."[14] But as Nietzsche adds: "He, however, has discovered himself who says, 'This is my good and evil',"[15] not what is good and evil for all, for the mass, for the majority, but what is good and evil for me. Man must reevaluate all existing values, create his own, and live by them courageously.

Nietzsche vacillates somewhat in taking a strong position on the truth and illusion theme, but he has Zarathustra tell us that man must learn to hang by slender threads. Apparently, the fewer the illusions the greater the strength. But Nietzsche does not say that we can have no illusions. In fact, there are some useful fictions. These fictions promote the will to power. Life is essentially a will to power, the feeling that one is in command of oneself and the future. But power and a new set of values are not desirable for their consequences but are good in themselves. For Nietzsche, history is not a linear process moving toward some ultimate end; instead it is cyclical, involving an eternal recurrence of people, things, and problems.

Nietzsche would be especially severe with the service ethic. Some of its values for the downtrodden, such as compassion and charity, are products of a herd mentality. Sympathy and pity are also weaknesses, not marks of virtue. He would likely view the service ethic as basically in the spirit of socialism, a type of "slave morality" in which people who are unequal are to be treated as equals.

The success ethics, from Nietzsche's perspective, tend to rationalize societal values, rather than to seriously question them in order to bring about a reevaluation of values. But because of hypocrisy and delusion, the rationalizers of societal values would likely adamantly resist Nietzsche's demands.

Each success ethic advocates "the way" to success: a generalized system that enables individuals to develop certain stipulated skills and requisite motivation. But according to Nietzsche, "the way" does not exist; each person must find his own way.

Nietzsche would also warn against the ostensible illusions of the success ethics, in their beliefs that by following certain formulas, observing certain rules, and sustaining a level of motivation, one could achieve success. The relative ease, and the profuse promises, of success, especially with the personality and mind power ethics, perpetrate illusions. For Nietzsche, it is an illusion that many have the potential to rise to the top, as Nietzsche views the world as consisting of rare overmen and the deluded masses.

Mill and the Greatest Good

John Stuart Mill (1806–1873), British philosopher and economist, was a precocious child whose father, James Mill, philosopher, economist, and historian, subjected him from the ages of three to sixteen to an extremely intensive education, which began with studies of Greek at three, Latin at eight, and by fourteen he had completed a rigorous classical education. Mill underwent a mental crisis in 1826, and owed his recovery in part to reading Wordsworth, learning that feelings should be cultivated as well as intellect. In 1823, he abandoned the study of law and began work for the East India Company, and was in charge of relations with East Indian states from 1836 to 1856. He served in Parliament from 1865 to 1868. Beginning in 1831, he cherished the intellectual companionship of Mrs. Harriet Taylor, whom he finally married in 1852, three years after her husband's death. He credited Mrs. Taylor for much of his own intellectual achievement. Mill's influence has been strong in economics, politics, and philosophy.

Utilitarianism is a system of normative ethics proposed by David Hume, but given definitive formulation by Jeremy Bentham and John Stuart Mill. In Mill's *Utilitarianism*,[16] he seeks to defend the view that acts are right and good which produce the greatest good for the greatest number. Pleasure and freedom from pain are the only desirable ends. Mill rejects the argument that Utilitarianism depicts human nature at the lowest animal level, as animals are incapable of experiencing many pleasures available to humans. Some kinds of pleasures are more valuable than others. Pleasures can be judged in terms of both quality and quantity. Based on wide experience, an individual can make a comparative judgment about the quality of pleasures, and any rational being should choose pleasures of higher quality. Mill asserts: "It is better to be a human being dissatisfied than a pig satisfied."

Actions are to be judged as right or wrong solely on the basis of their consequences. Second, the only thing that matters is the amount of happiness that such consequences bring about. Third, no one's happiness is to be counted as more important than anyone else's. Each person's welfare is equally important.

What things are good? What actions are right? We decide about the second question by answering the first one. Right actions are those that produce the most good, and the one thing that is good is happiness; all other things are desirable only as means to that end.

But why should anyone adopt these standards? Utilitarianism applies both external and internal sanctions. Desire of favor and fear of displeasure from others or from God are external sanctions. Feelings of affection for others or awe of God may motivate people to act unselfishly and adopt the Utilitarian morality. Conscience is the internal sanction. Mill views conscience as intense pain attendant on violation of duty. One's sense of obligation, he believes, is learned. Education and social arrangements can promote moral feelings toward virtuous activity. Mill attempted to show that human notions of obligation can be made compatible with the utility principle. With justice and obligation, humans can achieve the greatest happiness of the greatest number.

Mill's Utilitarianism highlights the fact that personality and mind power ethics do not advance the greatest good for the greatest number; instead they focus on the individual's achieving success in the system, and thereby fail to envision the system as a whole, and its overall effects. These two ethics, rather than promoting the greatest good, are more likely examples of ethical egoism. Universal ethical egoism states that everyone should always act in her own self-interest regardless of the interests of others unless their interests also serve hers.

Brian Medlin points out that ethical egoism is an inconsistent theory because the ethical egoist is likely to impair his own advantage by promulgating his doctrine, which encourages others to act exclusively in their own interest. Surely, the ethical egoist who seeks his own advantage must persuade them to do otherwise. But in order to be an ethical doctrine it must apply to others; thus ethical egoism, when carried out in practice, is reduced to individual egoism, which is not an ethical doctrine at all.[17]

Richard Brandt, on the other hand, believes that the charge of inconsistent attitudes is more damaging to ethical egoism than is Medlin's argument. Since ethical egoism demands that each person take the course of action that maximizes his own welfare, we must approve of the fact that *A* concerns himself with his own interests, and that *B* ignores the interests of *A*. When *A* is acting, his are the only interests that count; but when *A* is the recipient of actions, his interests do not count. Thus, when *A* is acting, he can sacrifice *B's* life in order to save himself from a scratch; and *B* can do the same when he is acting. Ethical egoism is guilty of directing action on the basis of inconsistent attitudes by asking us to be impartial to persons, but only in reference to their own acts. It directs us to have one attitude toward *A* when in *A's* presence but not in *B's*, and another toward *A* when no longer in *A's* presence but in *B's*.[18]

The doctrine of stewardship of wealth proposed by Andrew Carnegie would partly exempt his brand of the character ethic from these charges. Benjamin Franklin's list of virtues included justice, by which he meant doing no one wrong by doing injuries or omitting the benefits that are your duties. Other character ethic proponents in chapter 2, other than Stagg and Truman, could likely be charged with ethical egoism.

Marx and Capitalist Exploitation

Karl Marx (1818–1883), German social philosopher, was the chief theorist of modern socialism and communism. Marx studied law at Bonn and Berlin, but became interested in philosophy and took a Ph.D. degree at Jena in 1841. He joined the Communist League in 1847, and with Frederick Engels, wrote for it the famous *Communist Manifesto*, in 1848, which expressed the general view of class struggle. The failure of the revolutions of 1848 convinced him of the need for revolutionary parties. After his exile from most continental centers, he settled in England in 1849, and spent most of his life studying in the British Museum. Although he was able to earn some income as a correspondent for the *New York Tribune*, he was continually dependent upon Engels for financial aid. He helped found the International Workingmen's Association, in 1864, and published the first volume of his *Das Kapital* in 1867, which provided an exposition of Marxism and became the basis for international socialism.

Labor is the touchstone for self-realization in Marx's philosophy of human nature. Labor represents the efforts of individuals to create and satisfy their desires and to achieve happiness. Humans labor to create, to transform the world, and to make themselves at home in it.

Humans are not isolated from one another. One should speak of "men" and their relations in concrete behavior, so that, rather than talking about an abstraction of man inherent in each individual, Marx speaks of men always within a context of "the ensemble of social relations."[19]

The problems of individuals arise in their labor when the growing complexity of the division of labor and the advancement and application of technological knowledge alienate them from their work and serve as an increasingly dehumanizing force. Workers in capitalistic societies feel free when not at work and apart from themselves when working. Work becomes compulsion — not the satisfaction of genuine needs to create and relate oneself to the world, but merely a means to satisfy wants external to oneself. Hence, for Marx, one can only act freely in what he considers one's animal functions — eating, drinking, reproducing — while in the functions that make people human — one's work — one is nothing more than a work animal. The worker becomes a unit of labor cost, a saleable commodity, a thing. Alienation from labor and its concomitant dehumanization stem from the means of production, which established a division of labor that isolates persons from the community, and separates individuals and jobs from one another; and, through specialization, work narrows until it becomes inherently monotonous.

Marx borrowed the dialectic from Hegel, which attempted to account for the unfolding of events in nature as a result of the conflict of opposites and the development of negation, leading to a new synthesis. For Hegel, every state, condition, or proposition calls forth its own negation, which provokes the negation of the negation leading to a new synthesis. Marx joined the "Left Hegelians" early in his career at Berlin University, and subscribed to Hegel's logic while criticizing the political and religious implications of Hegel's philosophy. The Left Hegelians were concerned that Hegel's philosophy led to higher levels of self-consciousness, culminating in an absolute self-consciousness, thereby offering a metaphysical justification for Prussian absolutism. Marx then turned to the works of Feuerbach, and while keeping the Hegelian dialectic, reversed it by eliminating the idealistic content of Spirit and self-consciousness and substituting a materialistic content, the basis of which he borrowed from Feuerbach. By doing this, Marx developed the functional structure for his philosophy of history, which he called "dialectical materialism."

Marx probably developed his key concept of "class war" from his contact with French socialists of his time. Class war had usually symbolized, to the socialists, the conflict between rich and poor, but for Marx, it denoted the conflict between employer (bourgeoisie) and employee (proletariat) as it occurs in capitalistic societies.

Marx contends that the mode of production affects and conditions the whole of social, intellectual, and political life. Religion, art, and morality do not develop first, with the mode of production emerging from these factors; instead, they are determined by the mode of production. Man's social existence determines his consciousness, rather than the converse.[20]

One must still look at the theory of surplus value to comprehend Marx's view of capitalistic exploitation. Borrowing from the British economist David Ricardo, Marx held in *Das Kapital* that the value of the commodities consumed by a worker is less than the value of the commodities he produces; the difference, called "surplus value," represents the profit of the capitalist. It is labor-power rather than labor that the capitalist purchases. The natural price to pay for labor is that which allows the worker to subsist and continue his existence. But when labor-power is used it produces more value than it costs, because even though the worker may make enough for his maintenance in six hours, he has sold his labor-power, and thereby may be forced to work ten or twelve hours each day.

Marx differentiates capital into constant and variable, which corresponds generally to the distinction between machinery and wages. But since machines transfer their value, neither more nor less, to the product, machines yield no surplus value.

A belief related to surplus value was Marx's interpretation of the capitalist. He held that a capitalist was one who lived off the surplus value produced by the workers while he himself remained idle. To be a capitalist, one must secure sufficient surplus value that work no longer is necessary.

The seeds of its own destruction can be found in the capitalistic system, with its overproduction, its crises every ten years, and its unemployed workers. The capitalist waits to turn his products into capital before circulating them. But circulation is limited due to overproduction. The bourgeoisie are indicted for their incapacity to manage the productive forces of society.

The next historical stage is represented by socialism, wherein the proletariat revolt against and overthrow the bourgeoisie, leading to the "dictatorship of the proletariat," in which the agencies of production would be organized first by joint-stock companies, later by trusts, and then finally by the state. Socialized production, which has eliminated the abuses of capitalism, constitutes an interim stage, which will give way to communism, the final historical stage. The state will "wither away," and classes will no longer be necessary. Thus, whereas the capitalistic state seeks to perpetuate itself and maintain its power structure, the dictatorship of the proletariat deliberately prepares itself for its own demise by striving to abolish the class system. The alienation of labor endemic in capitalism will cease to exist when communism is reached. And the division of labor, which is the ultimate reason for the existence of classes, will be eliminated. Productive labor will become a creative and pleasurable activity by giving the individual the opportunity to develop his abilities, both physical and mental. Since no division of labor exists in a communist society, there is no one sphere of activity to which an individual will be limited, for he can perform one activity today and another tomorrow, hunting in the morning, fishing in the afternoon, and raising cattle in the evening, if he chooses.[21]

Three success ethics, other than the service ethic, uncritically embrace and extol capitalism and aspire for materialistic rewards within the system. From a Marxist perspective, these success ethics gravely ignore the great injustices and exploitation inherent in capitalism and, by instilling capitalistic goals for personal advancement, perpetuate the system and thereby sanction further abuses of the proletariat. These success ethics also grossly exaggerate the opportunities available for the working class to rise in the system.

In contrast, Marxism would depict the service ethic as resting on the ideology of liberalism and forms of humanitarianism. Liberalism, however, is little more than a palliative because it fails to get at the root of the problem — capitalism itself. It leaves capitalism largely intact while tinkering with working and living conditions. Thus, until the roots of the problem are extirpated, and capitalism eventually replaced with a classless society free of exploitation and injustice, widespread suffering and inequities will persist, although their severity will be obscured from public view by liberalism's nostrums.

Dewey, Individualism, and Community

John Dewey (1859–1952) was reared in Burlington, Vermont, and took his bachelor's degree at the University of Vermont. After teaching high school for two years in Oil City, Pennsylvania, he took his Ph. D. at Johns Hopkins University, where he came under the influence of Hegel's philosophy. He taught at the universities of Michigan and Minnesota, and from 1894 to 1904, he was director of the School of Education at the University of Chicago, where he first began to achieve renown, through the implementation of his ideas in the laboratory school. From Chicago, he went to Columbia University, where he remained until retirement. Dewey was a prolific writer who addressed himself to problems in art, religion, philosophy, politics, and education. Although not the founder of pragmatism, he became its best-known figure. Dewey is generally recognized as America's leading educational philosopher during the first half of the twentieth century and one of the most important influences on progressive education.

Aspects of Dewey's social and political thought are especially pertinent in reappraising the success ethics. Dewey observes that some investigators have searched for an all-embracing impulse that will explain the cause of human actions. "The point," according to Dewey, "is that appeal to certain alleged human motivations in a wholesale way, such as 'initiative,' 'independence,' 'enterprise,' at large, obscures the need for observation of events in the concrete."[22]

Other fallacies about human nature are committed whenever the individual is taken as supreme and cultural factors are negated, or vice versa. In the individualism of the eighteenth century, the individual was accorded greater importance than cultural factors. Other views reduce the individual, as Marx did in framing programs exclusively in terms of cultural conditions. It is erroneous, in determining the basis of social relations, to explain events "as if one factor or other in the interaction were the whole thing."[23] Dewey believes that to oppose the individual to society is to make an empty conceptual distinction.

Since no real dichotomy exists between the individual and the social, it is important not to confuse private acts with the former and public acts with the latter. Private acts are social in their consequences in many cases — they contribute to the welfare of the community or affect community relations. Thus, "any transaction deliberately carried on between two or more persons is social in quality. It is a form of associated behavior and its consequences may influence further associations."[24] Many private businesses, works of art, scientific discoveries, and other activities conducted as private affairs are social in their outcomes. Many acts of private philanthropy have been of untold benefit for many people, though no conscious intention to effect widespread benefit motivated them. Similarly, behavior is not necessarily socially valuable because it was conducted in the name of the public by private agents. Thus, the argument "has warned us against identifying the community and its interests with the state or the politically organized community."[25]

The distinctions between private and public are to be drawn in terms of the scope and consequences of acts that need social control. Certain characteristics bring a public into operation: "namely, the far-reaching character of consequences, whether in space or time; their settled, uniform recurrent nature, and their irreparableness. Each of these involves questions of degree."[26]

Dewey believes that it is necessary to explore the quality and char-acter of interpersonal relations in America in order to recognize the greatest threat to democracy. Our age, he claims, highly prizes mate-rial goods and places material gain ahead of human values. "We live as if economic focus determined the growth and decay of institutions and settled the fate of individuals. Liberty becomes a well-nigh obso-lete term; we start, go, and stop at the signal of a vast industrial machine. . . . Worth is measured by the ability to hold one's own or to get ahead in a competitive pecuniary race."[27]

The industrialist extols the virtues of machine technology and its work-saving devices to the extent of reverence for the machine itself and what it can do. The industrialist claims that the machine is used for humane and moral purposes. Industry and business conducted for profit are nothing new, but the machine has given them unprecedented power and scope. Human associations, law and politics, frequently are reduced to the influences of the machine and money. Equal opportu-nity, free association, and inter-communication are obscured and crowded out. Dewey observes that "there is a perversion of the whole ideal of individualism to conform to the practices of a pecuniary culture. It has become the source and justification of inequalities and oppres-sions. Hence our compromises, and the conflicts in which aims and standards are confused beyond recognition."[28] Various signs mark the dissolution of individuality: the quantification of life and an attendant disregard of its quality; standardization; and erecting technique as an end.

Dewey believes that the problem of developing a new individuality appropriate to our age is the deepest problem of our time. Nor should we seek to restore an individuality of a bygone age that relates to a radically different society. Instead, the individuality for the modern age should be determined by critical thinking, experimental investigation, and scientific inquiry.

Thus, for Dewey, the existence of community is necessary for indi-vidual development. He distinguishes between an association — an

organization of persons without common values or meaningful communication about their needs and aspirations — and a community that
results from shared goals and endeavors. Communities arise when
people recognize common problems and the need to cooperate. Such
mutual communication and cooperation are essential to democracy.
And the keynote of democracy is the participation of all citizens in the
formation of values that regulate social life.

Dewey's social philosophy serves as a critique of three success
ethics: character, personality, and mind power. Dewey attacked the
practices of a pecuniary culture. For the character ethic, being poor is
an evil to be overcome, and the accumulation of wealth is the end that
will confirm one as a successful person. Though Russell Conwell, for
instance, warns about the idolatry of money, and against hoarding it,
those who gain wealth are wise if they invest it and find purposes for
it. Proponents of the personality ethic were more interested in justifying material success than warning against the dangers of avarice; to
be successful, one must learn how to get others to do what you want.
As for the mind power ethic, O. S. Marden asserted that the Creator
did not intend for man to be poor or to suffer; one should learn to
attract luxuries. Marden held that morals had no connection with
money-making ability.

Dewey laments the obsessions of materialistic culture in the competitive striving for pecuniary gain, the reverence for the machine, and the
loss of individuality. The three success ethics are not only guilty of
conforming to the materialistic values of the culture (though differing
as to the most effective way to exercise them), but of aiding and abet-
ting in the dissemination of these values. Dewey believes that individualism has been perverted in order to comply with the goals of a materialistic culture.

The three success ethics have not overcome the dualism between
the individual and the social; instead, the dualism is magnified by the
emphasis on the individual over and against society. The focus is on
the individual exclusively, and how that individual can wrest desired
material goods and advantages from a recalcitrant and competitive
social order. Thus, the individual is viewed as supreme, and cultural
factors are endowed with less importance.

Finally, the three success ethics contribute to association, not
community. Each, with its own approach, shows how the individual,
arrayed against forces that might undermine him, can acquire wealth
and thereby become a successful person. But, for Dewey, the creation
of community is essential for sustaining a democratic way of life.

Niebuhr and the Will to Power

Reinhold Niebuhr (1892–1971), neo-orthodox theologian and political liberal, was a younger contemporary of Dewey. Both struggled to promote liberal social and political causes, yet they differed metaphysically: Dewey took a naturalistic approach and embraced a reassessed version of the Enlightenment's idea of progress, while Niebuhr took a supernaturalistic approach and adopted the Augustinian doctrine of original sin. Niebuhr was born in Missouri, and earned his B.D. and M.A. degrees at Yale. He held the only pastorate of his career for thirteen years in Detroit. His experience with workers confronted him with the dehumanization of factory work, and during this time he was notable for his support of the labor movement and pacifism. He spent most of his career teaching Christian ethics and theology at Union Theological Seminary in New York City, until his retirement in 1960.

Niebuhr holds that the basis of the human urge to survive is compounded in the "will-to-live." This is the fundamental drive in all individuals, although it finds different representations and expressions in each person. The will, for Niebuhr, is the self organized to attain either a short-range or long-range purpose. This requires an analysis of ends in view, and a comparison of their relative merit in terms of a system of values.

The will-to-live, however, is not as unaffected as it may at first seem. Whenever individuals strive to perpetuate their earthly existence, they are striving against other wills that have the same inclination. The will then surveys the situation to discover how it can increase its ability to continue in existence. Individuals tend to push forward their own interests, and this precipitates a struggle for power, prestige, and status. Niebuhr calls this tendency the "will-to-power." Each individual, no matter how uncorrupted that person's vision, is possessed of an inordinate amount of egoism, which invariably diverts nobler pursuits and ideals. "This egoism is stronger in men than in beasts precisely because man is the only finite creature who knows he is finite and he is therefore tempted to protest against his fate. One form that this protest takes is his imperialistic ambition, his effort to overcome his insignificance by subordinating other life to his individual or collective will."[29] Individuals hide their own interests behind universal or community values, which enables them to gain dominion while maintaining respectability.

Reason itself is not much help in averting the transmuting of the will-to-live into the will-to-power, because even the most rational persons are never quite rational when their own interests are at stake. Humans overestimate their finiteness and limited nature and are thereby guilty of pride; this pride is the Christian idea of sin. Through this pompous display, humans assert their tendency to play God. "Sin is occasioned precisely by the fact that man refuses to admit his 'creatureliness' and to acknowledge himself as merely a member of a total unity of life. He pretends to be more than he is."[30]

On all levels of behavior, the creative and egoistic aspects of human nature are curiously compounded in such a way that the more talented individuals in society can alternate these egoistic aspects and disguise them under the veil of creative selflessness and genuine interest in others' rights. Niebuhr suggests that we should learn to laugh at ourselves by recognizing our foibles and conceits in order that we may become humble in the face of God. "What is funny about us is precisely that we take ourselves too seriously. We are rather insignificant little bundles of energy and vitality in a vast organization of life. But we pretend that we are the very centers of this organization."[31]

What each self needs is the ability to rise above nature through religious faith and envision a universe where human personality is an ideal to be eternally cherished. In this way a sublimation of the admixture of these two wills may occur.

Human freedom, however, causes many problems. It causes humans to rebel against nature's necessities. Individuals, in their quest for power, may disrupt basic harmonies within a culture. Human ambitions render pure communism or pure democracy an impossibility. "This unique freedom is the generator of both the destructiveness and the creativity of men. Most of the efforts to manage the historical process would actually destroy the creativity with the destructiveness."[32]

History reveals that humans have achieved some measure of freedom over the ages, otherwise tribal communities would not have developed into empires and nations. "But there is no absolute freedom in history; for every choice is limited by the stuff that nature and previous history present to the hour of decision."[33] Modern man, however, holds a false conception of his freedom, and, consequently, cultures have built faulty perspectives. Niebuhr finds that modern man defies nature's laws by only interpreting nature from the viewpoint of his unique rationality. The individual fails to recognize the possibilities of the human spirit, which transcends both nature and reason.

The Christian interpretation of freedom in history seeks to give meaning to the maze of daily life. Sin arises from the improper use of freedom. Humans have a faulty perspective on their nature, and fail to recognize their unique roles as creators and creatures in history. The final form of this error is the modern belief that humans eventually will become the unequivocal masters of historical destiny. This error persuades modern man to reject all biblical concepts of divine providence as no longer relevant to his position of strength and power. Thus, not only is there an exaggeration of the degree of growth in freedom and power, but also the mistake of confusing freedom with virtue.

The biblical interpretation of freedom in history also accounts for evil in the world. Evil arises from the wrong use of human capacities, which is always some failure to recognize the limits of one's power, wisdom, or virtue. And humans must bear the responsibility for sin, for sin is the "consequence of man's self-centeredness and egotism by which he destroys the harmony of existence."[34]

How can humans find meaning in the confusing maze of historical events? Christianity provides intelligibility to the whole of history by viewing it in its universe of meaning. Christianity knows by faith of some events in history in which the transcendent and whole stream of history is revealed. This faith understands the sense of meaninglessness that enters history through the corruption of human freedom.

Niebuhr presents a severe and sobering perspective on human limitations and the individual's place in the cosmos. He would be critical of the unrestrained optimism that underlies the success ethics. A belief in the idea of progress is manifested insofar as the success ethics tacitly assume that the universe is essentially hospitable to human aspirations, and that if individuals will follow a prescribed way of life, their material and other goals will be realized. Niebuhr would find this to be a foolish and misleading picture, because it fails to consider human finitude, the transmutation of the will-to-live into the will-to-power, and the subsequent conflicts that arise when individual interests are at stake.

He would find the service ethic naive because of original sin and the difficulty of giving oneself to others and to causes outside oneself. One must guard against the altruism and selflessness in the service ethic becoming corrupted by a will-to-power over others. Proponents of this ethic may hide their real interests by invoking universal or community values to cloak their social projects.

Niebuhr would likely be skeptical that humans can actually acquire all the traits espoused in the character ethic. Though tempered by Andrew Carnegie's stewardship, the character ethic, with its ambitiousness and quest for wealth, is guilty of the sin of pride.

Niebuhr would not look more favorably upon the other two success ethics. O.S. Marden, in his approach to mind power, claimed that morals have no connection with money-making ability, and that one can learn, without strain, to attract luxuries. As for the personality ethic, it provided abundant advice on how to manipulate people and develop an attractive personal and physical appearance. Niebuhr's religious perspective would remind us that humans are creatures as well as creators of history, and that evil arises from the wrong use of one's capacities because of failure to recognize the limits of one's power, wisdom, or virtue.

Tillich and the Courage to Be

Paul Johannes Tillich (1886–1965), German/American theologian and philosopher, was born in Prussia (now Germany), received his Ph.D. from Breslau in 1911, the licentiate in theology in 1912, and in the same year was ordained in the Evangelical Lutheran Church. He served in the German army as a chaplain in World War I, and after the war he taught at universities in Berlin, Marburg, Dresden, Leipzig, and Frankfurt. Tillich's writings did not endear him to the Nazis, and he was the first non-Jewish professor to be removed from his post by the Hitler regime. He was invited to New York in 1933 by Reinhold Niebuhr, and became a naturalized citizen in 1940. He was a professor at Union Theological Seminary, Harvard University, and the University of Chicago, during which time he greatly influenced theology and the academic study of religion. He is basically an ecumenical theologian and a leading representative of existentialism in theology.

Tillich's aim is not to examine the religion of the churches, but rather, to focus on Christian faith in the larger culture. Theology exists for Tillich in the tension between revelational truth and the questions humans face in their daily existence. Augustine's conception of community underlies Tillich's thinking. Whereas Augustine speaks of supreme love as an orientation for human beings, Tillich speaks of an "ultimate concern." Communities are formed by an ultimate loyalty to some common object of love. Each culture has its own ultimate concern giving it its unique style of life. Out of anxiety, individuals generate their need for ultimate concern, and God is the name given to this ultimate concern that answers the questions of the meaning of existence. It is out of ultimate concern and the tension it generates that different conceptions of God have been created in history.

Tillich, in sharp contrast to traditional religious positions, rejects supernaturalism and the notion of a divine being outside and above the naturalistic world. Following Kant, he conceives reason as the structure of the mind that enables it to grasp reality. Reason, however, is finite; that which is ultimately significant — "being-itself" — cannot be known by reason. God is being-itself and is, manifestly, inexhaustibly in everything. One's finiteness is temporarily overcome not by reason but by revelation, which is an ecstatic, mystical experience whereby one is related in an immediate sense with the very "ground of being" — one's ultimate concern.

Religion traditionally has presented truth-claims about human beings, the universe, and God that in some sense are held to be true or warranted, and that provide a perspective that transcends the world of scientific phenomena. Believers accept a particular religious stance not only because it is emotionally satisfying, but also because it is thought to be the true position among the multitude of different religious systems. This, however, is not Tillich's position. Christianity would not be changed even if the historical Jesus had never lived, for Christian revelation is not based on a historic figure but on Jesus as the Christ. Religious symbols, in other words, need not be true; they need to be existentially effective, so that they evoke the power of being. All religious symbols have this power.

The principal existential concern for Tillich is for the courage of self-affirmation in the face of nonbeing. Courage has both an ethical and an ontological dimension, which must be united for an adequate interpretation. The ethical dimension expresses concrete action and signifies that one cares enough to decide to pursue a course of action despite opposition. The ontological dimension consists of affirming oneself despite the threat of nonbeing. Courage can best be understood when the ethical is rooted in the ontological dimension of one's being. Human beings are aware of the threat of nonbeing, through anxiety. Anxiety, in contrast to fear, has no specific object or situation on which to focus. Humans attempt to transform anxiety into fear in order to have a situation to confront and overcome. But the basic anxiety is the awareness of nonbeing, one's finitude. One's finitude is an irremovable part of one's being; thus, existential anxiety cannot be removed.

Anxiety becomes pathological when individuals can no longer affirm themselves in the face of nonbeing. Neurotics can only affirm themselves on a limited scale, because they refuse to accept their finitude. Therefore, for Tillich, a neurosis is "the way of avoiding nonbeing by avoiding being."[35] The actualization of being implies the acceptance of finitude and existential anxiety; therefore, because of the inability to accept nonbeing, the neurotic's response is limited to a weak self-affirmation.

Tillich delineates three types of anxiety: 1) ontic anxiety, or the anxiety of fate and death; 2) moral anxiety, or the anxiety of guilt and condemnation; 3) spiritual anxiety, or the anxiety of emptiness and meaninglessness. Although these three forms of anxiety are present in every age, one form tends to predominate during a particular cultural period. Thus, ontic anxiety was predominant during the terminal stages of ancient civilization, moral anxiety at the end of the Middle Ages, and spiritual anxiety at the end of the contemporary period.

The neurotic is caught up in an inability to handle these three types of anxiety. In confronting the anxiety of fate and death, self-insulation is used to build security from the threat of existence. The neurotic expresses an unrealistic perfectionism when confronting the anxiety of guilt and condemnation. These defense mechanisms limit the range of moral experience and restrict the ability of self-affirmation. Finally, in the face of anxiety of emptiness or meaninglessness, the neurotic seeks certitude in beliefs by immersing in the absolute authority of a social or religious institution or a fanatical leader. This leads to a refusal to entertain doubt, engage in independent thinking, and face courageously the existential dimension of meaninglessness.

A basic polarity of being exists between participation and individualization. The danger of the first is the loss of the self in the collective; the danger of the second is the loss of oneself from the world. Tillich believes that these polarities can be united by transcending them, through absolute faith. (Absolute faith is prescribed by Tillich even though he is critical of collective absolutes and of God viewed as an absolute in object form.) This absolute faith can conquer the three forms of anxiety. The courage to be must be rooted in being-itself, which transcends the self and the world, and unites the polarities of participation and individualization. Tillich rejects the traditional theological notion contained in the subject-object view, whereby God is an object to man. Such a God, Tillich believes, would become a tyrant who would destroy human freedom. Nietzsche has already pronounced the death of the God of traditional theology. Tillich's being-in-itself, or the ground of being, unites and transcends the courage to be as oneself (individualization) and the courage to be a part (participation). Thus, God is being-itself, the structure of all being but not determined by the structure itself.[36]

Tillich's formulation of the courage to be relates directly to the mind power ethic in terms of the human condition. According to O. S. Marden, it is not laziness that impedes success but diffidence, worry, and discouragement. When people worry, they defraud themselves; thus, one needs both freedom from fear and self-confidence, to release money-making powers. Marden recommended visualizing yourself radiating magnetism, and picturing yourself as gregarious, unselfish, generous, and tolerant.

Similarly, Norman Vincent Peale's message is that the way you think can create failure and unhappiness, but it can also bring you success and happiness. Those who think negatively get negative results; therefore, believe and succeed. Thus, he asks that you make an indelible stamp on your mind as succeeding, and always picture "success," no matter how badly conditions are at the moment. Affirm aloud, "God is now giving me success. He is now giving me attainment."

From Tillich's perspective, Marden and Peale ignore existential concerns of life and death. Life must be courageously faced so that it does not become a form of pathological anxiety in which individuals can no longer affirm themselves when confronted with non-being. Thus the mind power ethic, in its eagerness for material success, ignores essential features of the human condition.

Postscript

Much of the debate surrounding philosophical, especially ethical, responses to the various success ethics has been shown to concern perennial issues of egoistic versus altruistic intention and action. Is well-being realized in one's self, as many proponents of the character, mind power, and personality ethics seem to maintain? Or is the greatest degree of benevolence for everyone the measure of moral thought and action, as most advocates of the service ethic appear to hold? Of course, adherents to the service ethic will still have to avoid inevitable charges of paternalism if their philosophical position is to carry the day.

Despite its manifest weaknesses, the service ethic does necessitate that one give moral reasons for being moral. Unlike the other success ethics, it does not merely grant that human beings may take prudential steps only, and thus may choose to opt out of fuller moral community. For the service ethic, the good of everyone is ultimately more important than the long-term enlightened self-interest of any one individual. It is for this reason that the service ethic offers perhaps the most viable opportunity to broaden the idea of success toward communitarian concerns beyond those of acting to one's own greatest advantage.

9

Social Perspectives

Advanced industrial societies are immensely complicated organisms with many specialized — and sometimes seemingly intractable — parts and elements. As such, they are always caught up in diverse patterns of differentiation, disorganization, integration, and restructuring. All this makes problematic any simple plea that invokes the success ethic as a panacea for various and sundry social ills. As Pitirim Sorokin puts it: "In [social] systems with a large number of main variants the rhythm is so complex, consisting of so many phases, that we can hardly grasp its nature or observe its recurrence."[1] Despite this enormous sociological task, an almost equally large number of social thinkers have evaluated, in significant and relevant ways, how the success ethic has stultified individual lives in American culture.

Thus, the principal aim of this chapter is to present and analyze some major social perspectives that offer particularly forceful critiques of the success ethic. It is expected that these perspectives, derived from both scholarly and popular sources, will cast additional illumination on education and the American Dream as well. They will also show how the success ethics have become crystallized or redefined over the changing course of American society. The main themes and currents of thought to be discussed include the money culture, inner- and other-directed characters, organization men and women, status-seeking, one-dimensionality, and the nation's withering habits of the heart.

The Money Culture

The various success ethics expend much energy in judging the worth of material wealth, whether it be spent in the service of society (the character ethic) or the pursuit of personal happiness and prosperity (the mind power ethic), or used as the cardinal measurement of success in the external world (the personality ethic) — or denounced outright for contributing to the social sins of greed and avarice (the service ethic). Whatever their perspective, proponents of success need to be aware that obsession with money can serve to build walls between people. In a money culture, individuals can become alien to each other. Amorphous parts in an exchange-value system, they can ultimately objectify themselves into thinghood and generate alienated existences. As the social theorist Georg Simmel warns, "Money is . . . the vehicle for a movement in which everything else that is not in motion is completely extinguished."[2]

For Karl Marx, egoistic needs stemming from the acquisition of private property are the primary source of alienation in advanced industrial capitalism. "Private property has made us so stupid and partial that an object is only [felt to be] ours when we have it, when it exists for us as capital or when it is . . . *utilized* in some way." Because of the antagonistic relations engendered by private property in civil society, human labor and its products become alienated. Accordingly, Marx's utopian vision and logic for social change is made manifest: "An organization of society which would abolish the preconditions and thus the very possibility of huckstering, would make the [egoist] impossible."[3]

The fetishism of money is most striking in the personality ethic practiced by the likes of Willy Loman and F. Ross Johnson. For them, personality is the quality of being somebody; and it is largely the accumulation of money assets that brings that "Somebody" into being. Yet their pursuit of the money culture by means of the force of their personalities and sociability has the ironic effect of diminishing their authentic personhood and their relations to others:

> Since sociability in its pure form has no ulterior end, no content and no result outside itself, it is oriented completely about personalities. . . . But precisely because all is oriented about them, the personalities must not emphasize themselves too individually.[4]

The fundamental flaw in using money as the standard for success is that it instantiates material wealth as the overriding motivation for human activity. Furthermore, it tends to create additional wants that may not be necessary to the good life. "When we use [money] as an inducement," argues Philip Slater, "people often forget what they wanted it for and it becomes an instrument of personal or collective narcissism."[5] In pragmatic terms, money thus persuades us to do certain things that might well be artificial, immoral, or otherwise unthinkable.

In still other ways, the money culture has served as a psychological vehicle for several other success ethics. For some advocates of the character ethic, most notably Andrew Carnegie and Russell Conwell, it has permitted them to use their philanthropy for public purposes and for the personal soothing of any guilt feelings accruing from their accumulated fortunes. And if one is devoted to mind power, one need only heed Napoleon Hill's brief therapeutic advice: put your sense of purpose in order, imagine dollar signs, and you, too, shall have the opportunity to rise up the ladder of material success. Or, once one is really rich, one can blithely decide to "buy out of social problems, leaving the poor to choose between short-term suffering and long-run suffering" in a world carved out of the remnants of competitive success and failure. That cruel gap between the reality and fantasy of our national life is what Slater refers to as "American culture at the breaking point."[6]

Inner- and Other-Directed Characters

In their modern sociological classic, *The Lonely Crowd* (1950), David Riesman and associates argue that the "inner-directed" characterology that traditionally dominated America's push toward individualistic self-reliance has increasingly given way to the orientation of "other-directed" persons who are spurred chiefly by outward appearances and peer influences. Interestingly, Riesman's typology closely parallels the developmental structure and contours of the character ethic (inner-direction) and the personality ethic (other-direction).

Riesman's inner-directed persons deeply introject adult authority early in life, and hone the moral lessons taught by their elders throughout their growth. These teachings enable them to establish life plans that fuel such traits as competitiveness, conscientiousness, and pioneering spirit. As such, the inner-directed child is prodded "to live up to ideals and to test his ability to be on his own by continuous experiments in self-mastery." This pedagogic regimen calls for explicit, conscious character training by parents, who instill in their charges the proposition that human development is both demanding and "something to be worked on" all their lives.[7]

One quickly detects striking parallels in the formation of the character ethic and the construction of Protestant ethic traits of industry, frugality, sobriety, perseverance, reliability, punctuality, thoroughness, and initiative. Inner-directed people are likewise stirred by appeals to ambition, hard work, and self-discipline. Like Benjamin Franklin and Andrew Carnegie, they long to become inventors and pioneers in whatever enterprise they choose as their life's work. Typically, like Franklin and Carnegie, inner-directed youth would apprentice themselves to adult mentors in occupations and professions to mold their future. Indeed, Riesman contends that the modus vivendi of inner-direction may be best expressed in the schoolbook proverb, *ad astra per aspera:*

> The stars were far away, but still he aimed for them, in terms of a lifetime of effort. . . . He wanted money or power or fame or some lasting achievement in the arts or the professions. He wanted to leave a reputation, a memorial.[8]

Teachers also play an important role in transmitting cultural and cognitive knowledge, as well as decorums of behavior, to the inner-directed pupil. Furthermore, his schooling takes on an impersonal tone, explicit sexual segregation, and a conscious avoidance of any education of the emotions. Curriculum content, individualist competition, and study as hard work become the cornerstones for classroom practice. Such pedagogy "affirms to the child that what matters is what he can accomplish, not how nice is his smile or how cooperative his attitude." While attractive appearance and personal conviviality mark the persona of the other-directed character, inner-directed youth prepare for life goals that are clearly attached to meritocratic aims and aspirations.[9]

Admittedly, inner-direction reinforced many of the traditional Horatio Alger portraitures of success in American culture. At the same time, its images and byproducts were fraught with adverse effects. The perpetual "struggle for self-approval" implicit in its orientation left its supplicant "to feel as if he had constantly to hold on to himself; that without ceaseless vigilance he would let go and drift." That is to say, the inherent propensity of inner-direction "is to protect the individual against the others at the price of leaving him vulnerable to himself."[10]

Meanwhile, Riesman's other-directed men and women learn that "it is only the process of striving itself and the process of paying close attention to the signals from others that remain unaltered throughout life."[11] Thus, other-direction does necessitate substantial sensitivity to other people's desires. More negatively, it invites the distinct possibility that conformism might become one's lifestyle. Like Willy Loman, other-directed personalities strive to be well-liked at all costs. The ability to smile and the energy to make personal connections become the main entrees to future success. Outward striving through external appearance and attractiveness becomes the principal vehicle for getting ahead in a world of flux and impermanence.

In a capitalist society, both other-directed persons and those driven by the personality ethic tend to place a marketing mentality above any pure interest in productivity. As Riesman puts it, "All little pigs go to market; none stay home; all have roast beef, if any do; and all say 'we-we.'" Riesman refers to such strivings as characteristic of "antagonistic cooperation," in which short-term social relationships are seen as more significant than long-term goals. Weaned on supposedly progressive tenets of education that foster group dynamics, social skills, and superficial forms of interdependence, other-directed personalities can paradoxically "be strikingly insensitive to problems of character . . . [and] personal development." Because they are seldom alone, they forget how to ruminate, create, or "dream unsupervised dreams." Instead, they learn how to manipulate other people for the benefit of their own rise up the market ladder. In the process, they tend to feel guilty for any unintentional harm they might do to others.[12]

Consequently, neither inner- nor other-directed personalities, if true to their pure form, typically lead full, enriching lives. Inner-directed persons, like their character ethic counterparts, struggle to sustain a rather stoic existence founded on internalized ideals of success built upon the Puritan and Protestant ethics. Other-directed people may duplicate the personality ethic's failure to come to terms with genuineness and authenticity in creating meaning for their lives. While inner-directed types run the risk of becoming dried-up, repressed personalities, other-directed men and women may never know who they really are.

Organization Men and Women

William H. Whyte, Jr.'s *The Organization Man* (1956) reinforces Riesman's grim picture of how American life has been transformed under the "protection" of large organizational structures. With the ebbing away of Protestant ethic virtues and the values of inner-direction, Americans have continued to turn more other-directed in their search for security and advancement. Whyte argues that modern men and women have largely forsaken their own development for a new kind of invidious belief system:

> A belief in the group as the source of creativity; a belief in "belongingness" as the ultimate need of the individual; and a belief in the application of science to achieve the belongingness.[13]

Whyte directly counters Elton Mayo's early-twentieth-century human-relations model of business and industry, which extolled the presumed power of belongingness and associated work activities. Whyte's main concern is that any falsely conceived sense of collectivization might rapidly erode personal creativity and the human capacity to think beyond group boundaries:

> All creative advances are essentially a departure from agreed-upon ways of looking at things, and to over-emphasize the agreed-upon is to further legitimatize the hostility to that creativity upon which we all ultimately depend.[14]

Indeed, Whyte worries that group means may eventually become so rooted in corporate enterprise that both leaders and workers might neglect to refer to ends and goals themselves.

Reiterating Riesman's portrait of the other-directed character and the implicit dangers in adopting any full-blown personality ethic, Whyte fears that contemporary culture has begun to define "making good" as synonymous with "making friends." Like Riesman, he bemoans deficient forms of progressive education that unduly stress group cooperation. For Whyte, the school's "unquestioning emphasis on intellectual ability is profoundly important in shaping the inner-directed character. It affirms to the child that what matters is what he can accomplish, not how nice is his smile or how cooperative his attitude." At bottom, he is also concerned that students lacking critical thinking skills and a broadly based liberal education might be less immune to corporate indoctrination in the workplace environment.[15]

Citing academic administrators who seek "gregarious" and "active" types of students (akin to F. Ross Johnson during his collegiate years), Whyte quotes one dean of freshmen to this effect: "We find that the best man is the one who's had an 80 or 85 average in school and plenty of extracurricular activity. We see little use for the 'brilliant' introvert who might spend the rest of life turning out essays on obscure portions of D. H. Lawrence's letters." Likewise, he castigates the fact that 19.3 percent of all undergraduates in 1954–55 were majoring in business and that most of the rest were preparing to become "technicians" (12.3 percent in engineering, 8.1 percent in education, and 3.8 percent in agriculture). Whyte is particularly critical of the over-specialization he sees in schools of commerce, their apparent slighting of the humanities, and their penchant to offer such courses as "Personality Development," "Mental Hygiene," and "Psychology Applied to Life and Work." Almost in exasperation, he gleans a singular and inviting common denominator in such programs of study:

> Dangled before the student is the secret of happiness, for the courses explicitly instruct one in the skills of manipulating other people or the skills of adjusting oneself. The student can hardly be blamed if he passes up an opportunity of poring through William James.[16]

It is noteworthy that Whyte devotes several chapters of *The Organization Man* to a biting critique of "the practical curriculum," "business influence on education," and the woeful demise of the "well-rounded" man in corporate America. Making use of themes from the popular novel and film *The Man in the Gray Flannel Suit* to drive home his points, Whyte ridicules the conformist blandness that our educational and commercial organizations appear to be instilling in America's future leaders: "He will, in sum, be the apotheosis of the well-rounded man: obtrusive in no particular, excessive in no zeal. He will be the man in the middle."[17]

Once they are participants in the organization's life, corporate men and women are put through the paces of endless checking for conformity, from personality testing to choosing which spouses best fit the organization's requirements and specifications. Genius, originality, and exceptionality — all potential hallmarks of inner-direction and the character ethic — are typically cast asunder under the relentless sway of the organization's preeminent other-directed, personality-based mind set.

In pointed ways, Whyte also notices a subtle, but profound, shift in the manner in which self-help writers of his time market their ideas of success. The psychology of adjustment had become the order of the day. Instead of promoting mind power or character development,

> what they tell you to do is to adjust to the situation rather than change it. . . . The picture they present is one of an essentially benevolent society, and the peace of mind or the positive thinking extolled is a kind of resignation to it.[18]

Whyte especially criticizes Norman Vincent Peale for the curious way in which he attempts to wed a secular sense of belongingness to the older Protestant ethic. In fact, he accuses Peale of painting a starkly profane image of the relations between divinity and humanity:

> [According to Peale], God likes regular people — people who play baseball, like movie nuns [in *A Man Called Peter*]. He smiles on society, and his message is a relaxing one. He does not scold you; he does not demand of you. He is a gregarious God and he can be found in the smiling, happy people of the society about you.[19]

Whyte granted that organizational life had made men and women more mobile, but in the process they had become increasingly alienated and unrooted. Repeated job transfers had transported them to such sites as Park Forest, Park Merced, Drexelbrook, or Levittown. Yet each town and city resembled the other, and the "outgoing" nature of the new denizens remained the same. No matter the place or climate, one could get along if one practiced the psychology of adjustment. Nevertheless, darker sides of American living, e.g., racial segregation and classism, continued to divide this growing transient populace. "The new suburbanites," writes Whyte, "do indeed obscure some harsh realities when they talk of their democratic ideals, yet their unwillingness to concede class divisions is itself a very powerful factor in keeping the divisions from crystallizing."[20]

Though, like Riesman, Whyte speaks in terms of pure types that rarely exist in such pristine form in real life, his admonitions against the other-directedness personified in the personality ethic are still worth considering in contemporary times. In the final analysis, he is actually propounding a serious moral thesis in the guise of sociological reporting.

Perhaps Whyte best articulates his fundamental ethical argument in the following lines:

> The suburbanites are more troubled, for they experience the double-barreled effects of belongingness, and in highly practical, immediate ways. It is not the question of conformity, though many speak of it as such. It is, rather, the question of determining *when* one is conforming, when adjustment is self-lessness, or surrender. It is a moral dilemma — the one, I believe, central to the organization man, and while the suburban group affords the most concrete illustration, the underlying problem will not be shed when he moves on.[21]

Status Seeking and the American Dream

Shortly after the publication of *The Lonely Crowd* and *The Organization Man*, Vance Packard, a noted journalist and social critic of current trends in human behavior, drew upon eight investigations he had made across the United States on various aspects of status and class structure. His *The Status Seekers* (1959) concluded that the American Dream was being spawned in troubled waters. Penetrating beyond the surface of traditional rhetoric about equal opportunity and open access to the proverbial ladder of success, Packard's epigrammatic study portrayed a gloomier view of a rather rigid class system.

According to Packard, myriad hidden barriers profoundly affect one's ability to rise or fall in our highly stratified society:

> Most of us surround ourselves, wittingly or unwittingly, with status symbols we hope will influence the raters appraising us, and which we hope will establish some social distance between ourselves and those we consider below us. The vigorous merchandising of goods as status symbols by advertisers is playing a major role in intensifying status consciousness. Emotionally insecure people are most vulnerable.[22]

Some of the many considerations that provide "social distance" and divide Americans include the following: Becoming a member of the "diploma elite"; entering a prestigious profession; choosing a "proper" address, a fitting mate, and appropriate friends; shopping for status goods; and joining the "right" church, club, lodge, and political party.

This laundry list of success tools amounts to a social bag of tricks particularly useful for those motivated by the personality ethic. However, the distinguished sociologist C. Wright Mills detects more ominous signals in such status-packaging:

> When white-collar people get jobs, they sell not only their time and energy, but their personalities as well. They sell by the week, or month, their smiles and their kindly gestures, and they must practice the prompt repression of resentment and aggression.[23]

The potential for resentment and aggression runs high for those who do not, or cannot, buy into status-seeking circles. And the doors for access into such enclaves are, indeed, restricted. They include significant doses of wealth, education, powerful occupation, Anglo-Saxon origin, high-brow religious affiliation, and assiduously graceful lifestyle.

Why had opportunity for achieving the American Dream so dwindled by the mid-twentieth century? Packard cites a number of societal pressures that apparently contributed to those withering realities. First, he claims that "steppingstone" jobs had been shrinking at a rapid rate. No longer could one so easily expect to work his way up from the bottom of his company and hope to rise to the top rungs of the corporate ladder.

Second, industry had begun earmarking specialized jobs for those with collegiate preparation. Third, job skills had become narrowly fragmented, thus allowing management the opportunity to hire semi-skilled, lower-paid employees whom they could train more cheaply on the job. Fourth, there had been a burgeoning of bureaucracy throughout business and government, accompanied by greater use of vertical chains of authority, impersonal methods, and rule-making orientations toward management procedure. "The system of rules," notes Packard, "often breeds contempt or resentment toward the organization. The hierarchy of authority . . . leaves those of low status and power feeling intensely unequal, and inclined to have little interest, initiative, and loyalty. And specialization tends to set up a tight pattern of stratification."[24]

Adding to workers' sense of alienation from their labor, according to Packard, were the following negative trends: Widening isolation between employees and management; and more monolithic forms of unionization, which sap workers' independence. Packard's prognosis for the future of the American Dream was thus downright pessimistic: "The result of all these pressures toward rigidity in the work lives of most people . . . in America is a diminishing upward mobility, and a slackening of ambition. . . . For those frozen into the lower layers, frustration is a commonly felt emotion." Perhaps even more bleakly, he summarized any realistic "opportunities" for upward mobility as follows:

1. You can marry off an attractive daughter to a higher-status male. That's still being done occasionally.
2. You can try to see that your children get a college education. That doesn't guarantee anything, but does at least qualify them for consideration for semi-upper-type jobs and friends.
3. You can create the feeling that you are getting somewhere by stepping up your consumption of material goods.[25]

Such limited possibilities leave one with these questions to bear in mind: Should I purchase a Ford or a Buick? Which affords greater sex appeal? Should I join the Kiwanis or Rotary? Which will buy more business contacts and clients? However one responds, he or she is surely kissing air with those already immersed in the cult of the personality ethic.

One-Dimensional Society

Whatever form any discrete success ethic might take, it runs the risk of oversimplification, thereby restricting one's critical capacity for raising important questions and challenging existing forms of knowledge, valuation, and social organization. Integrative approaches to social theory and social criticism become especially problematic in most versions of self-help literature. Compounding this proclivity toward one-dimensionality is the distinct possibility that we inhabit a terribly fragmented culture that rarely prods us to transcend any given phenomenological parade of "facts" and "events." Indeed, some recent social thinkers, most notably Herbert Marcuse and the Frankfurt School, have analyzed social issues by beginning with the assumption that our societal structures have already been made thoroughly irrational and repressive.

For Marcuse, human knowledge is historically conditioned, and therefore amenable to social change. With Marx, he contends that growing intellectual and material resources should increasingly allow us to expunge irrationality and repression from existence. However, modern men and women appear to be overwhelmed by the very social forces that might be used for human liberation:

> The institutions man founds and the culture he creates develop laws of their own, and man's freedom has to comply with them. He is overpowered by the expanding wealth of his economic, social and political surrounding and comes to forget that he himself, his free development, is the final goal of all these works; instead he surrenders to their sway.[26]

From *Reason and Revolution* (1941) to *One-Dimensional Man* (1964), Marcuse focuses upon the stimulation of conscious awareness as a necessary precondition for socio-historical transformation. "[Any significant] change would *presuppose* that the laboring classes are alienated from this universe in their very existence . . . so that the need for qualitative change is a matter of life and death." Paradoxically, then, alienation becomes a positive force by acting to negate the negativity in social life. In addition, Marcuse argues that the use of Reason is essential to individual and social growth. However, the historical role of Reason has been largely dysfunctional and surplus-repressive, i.e., "to repress and even destroy the urge to live . . . or to postpone and put an exorbitantly high price on [its] fulfillment." Life-growing (libidinal) forces have not adequately merged with Reason because the latter has been effectively usurped and conditioned by repressive societal identifications (mimesis). When one immediately identifies with one's social apparatuses, one begins to treat them as independent monoliths. In the process, one's own wishes and desires become repressed; he introjects the needs and wants of the overarching social structure as one's own.[27]

In effect, Marcuse is bothered by the irrationality of a technocratic social system that actually forestalls social change and needlessly closes new dimensions to self-determination in the name of Reason and Progress. The general impact of such repressive socio-historic Reason and Progress is to submit human beings to distorted

> facts of life, and to the dynamic capability of producing more and bigger facts of the same sort of life. The efficiency of the system blunts the individual's recognition that it contains no facts which do not communicate the repressive power of the whole. If the individuals find themselves in the things which

shape their life, they do so, not by giving, but by accepting the law of things — not the law of physics, but the law of their society.[28]

Due to this one-dimensional world of unreason, one's rational options become unnecessarily restrictive: "Choices are limited to 'reasonable' choices and . . . reasonable choices are prescribed within or at least in terms of one universe of discourse."[29] Marcuse thus characterizes such technological Reason as an omnipresent "logic of domination." Its values and goals circumscribe personal independence; the "objective order of things" becomes the order of the day.[30]

In Marcuse's analysis, each variety of the success ethic, since it offers simply a superficial palliative to widespread social alienation, serves only to intensify already subtle forms of social unreason. For him, each represents a "bourgeois ideology," which still "smacks of repression, though of refined and [sometimes] sophisticated repression, of internalization, sublimation of freedom and equality."[31] No matter how superficially inviting, success ethics permit men and women to partake of the "false consciousness" that they are free, or becoming free, when in reality they are repressed. Thus, in their idealization of such questions as power and control, they camouflage the ubiquitous harshness of social repression. In the end, then, the many calls to success usher in the "repressive idea of the person or personality who can 'fulfill himself' without making excessive demands on the world, by practicing the socially required degree of resignation."[32]

Writing at a time when America's economic fortunes were more promising, Marcuse claimed that its blue-collar and professional classes were typically co-opted by a society of relative abundance. In the present age of increasing scarcity and declining dreams, his New Left message appears out of step with some current social realities.[33] For Marcuse, the American Dream was merely a soothing narcotic, to be dreamt about at one's peril. For today's young Americans, it seems unrealistic to assume that their standard of living will equal that of their parents in the very near future.

Withering Habits of the Heart

Robert N. Bellah and associates' *Habits of the Heart* (1985) is based on qualitative social research conducted over a five-year period in various American communities. It has quickly gained acclaim as a landmark study of how American character and values have changed over the centuries. The main thrust of Bellah's argument is that many Americans have become too steeped in the language and deeds of individualism — so much so that they have come frighteningly close to losing a genuine sense of commitment to communitarian ideals and any semblance of stable moral equilibrium.

Bellah and associates have much to say about the apparently uncritical leaps of faith that those seeking upward mobility tend to make in their daily lives:

> The ambiguities of individualism for the middle-class person arise precisely from lack of certainty about what the "best" we are supposed to make of ourselves is. . . . Middle-class individuals are thus motivated to enter a highly autonomous and demanding quest for achievement and then left with no standard against which achievement is to be measured except the income and consumption levels of their neighbors, exhibiting anew the clash between autonomy and conformity that seems to be the fate of American individualism.[34]

Long forgotten are the more enlightened, vibrant success ethics, articulated in biblical religion by John Winthrop (1588–1649), and in the poetic "expressive individualism" of Walt Whitman (1819–92). Appealing to an ethical concern for community, Winthrop spoke of moral freedom "in reference to the covenant between God and man," i.e., a liberty "to that only which is good, just and honest."[35] In his "deeper cultivation of the self," Whitman eschewed the life of material wealth for "a life rich in experience, open to all kinds of people, luxuriating in the sensual as well as the intellectual."[36] Transcending conventional societal constraints, he headed down "the long brown path before me, leading wherever I choose."[37] Yet, for all his fiery individualism, Whitman's philosophy of life was liberally tempered by his devout allegiance to republican virtues, perhaps best expressed in his *Democratic Vistas* (1871).[38]

In *The Good Society* (1991), the authors of *Habits of the Heart* update their social chronicle to include policy recommendations for improving America's domestic agenda. In so doing, they reiterate and expand upon their former conclusions about the status of success in our nation's cultural existence: Rampant individualism and loss of community feeling have shattered any real sense of social and economic opportunity. In the process, the American Dream has become a hollow ideal for those living in despair, desperation, and squalor. Increasingly devoid of hope, they are more and more likely to lash out in self-destruction (drugs, alcohol, suicide) and antisocial activities (vandalism, crime). For Bellah and associates, the once glorious Dream has been unequally played out within an unholy amalgam of Lockean liberalism and Social Darwinist ideas whose "effect is to make people anxious about defending their perilously fragile dignity." In fact, we have turned traditional Lockean politics into a crass Hobbesian world view of a struggle for existence which can be decidedly nasty, brutish, and short.[39]

What implications emerge from Bellah's analysis for the various success ethics? For one, the authors of *Habits of the Heart* and *The Good Society* would be quite leery of the character ethic's emphasis on the individual's own efforts as the prime factor in attaining upward mobility. They would generally approve of its appreciation for moral and political stewardship and philanthropic intervention, though they would doubtless prefer to enlarge those concerns in a fuller communitarian fashion. They would be harshly critical of the mind power ethic's penchant for personal acquisitiveness and its predilections toward merely mentalistic, and sometimes narcissistic, forms of psychic renewal. And they would be deeply offended by the personality ethic's stress on superficial expressions of physical appearance, group dynamics, winning people over, and any headlong crusades simply to be "somebody." The latter characteristics would underscore a certain contempt for the brotherhood and sisterhood of human beings, and thus would appear to reside outside the communitarian circle of Bellah's social program.

More positively, Bellah and associates would find greater cause for hope in the arguments of the service ethic. Bolstered by amelioristic humanitarian claims, which make cultural progress seem a realistic possibility, proponents of the service ethic would come closest to meeting the aims and goals of Bellah's "good society." At the same time, Bellah would want such advocates to infuse their Winthropian spirit for community with a Whitman-like effervescence for all of life's sensate and ideational bounties. This is no mean balancing act, and its problematic nature perhaps best reflects the sometimes semi-utopian flavor of Bellah's vision for social change.

Postscript

Though Riesman, Whyte, Packard, and Bellah largely mirror the white, male, upper-middle-class American society that they presume

to criticize, many of their insightful observations have aptly eluci-
dated any number of theoretical dilemmas and practical deficiencies
in the scope and function of the various success ethics in our culture.
Marcuse's acutely historical dialectic has also contributed enormously
to our understanding of the ideological roots of those same success
ethics and the surplus-repressive social logic that has enabled them
to thrive in advanced Western civilization. And although some of
their more transitory notions now seem destined to become museum
pieces in the history of American ideas, they have all served us well
by compelling success activists to prove whether their views are really
consistent with the activity and good which they promulgate to prospec-
tive audiences.

10

The Future Success Ethic in American Culture

A new success ethic is likely to emerge in the early twenty-first century, resulting from vast changes in the past several decades. These changes include social disorganization, value erosion, the rise of a global culture, the growth of postmodernism, expansion of information technology, and large-scale political and economic changes. This does not mean that the success ethics presented earlier will suddenly disappear; rather, it suggests that they may become less salient and influential. The new success ethic, it is hypothesized, will be based on certain civic virtues and intellectual attributes, and is therefore called the *civic internationalist ethic*. As the global economy is transformed, this ethic is likely to influence knowledge workers first and other workers later. But before presenting two dominant features of this ethic, attention is given to social disorganization and value changes, as some of the precipitating reasons for the ethic's emergence.

Social Disorganization and Value Erosion

The United States' poverty rate for children is more than double that of any other major industrialized nation, UNICEF researchers have noted. While other industrialized nations have been bringing children out of poverty during the past twenty years, only the United States and Britain have slipped backward.

A report from the United Nations Children's Fund, titled "The Progress of Nations," provides evidence that the United States is one of the most dangerous places in the world for young people. And while many other places are improving, the United States is worsening. The report said that nine out of ten young people murdered in industrialized countries are slain in the United States. The United States' homicide rate for young people between 15 and 24 is five times that of its nearest counterpart, Canada. Violence has reached such proportions that the national Centers for Disease Control and Prevention recently issued a report citing violence as an epidemic.[1]

Children watch an average of 8,000 murders and 100,000 violent acts on television before finishing elementary school, according to the American Psychological Association. All that violence is numbing, and even suggests that violence is normal. A surfeit of violence also increases children's fear of becoming victims, thereby making them interpret others' intentions as threatening and conditioning them to respond aggressively.[2]

Various proposals to regulate television violence include the encouragement of a voluntary code to inform parents about program content, exercise of political and economic pressure on corporations that sponsor violent programs, and application of more stringent regulations through the Federal Communication Commission over the television industry. Reform of the criminal justice system and gun control legislation are other actions for curbing the rampage of violence. Proposals for reducing childhood poverty include reforming welfare, decreasing teenage pregnancy, and expanding sex education. But in addition to these measures, a more complete plan is presented in the next section.

The erosion of values is depicted in a national survey of more than two thousand Americans interviewed in fifty locations, each of whom was asked to answer over 1,800 questions, while thousands more responded in telephone interviews.[3] It was found that people across the country are less interested in changing their inner selves, including their intelligence or personality, than in changing their outward appearance. Women, more than men (63 percent versus 38 percent), would change their faces and bodies. Only one in four thinks that America will be better off a year from now, but the majority believe that they personally will be better off.

Workers admitted spending twenty percent of their time on the job loafing, while half confessed to chronic malingering. Only one in four gave his or her best effort, and only one in four works to realize his or her human potential. The belief in hard work embodied in the character ethic is not strong among respondents, as half of them claimed that one gets ahead not through hard work but through politics and cheating. Of all adults surveyed, ninety-one percent admitted to lying regularly, and two out of three believe there is nothing wrong with telling a lie.

High-school seniors proved more cynical than business executives. On each of a dozen questions, seniors held to a much lower standard than executives. A sample of sixth-grade boys and girls found that while some girls chose helping occupations as career goals, none of the boys did. Asked about their one wish, nearly every boy chose money. Their dream: "Five million dollars and two days at the mall." Their elders were hardly better. In questioning adults, twenty-five percent would abandon all of their friends for $10 million, while a similar percentage would turn to prostitution for a week. But some would go further — change their race, have a sex-change operation, or murder. In fact, seven percent said they would murder someone for money.[4] As the researchers concluded: "It's been said that an era comes to an end when its dreams are exhausted. America's dreams are wearing extremely thin — at least the kind of dreams that can sustain a great nation."[5]

Civic Virtues

Our premise is that a democratic society, if it is to be viable, requires certain civic virtues, which presently are in relatively short supply. Our predicament was expressed lucidly by Benjamin Barber: "Certainly there will be no liberty, no equality, no social justice without democracy, and there will be no democracy without citizens and the schools that forge civic identity and democratic responsibility."[6]

John Dewey viewed democracy as more than a form of government; he saw it as primarily a mode of associated living.[7] He established two tests for the worth of social life: the number and variety of interests shared by a group, and the freedom of interplay with other groups. Undesirable societies establish barriers to the free exchange of ideas, whereas a democratic society has a place for all members and uses their thinking to make changes in social life.

R. S. Peters claims that a number of presuppositions distinguish democracies from other forms of government.[8] One thing that is implied is that citizens who suffer from state action can be consulted, decisions can be made, and their opinions can be heard. Governments rule by "advise and consent" in accommodating themselves to the demands of major interests. An institutional requirement is to provide safeguards for the expression of public opinion; therefore, freedom of expression and association should be guaranteed. In addition, procedures of public accountability are necessary in order to change democracy without resorting to revolution. A precondition for democracy is that people should have had some relevant experience in which they can apply abstract principles (e.g., fairness, liberty, respect for persons), so that such principles can be applied intelligently. Another precondition is that there should be a large measure of consensus on procedural principles by which people seek cooperation, reasonableness, and tolerance, otherwise democratic institutions would be little more than a formal facade. A final precondition is a willingness to participate in public life.

What does democracy at the community level entail? "Communities speak to us in moral voices," says Amitai Etzioni. "They lay claim on their members," and therefore, "what we need now is less 'how to win friends and influence people' and more how to restore the sway of moral voices."[9] He adds that claiming rights without assuming responsibilities is unethical and illogical, even though with some responsibilities we derive no immediate benefits or long-term payoffs. Actually, no society can function well unless most of its members, most of the time, voluntarily heed their moral commitments and social responsibilities. He believes that we must be ready to express our moral sense if we hope to attain a higher level of moral conduct. Moral values will find support as we assume more responsibility for children, elderly, neighbors, environment, and community. He believes that the alternatives are bleak: either a police state or a moral vacuum.

Democratic citizenship, according to Richard Pratte, involves a moral compact promotive of a civic consensus directed toward reaching the public good.[10] Certain civic virtues come into play. A community requires members to accord others consideration, compassion, and tolerance. It also requires a sense of self-identity, protection of privacy, and moral autonomy. The ethic of obligation involves concern, caring, and tolerance. This means that service embodies the ethical obligation to exhibit concern toward others, a willingness to care about them and to show tolerance for other citizens in shaping the life of the community. Civism, or good citizenship, for Pratte, is political activity taken as the fulfillment of human powers, as the object of personal self-development.

Education for civism teaches us not to take our self-interests too seriously, and to develop a healthy sense of belonging and interconnection, in which one is willing to serve others. Pratte envisions three goals for civic education: (1) the development of historical perspective; (2) the development of social action skills; and (3) the reduction of ethnocentrism. Certain desirable traits are cultivated as one fulfills each goal. Fulfilling the first goal develops a knowledge of cultural traditions, including the learned disciplines. The second goal promotes the ability to confer, discuss, debate, plan, and compromise, as well as a range of communication skills. Finally, the third goal develops skills in detecting prejudice in thought and action.[11]

Benjamin Barber, in focusing on a university setting, envisions democratic education as related to freedom insofar as where freedom exists and the community is open and inclusive, there is both democracy and more learning.[12] In such an environment, knowledge is always provisional and conditionally agreed upon, where no argument will be accorded merit merely because of its source. Democracy and education, he says, intersect at the point we call community. If in today's universities there is insufficient learning, the problem may be in too much solitude and too little community. In fact, community is central to both education and democracy. Learning communities function effectively only when their members are empowered to participate fully in common activities that define the community. The university, he insists, has a civic mission: the cultivation of a free community. This means the creation of both a democracy of words (knowledge) and a democracy of deeds (the democratic state).

Pratte believes that community service can be the unifying force for a moral civic education. Service, however, should not be considered a form of charity. Community service should also be separated from career training, even though there may be some side benefits to explore careers. If community service is to begin in the elementary grades, it is important that teachers and parents assume responsibility by closely monitoring the community experiences of students.[13] Ernest Boyer recommends a new Carnegie unit where students would invest not fewer than thirty hours a year, a total of 120 hours over four years, in order to qualify. Students could tutor younger students and assist in the school office, cafeteria, and other areas of the school. Outside of school they could serve in libraries, hospitals, parks, museums, nursing homes, day-care centers, and other places.[14] But, as Barber admonishes, the aim of service should be neither voluntarism nor a spirit of altruism, because if service is considered supererogatory it cannot be required, and if it is voluntary it is an oxymoron and makes little pedagogical sense. Instead, the ultimate goal of service is to learn to be free, which entails being responsible to others.[15]

The civic virtues, then, cut across and draw upon the cognitive, moral, and conative domains. The cognitive civic virtues consist of developing a historical perspective on one's society and government, acquiring a knowledge of cultural traditions, and cultivating skills in detecting prejudice. They also include the ability to grasp abstract principles and understand how they can be applied to political situations.

The moral civic virtues involve developing empathy, compassion, and a caring attitude toward others. Individuals learn to assume responsibility for their own actions rather than displacing blame on others, groups, or institutions. Ultimately, the individual strives to move toward greater moral autonomy.

The conative civic virtues involve those parts of the personality which can be characterized by purposive behavior and the impulse to act. One must first overcome the hiatus that is usually experienced between knowing the good and doing the good. This is difficult for some people to achieve because of moral weakness and backsliding. One must learn to heed moral commitments. Certain social and communication skills are also needed to participate effectively in public life. Skills and attitudes required are the abilities to confer, to plan, to cooperate, to be reasonable, and to show tolerance of others' views. Moreover, one also should be able to share interests and exchange ideas with others, as well as successfully apply abstract principles in political situations.

Our educational institutions should help produce these abilities, and communities should provide sufficient freedom to practice and apply the requisite skills. The above civic virtues are one of the two dimensions of the civic internationalist ethic. These civic virtues will be utilized not only in one's native society but in other cultures of the world where one may serve, and these virtues will need to be adapted to the prevailing cultural norms. The global community will require successful individuals to live effectively in diverse societies as part of their economic, political, or professional assignment. The types of developments and anticipated changes likely to bring about the internationalist virtues are presented next within the context of future global changes.

Internationalist Attributes

Some observers claim that the United States, Japan, Canada, and several other economically developed countries have changed from industrial to post-industrial societies. A number of dramatic developments have precipitated these changes, most of which have occurred since World War II. Among these developments are the invention of nuclear energy, automation, the space age (beginning with the launching of Sputnik), the development of digital and analog computers, and the emergence of biological discoveries promising to unlock the genetic code.

These remarkable changes have ushered in the post-industrial age. This stage of development is not only different in degree but in kind; it is further distinguished from the industrial age by the rate of change. Although industrialism brought about greater economic interdependence, post-industrialism has witnessed a growing interdependence not only in economic life but in social, political, and educational aspects of society as well. This trend has been heightened by the amazing developments in transportation and communication, so that the world today, in Marshall McLuhan's terms, is becoming a "global village." Earlier changes were primarily in technology; only slowly, over many decades, did these changes exert a profound effect on social life and value systems. Today, these changes are having a great impact on the way people live and relate to one another, their beliefs and values. The inability to cope with such rapid changes has led to what Alvin Toffler has called "future shock" — the disorienting effect of subjecting people to great changes in too short a time to be able to adapt to them. Since the present rate of change is likely to accelerate in the next twenty-five years, the civic internationalist ethic must find new means of understanding and coping with rapid changes.

The post-industrial society which, according to Daniel Bell, began in the 1945–1950 period and will see its full emergence in the subsequent thirty to fifty years, has a number of significant characteristics. The economy shifts from manufacturing to service. The professional and technical classes become preeminent, with the centrality of theoretical knowledge as the source of innovation and policy formation. The critical difference between industrial and post-industrial society is the switch from empirical knowledge to theoretical knowledge. The chief resource is scientific personnel, and a major problem is the organization of science. Such a society requires more expertise and greater guidance of social and political affairs. Comprehensive overhaul and modernization of government structures are necessary in order to find the appropriate size and scope of units to perform essential tasks.[16] Telecommunications will be decisive in terms of economic and social exchanges, the way knowledge is created and retrieved, and the characteristics of occupations.[17]

The post-industrial society offered a fertile field for the growth of postmodernism. Postmodernism is a controversial term for suggesting the overall character of direction or experimental tendencies in Western art, architecture, and other fields since the 1940s or 1950s, especially recent events associated with post-industrial society. Postmodernism is related to a revolt against authority and signification, a tendency toward pastiche, parody, quotation, self-referentiality, and eclecticism. In painting, its form is abstract expressionism; in music, the works of Stockhausen, Messiaen, and Cage; in theater, total theater and theater of the absurd; in philosophy, deconstruction; in literature, nouveau roman, anti-novel, concrete poetry, the new Gothic, and horror show.

No consensus exists on the meaning and scope of postmodernism. Charles Jencks holds that postmodernism means the end of a single world view, a respect for differences and a celebration of the regional, local, and particular. An essential goal is to further pluralism, to overcome elitism in the earlier paradigm.[18] In contrast, Aronowitz and Giroux do not believe that postmodernism represents a drastic break from modernity so much as a shift to social conditions that are reconstituting the world while simultaneously producing new forms of criticism, as well as an emerging set of conditions that characterize the age of global capitalism.[19] J. F. Lyotard, an early observer of the postmodern condition, speaks of a postmodern artist or writer as not governed by pre-established rules and familiar categories. The rules and categories are what the work of art is seeking; the artist and writer, therefore, work without rules to formulate what will have been done.[20] Fredric Jameson defines postmodernism as the "cultural logic" that represents the third great state of late capitalism, as well as the new cultural form in Western societies. It represents remapping of social space and the creation of different social formations that call for transformed cognitive maps.[21]

In postmodernism, a number of traditional differentiations are seriously questioned: between literary and other types of discourse, high and low culture, artist and critic, signifier and signified. The purpose is to undo a privilege that one side of the pair has over the other by a logic of separation. Also opposed is the modernist obsession with purity; instead, heterogeneity is celebrated. The humanist self is rejected because it denies that the self is socially constructed and, in the very act of construction, such a self represses such heterogeneous elements as the feminine and utilitarian.

The modernist belief in artistic autonomy is discarded because it is neither possible nor desirable, since the alienated artist cannot occupy a place outside of capitalist society, because to do so would isolate the artist from the culture and from a larger audience. Thus, engagement is proposed as an alternative to alienation. This view would be in keeping with a global culture's emphasis on participants in various specialties contributing directly and tangibly to the culture's advancement.

Against modernist truths of liberal or communist ideology, postmodernism focuses on smaller groups and local diversity, or a commitment to de-centered pluralistic visions. It has disavowed the modernist attachments to structuralism, perennialism, traditional liberal arts notions, and seeks heterogeneity and pluralism, which take such diverse forms in education as schools of choice, multicultural education, non-Western literature, and values clarification. Popular culture, largely rejected by high-culture proponents in the modernist period, is accepted by postmodernists as worthy of study and participation.

Postmodernists oppose theories that seek essential and necessary truths, and instead attempt to legitimate knowledge claims on the basis of human practices. Thus, they attack foundationalism, humanism, Western rationality, and autonomy. Western reason is depicted as seeking social domination of nature that requires control mechanisms over individual impulses and increasing organization and administration of society.

Instead of studying the form and content of a text and searching for universal values, postmodern literary theory focuses on the reader or audience response. Reader-response criticism conceives a literary work and its meanings as produced by the evolving responses of a reader to a given text. Wolfgang Isser claims that reading causes the literary work to unfold. Literary texts are full of unexpected twists and turns that frustrate expectations. Whenever the flow of a tale is interrupted by moving in unexpected directions, the reader can establish connections missing in the text itself. A given text, he says, is capable of different realizations, and no reading can exhaust its full potential because each reader determines how to fill in the gaps. In doing so, the reader implicitly acknowledges the inexhaustibility of the text, and it is this inexhaustibility that compels the reader to make decisions.[22]

The prevailing philosophy of language of postmodernism is deconstruction. The deconstruction of a text consists of teasing out the conflicting forces of signification in the text itself. If anything is destroyed, it is not the text but the claim to unequivocal domination by one mode of signifying. Derrida sought to refute the assumption that a text has "a" meaning, which industry, application, and attention will winnow out. Meaning is not encased in language, but is coextensive with the play of language itself. Derrida attempts to show that meanings of a text are disseminated across its entire surface, and there is no single guaranteed meaning which inhabits a text that constitutes its "presence." Thus, a text possesses so many meanings that it cannot have "a meaning." Derrida's concept of *différance* combines "difference" with "deferral" to suggest the endless deferral of meaning.[23] Deconstruction was welcomed in some literary circles because it placed literary problems of figurative language above philosophers' and historians' claims to truth, and also opened unlimited possibilities of interpretation.

Rather than nationalistic views, the postmodernist outlook relates more to a global culture. Immamuel Wallerstein holds that "the capitalist world economy is a world-system, and for some time now one that has expanded to cover the entire globe...."[24] To speak of a global culture does not mean that it rests upon a world state or that it entails the dissolution of the nation-state. It means instead that transitional cultural processes can be observed that take a variety of forms which sustain the flow of goods, people, knowledge, and information.

Education is increasingly viewed as an instrument of economic development and a means to embrace a nation's human capital. National economies are internationally interdependent, insatiable in their quest for technological innovation, and critically dependent on human talents. Educational institutions are being scrutinized by government officials in terms of new educational policies to meet social and economic imperatives. Specific outcomes of the globalization process are the expansion of school and college populations, national educational objectives, greater use of standardized tests, growing efforts to link colleges and industry, centralized curricula, and increased expectations for mathematics and science instruction.[25]

Globalization is today a significant economic trend challenging American industry. Ideas, technology, equipment, new inventions, money, and factories now move around the globe, a process that tends to diffuse economic power. American corporations are less connected to this country, and the major ones have more sales and larger operations outside of the United States. Thus, their concern about the U.S. economy is in terms of whether it is a major market for them.

The automobile industry no longer thinks only of domestic markets but in terms of the global market. It would now be difficult to find a car produced with materials and components from only one country. Some firms in the food industry attempt to sell their products throughout the world. Mergers in the media and entertainment industry, as with

Time Inc. and Warner Communications, increase the ability to compete in the global market. The market for jobs has moved to countries with low labor costs, and service jobs shift to those countries with low labor costs and relatively high levels of education. Although in some cases American companies may have lost shares of the domestic market to cheap labor, this factor may be overrated since U.S. firms historically never had the advantage of cheap labor. Other factors as important as cheap labor are good management, efficient use of capital, new technology, and trained (rather than cheap) labor.[26]

Technology is a critical area in America's international competitiveness. Successful competition in technology requires managers with technological understanding; business traditions and financial incentives that encourage long-term investments; a well-educated work force; committed engineers and scientists; and institutions engaged in research and development.[27]

Robert Reich claims that the "knowledge workers," the top twenty percent of American workers, are competing quite well in the international economy. These are the workers whose job is to manipulate abstract symbols, such as research scientists, engineers, investment bankers, lawyers, management consultants, filmmakers, musicians, writers, publishers, and others. As the global market becomes more integrated, knowledge workers can sell their designs, financial analyses, formulas, and prototypes throughout the world.

But the other two categories of American workers find their positions are becoming more precarious. "Routine production workers," the blue-collar workers or the data processors working on global computer networks, are becoming less competitive because they must compete with workers in other countries with lower wage scales. Global corporations tend to move routine work to locations where wages are lowest.

The third category consists of service workers, ranging from retail sales clerks to security guards. These workers, in contrast, are not engaged in international competition, but compete for their jobs against labor-saving machines. In order to improve the condition of these two groups (the bottom eighty percent), their productivity will need to increase; otherwise, they will be unable to compete with low-wage workers in other countries. Moreover, the only ones who can afford to make an investment in education and training of these two groups are the knowledge workers. Reich, however, doubts that the latter will do so because they are no longer dependent on the bottom eighty percent; rather, the converse is the case.[28]

Economist Lester Thurow views the labor situation somewhat differently than Reich. While the education of the top twenty-five percent of the labor force is critical because they are the ones who invent new products, the bottom fifty percent moves to center stage if the route to success lies in producing the cheapest and best products. To accomplish this goal will require the average worker to have a higher level of education and skill than ever before. Every production worker must be taught some simple operations research in order to employ statistical quality control. Today's high-density semiconductor chips can be invented but cannot be built without every worker acquiring a level of basic mathematics far beyond that achieved by most American high school graduates. A worker in a global economy has one of two things to offer: skills or the willingness to work for low wages. The unskilled in wealthy societies must work for the wages of the unskilled in poor societies. If they are unwilling to do so, the jobs are simply transferred to poor countries. Thus, Thurow claims, the skills of the bottom half of the population affect the wages of the top half, since if the bottom half cannot staff the processes to be operated, the management and professional jobs attached to these processes disappear.[29]

Paul Kennedy notes that while the United States possesses the world's greatest array of research universities and scientific institutes, serious problems arise at the K–12 level in terms of Scholastic Aptitude Test scores, dropout rates, and functional illiteracy. America spends a disproportionate forty percent on higher education, while the share allocated to the rest of education is less than other countries. American students attend school for fewer days each year (175 to 180 days) than Europeans (200+) and Japanese (220+). By the age of eighteen, the average Japanese or South Korean student has had three or four years more schooling than the average American.[30] Our educational crisis, asserts Benjamin Barber, "stems from a dearth of democracy: an absence of democratic will and a consequent refusal to take our children, our schools, and our future seriously."[31] Local governments, according to Lester Thurow, do not want to pay for first-class schools because less than half the population has children in school at any given time, students graduate and may take their skills elsewhere, and high taxes to pay for good schools may drive industry away. Firms can locate in adjacent geographical areas and utilize the well-educated work force.[32] To improve school finance, Reich proposes reducing military spending by three percent each year for the next ten years (which would yield half a trillion dollars over a decade). These funds would be invested in education and the infrastructure, because they would foster greater future productivity. By making these investments, corporations will view the United States as an attractive place to invest, and will create higher value-added jobs that will increase U.S. wealth and pay off budget deficits.[33]

The United States, Thurow indicates, is unique among industrial countries in lacking an organized postsecondary education system for the non-college bound. Britain, France, and Spain spend more than twice as much as the United States for developing post-secondary skills of the non-college bound; Germany spends more than three times as much; and Sweden nearly six times as much. Thus, in the United States, too much training occurs on the job and is unsystematic. He believes that, in order to improve standards and compete better internationally, the high school day should be lengthened by a couple of hours per day and the school year extended to 220 days. Administrative costs should be reduced, and teacher salaries should be raised to the level of those in Germany and Japan.[34]

The internationalist needs to acquire certain desirable attributes; yet, in order to do so, programs must first be improved. A national survey of three thousand college students by the Educational Testing Service found only a small proportion of college students have an adequate understanding of global situations and processes. At most, five percent of the four-year college programs are devoted to global knowledge. Political science textbooks lack an adequate global perspective. Moreover, the Department of Education spends less than 1.5 percent of its budget on international programs.[35]

Gordon Ambrich perceives that the focus of the 1990s will be on preparing students for a worldwide marketplace, in which emphasis will be placed on foreign languages and citizenship responsibility in democratic government. He also believes that attention will be given to cross-national comparisons of education and the use of education to provide global action on peacekeeping and environmental problems.[36] Austin and Knight Kiplinger envision a college core curriculum in which courses will be placed in a global context regardless of the student's major. Most all professions will require some knowledge of geography, economics, languages, and cultures.[37]

These changes have already begun at some universities. Stanford University has seventeen courses that have a global dimension, including a seminar on East-West economic relations. It also sends students on study trips to Japan, the Soviet Union, and Mexico.[38] Purdue University is adopting curriculum changes that will internationalize the outlook of its students. Languages now include Japanese and Chinese, and

Purdue has new affiliations in China and Europe. Engineering students will take courses in foreign languages and general culture to make them more marketable.[39] These are a few of the initial changes to meet the challenges of globalization.

Most jobs, according to Arthur C. Clarke, will involve the creation, transmission, and processing of ideas and information; therefore, education will need to focus on how to think and how to learn.[40] The growth occupations are shifting to sectors that require high-level problem-solving communication, reading, writing, and mathematical skills.[41] John Naisbitt believes that we will need to return to the ideal of a generalist education. Those who overspecialize will find their specialty becoming obsolete, whereas a generalist is committed to lifelong education, and can change more readily. Long-range forecasting skills, he believes, will also be increasingly valued.[42] Change is rapid in knowledge production, as the volume of information doubles every two years; therefore, periodic upgrading of qualifications will become routine.[43]

Learning how to learn will need greater emphasis. According to R. F. Dearden, such skills are a cluster of second-order learning skills having wide application to first-order operations. Specific content is a first-order operation; second-order learning consists of activities such as investigating how to investigate and thinking about how to think effectively. Learning how to learn, he claims, consists of four types of second-order skills: information-finding skills; general substantive principles (scientific principles, moral principles, or other types); formal principles of inquiry (that is, methods of inquiry in the various disciplines); and self-management skills. Information-finding involves such skills as learning how to ask questions to gather needed information, learning how to listen carefully, and learning how to pay attention and concentrate on the task at hand.[44]

The internationalist needs critical thinking skills. Such skills include the ability to identify premises, assumptions, and hypotheses; evaluate information and evidence; assess the reliability of observations; discern fallacious arguments; and test hypotheses. Most educators believe that such skills should be taught, but disagree over how best to teach these skills. One study lists over fifteen different programs from which to select.[45]

One or more generic modes of inquiry should be utilized. The three most important ones are analytical, empirical, and valuational. Analytical inquiry is deductive and conceptual, and is conducted independently of empirical findings; mathematics, logic, metaphysics, epistemology, and theory construction in the various disciplines are examples. Empirical inquiry includes studies in the social sciences and the natural sciences. Valuational inquiry focuses on the worth, goodness, or appraisal of some object, process, experience, or interpersonal relationship; it may occur in aesthetics, ethics, some religious studies, and aspects of economics.

Broad and significant life experiences are also necessary for developing the internationalist. Probably the most important experiences are those that eventually enable the individual to break away from provincialism, ethnocentrism, dogmatism, and stereotyped thinking, experiences that enable the individual to understand and appreciate diverse cultural patterns. Classroom studies need to be supplemented with experiential education that involves service learning and cross-cultural experience. Service learning emphasizes serving others in supervised work with public service agencies, local or state government, community problems, and the like. Cross-cultural experience stresses foreign study or intra-cultural programs, with the former focusing on international differences and the latter on differences in one's own culture. Foreign study requires students to retain their student role in a new setting, while intra-cultural programs require living in a subculture and assuming a participant-observer role. Such experiences would broaden one's understanding of cultural patterns, enhance interpersonal skills, and promote the ability to think more deeply about significant cultural and global problems.

Current fragmentation of the curriculum poses a serious problem for the viability of such programs. This problem can be alleviated by enlisting the faculty in a cooperative process of thinking globally and structuring their course offerings to relate directly to this curriculum pattern. Programs for both general and professional education should offer a significant focus on global education. Within such programs experiential education will be provided that includes both service learning and cross-cultural experiences. Professional education would tailor these experiences to the type of future employment situations available internationally to graduates.

Just as the civic virtues contain a strong moral dimension, the internationalist would be an ethical person. Internationalists are likely to be able to resist social pressure to choose an alternative that they would not select if left to their own devices. They are able to appraise their action on the basis of a consistent set of principles that have been developed as a guide to life's direction. The principles are generated from a philosophy of life. Such persons are flexible and capable of reinterpreting principles in light of conflicting situations, they can envision the social consequences of their acts and modify their behavior accordingly, and can reconstruct their behavior because their openness to experience provides them with alternative modes of action. Internationalists are not closed off from others' ideas and diverse moral systems; yet ultimate decisions for their actions are their own and they assume responsibility for their acts. Universities should see that applied ethics is an integral part of students' programs at both undergraduate and professional levels.

Postscript

In summary, the internationalist is globally educated, possesses critical thinking skills, second-order skills to learn how to learn, and broad and significant life experiences in service learning and cross-cultural experiences, and is an ethical person. These attributes would be combined with the cognitive, moral, and conative civic virtues (presented earlier) in order to complete the total personality of the civic internationalist, a person who embodies the characteristics of a future success ethic, one that will enable the individual to live effectively in a global society. Of course, it may be said that such a paragon of virtues is unrealistic and unlikely to be achieved. The civic internationalist, however, is actually an ideal type, a hypothetical construct formed from real phenomena drawn from the demands of a global economy and having explanatory value. It serves as points toward which to aim and valuable directions to be taken, rather than as a literal blueprint.

Yet success alone is not enough; there should also be time for love, leisure, and happiness. Aristotle claimed that "human good turns out to be activity of soul in accordance with virtue, and if there are more than one virtue, in accordance with the best and most complete. But we must add 'in a complete life.'"[46] Ultimately, success alone is insufficient for a full and complete life. As Wordsworth observed:

When good men, disappointed in the quest
Of wealth and power and honours, long for rest;
Or, having known the splendors of success,
Sigh for the obscurities of happiness.[47]

Notes

Preface

1. Richard M. Huber, *The American Idea of Success* (New York: McGraw-Hill, 1971).
2. C. Wright Mills, *The Sociological Imagination* (New York: Oxford University Press, 1959), p. 21.
3. Mills, *The Power Elite* (New York: Oxford University Press, 1956), p. 318.
4. Mills, *The Sociological Imagination*, p. 9.

Chapter 1. The Pursuit of the American Dream

1. Max Weber, *The Protestant Ethic and the Spirit of Capitalism*, trans. Talcott Parsons (New York: Charles Scribner's Sons, 1930).
2. Richard Tawney, in *Religion and the Rise of Capitalism* (New York: Harcourt, Brace, 1926), reverses Weber's emphasis by contending that the Protestant ethic was a byproduct of modern capitalism.
3. Ralph Henry Gabriel, *The Course of American Democratic Thought* (New York: Ronald Press, 1940), ch. 13.
4. James Truslow Adams, *The Epic of America* (Garden City, N.Y.: Blue Ribbon Books, 1931), p. 404.
5. *Ibid.,* 405, 411, 415.
6. Howard L. Nixon, II, *Sport and the American Dream* (New York: Leisure Press, 1984), pp. 10, 17.
7. *The American Dream: A National Survey by the Wall Street Journal* (New York: Dow Jones, 1987), pp. 9, 84.

189

8. John Hardin Best, "The Retreat from Equity in American Education." Paper presented at the annual convention of the International Studies Association, Washington, D.C., March 5–9, 1985.

9. Maxine Greene, "On the American Dream: Equality, Ambiguity, and the Persistence of Rage," *Curriculum Inquiry* 13 (Summer 1983): 179–93.

10. William Proefriedt, "Education and Moral Purpose: The Dream Recovered," *Teachers College Record* 86 (Spring 1985): 399–410.

11. Wellford W. Williams, "Captured by the American Dream: Vocational Education in the United States." Paper presented at the Vocationalizing Education Conference, London, England, May 7–9, 1986.

12. Stephen E. Baldwin, "Moving Toward a Higher Value-Added Economy: What Is the National Need for Economic Growth and Work Improvements?" Monograph Series Vol. 1, No. 9. Washington, D.C.: National Commission for Employment Policy, 1987.

13. "Fixing America's Economy," *Fortune* 126 (October 19, 1992): 48–100.

14. Joseph I. Lipson and Kathleen M. Fisher, "Technologies of the Future," *Education & Computing* (1985): 11–23.

15. Thomas P. Steward, "The New American Century: Where We Stand," *Fortune* 123 (Spring/Summer Special Issues, 1991): 12–23.

16. "A Chat with the Dean of American Business History," *Financial World* (June 25, 1991): 42.

17. *Ibid.*

18. Steward, "New American Century."

19. Kevin Phillips, *The Politics of Rich and Poor* (New York: Random House, 1990).

20. *Ibid.,* xii.

21. "Portraits of the Boss," *Business Week* 3287 (October 12, 1992): 108–9.

22. "The Halting Progress of Blacks in the Last Generation," *U.S. News & World Report* (January 22, 1990): 28.

23. "Few Gains Made in 'Decade of Hispanic,'" *American Statesman* (December 16, 1989): A1, A5, A9.

24. "Changing Face of Poverty Behe's Assumption," *American Statesman* (October 22, 1992): A9.

25. "The Young and Restless," *American Statesman* (September 30, 1992): G5.

26. *The American Dream,* p. 79.

27. Robert B. Heilman, "The Dream Metaphor: Some Ramifications." In *American Dreams, American Nightmares,* David Madden, ed. (Carbondale: Southern Illinois University Press, 1970), pp. 1–18.

28. Martin Luther King, Jr., "I Have a Dream." In *The Annals of America,* vol. 18 (Chicago: Encyclopedia Brittanica, 1968), pp. 158–59.

29. David McCullough, *Truman* (New York: Simon & Schuster, 1992).

30. Elliot Carlson, "Remembering 'the Real' Harry," *AARP Bulletin* (October 1992): 20, 13.

31. Robert N. Bellah, Richard Madsen, William M. Sullivan, Ann Swidler, and Steven M. Tipton, *The Good Society* (New York: Alfred A. Knopf, 1991), pp. 270, 272.

32. Ayn Rand, *The Fountainhead* (Indianapolis: Bobbs-Merrill, 1943).

Chapter 2. The Character Ethic

1. Warren I. Susman, "Personality and Twentieth Century Culture." In *New Directions in Intellectual History,* John Higham and Paul L. Conkin, eds. (Baltimore: Johns Hopkins University Press, 1979), pp. 212–26.

2. "Introduction." *The Autobiography of Benjamin Franklin* (Boston: Houghton Mifflin, 1923), p. xxiv.

3. *The Autobiography of Benjamin Franklin and Selections from His Other Writings* (New York: Random House, 1950), pp. 232–34.

4. *Ibid.,* 217.

5. *Ibid.,* 93–95.

6. Carl Van Doren, *Benjamin Franklin* (New York: Viking Press, 1945), p. 91.

7. David Riesman (with Nathan Glazer and Reuel Denney), *The Lonely Crowd* (Garden City, N.Y.: Doubleday, 1953).

8. Andrew Carnegie, *The Empire of Business* (Toronto: William Briggs, 1902).

9. Pitirim Sorokin, "American Millionaires and Multi-Millionaires," *Journal of Social Forces* (1925), 634, 639.

10. Carnegie, *Empire of Business.*

11. "The Road to Business Success," *ibid.,* 3–18.

12. "How to Win Fortune," *ibid.,* 110.

13. *Ibid.,* 122.

14. "Wealth and Its Uses," *ibid.,* 129.

15. See Seymour M. Lipset and Reinhard Bendix, *Social Mobility in Industrial Society* (Berkeley: University of California Press, 1967); Melvin M. Tumin, *Social Stratification: The Forms and Functions of Social Inequality,* 2nd ed. (Englewood Cliffs, N.J.: Prentice-Hall, 1985).

16. Francis W. Gregory and Irene D. Neu, "The Business Industrial Elite in the 1870s: Their Social Origins." In *Man in Business,* William Miller, ed. (Cambridge, Mass.: Harvard University Press, 1952).

17. Mabel Newcomer, *The Big Business Executive* (New York: Charles Scribner's Sons, 1955), p. 69.

18. Carnegie, "Wealth and Its Uses."

19. Carnegie, "Thrift as a Duty," 99.

20. Elbert Hubbard, *A Message to Garcia* (East Aurora, N.Y.: The Roycroft Shop, 1899), p. 3.

21. *Ibid.,* 10.

22. *Ibid.,* 13–14.

23. Richard M. Huber, *The American Idea of Success* (New York: McGraw-Hill, 1971), p. 82.

24. George H. Lorimer, *Letters from a Self-Made Merchant to His Son* (Boston: Small, Maynard & Co., 1902).

25. *Ibid.,* 29.

26. *Ibid.,* 246.

27. *Ibid.,* 16.

28. *Ibid.,* 47.

29. *Ibid.,* 62.

30. *Ibid.,* 143.

31. *Ibid.,* 184.

32. Russell H. Conwell, *Acres of Diamonds* (New York: Harper & Brothers, 1915).

33. *Ibid.,* 21.

34. *Ibid.,* 26.

35. *Ibid.,* 44.

36. *Ibid.,* 59.

37. Robert Shackleton, "His Life and Achievements." In *ibid.,* 103.

38. Tom Perrin, *Football: A College History* (Jefferson, N.C.: McFarland & Co., 1987), p. 11.

39. Amos Alonzo Stagg, *Touchdown!* (New York: Longmans, Green, 1927), p. 163.

40. *Ibid.,* 213.

41. *Ibid.,* 228.

42. *Ibid.,* 272.

43. *Ibid.,* 278.

44. *Ibid.,* 174.

45. Perrin, *Football,* p. 1.

46. Hank Nuwer, *Strategies of the Great Football Coaches* (New York: Franklin Watts, 1988), p. 19. Other Stagg innovations include: having the quarterback stand over center to receive the snap, spread punt formation, fake kick, Statue of Liberty play, the reverse, the lateral; and on defense, the 72–2, the 6–2–1–2, and the 5–2–1–2–1 formations. He also invented the tackling dummy and the playbook.

47. David McCullough, *Truman* (New York: Simon & Schuster, 1992), pp. 192, 671.

48. *Ibid.,* 567.

49. Merle Miller, *Plain Speaking: An Oral Biography of Harry S. Truman* (New York: Berkley Publishing Corp., 1974), p. 35.

50. *Ibid.,* 24.

51. *Ibid.*, 111.

52. *Ibid.*, 57, 64.

53. *The Autobiography of Harry S. Truman,* Robert H. Ferrell, ed. (Boulder: Colorado Associated University Press, 1980), p. 36.

54. Miller, *Plain Speaking,* p. 10.

55. *Autobiography,* p. 33.

56. McCullough, *Truman,* p. 181.

57. *Ibid.*, 282.

58. *Autobiography,* p. 120.

59. Miller, *Plain Speaking,* p. 227.

60. McCullough, *Truman,* pp. 630–31.

61. *Autobiography,* p. 116.

62. Miller, *Plain Speaking,* p. 367.

63. *Autobiography,* p. 121.

64. McCullough, *Truman,* p. 141.

65. *Ibid.*, 247.

66. *Ibid.*, 991.

67. Dennis Gilbert and Joseph A. Kahl, *The American Class Structure,* rev. ed. (Homewood, Ill.: Dorsey Press, 1982), pp. 170–74.

68. Seymour Martin Lipset and Reinhard Bendix, *Social Mobility in Industrial Society* (Berkeley: University of California Press, 1967), p. 25.

69. David L. Featherman and Robert M. Hauser, *Opportunity and Change* (New York: Academic Press, 1978).

70. Peter M. Blau and Otis Dudley Duncan, *The American Occupational Structure* (New York: Wiley, 1967), p. 28.

71. Charles Hirschman and Morris G. Wong, "Socioeconomic Gains of Asian Americans, Blacks, and Hispanics: 1960–1976," *American Journal of Sociology* 90 (1984): 584–607.

72. Patricia Madoo Lengermann and Ruth A. Wallace, *Gender in America: Social Control and Social Change* (Englewood Cliffs, N.J.: Prentice-Hall, 1985).

73. Edward F. Denison, "Appendix to Denison's Reply," *The Residual Factor and Economic Growth* (Paris: Organization for Economic Cooperation and Development, 1964), pp. 86–100.

74. Christopher Jencks, et al., *Who Gets Ahead: The Determinants of Occupational Status in America* (New York: Basic Books, 1972).

75. Charles S. Benson, "Economics of Education: The U.S. Experience." In *Handbook of Research on Educational Administration,* Norman J. Bryan, ed. (New York: Longman, 1988), pp. 360–61.

76. W. W. McMahon and A. P. Wagner, "The Monetary Returns to Education as Partial Social Efficiency Criteria." In *Financing Education: Overcoming Inefficiency and Inequity,* W. W. McMahon and T. G. Geske, eds. (Urbana: University of Illinois Press, 1982), pp. 150–87.

77. Christopher Jencks, et al., *Inequality: A Reassessment of the Effect of Family and Schooling in America* (New York: Basic Books, 1972).

78. "White Collar Wasteland," U. S. News & World Report 114 (June 28, 1993), 42–45.

79. Frances Moore Lappé and Paul Martin DuBois, *The Quickening of America: Rebuilding Our Nation, Remaking Our Lives* (San Francisco: Jossey-Bass, 1994), p. 23.

Chapter 3. The Mind Power Ethic

1. William James, *The Varieties of Religious Experience: A Study in Human Nature* (New York: Collier Books, 1902; 1961), pp. 92, 95, 120.

2. Horatio W. Dresser, *A History of the New Thought Movement* (New York: T. Y. Crowell Co., 1919), p. 216.

3. *Ibid.*, 267, 279–280.

4. Richard M. Huber, *The American Idea of Success* (New York: McGraw-Hill, 1971), p. 135.

5. William Walker Atkinson, *New Thought: Its History and Principles* (Holyoke, Mass.: Elizabeth Towne, 1915), pp. 3–37.

6. Huber, p. 136.

7. Prentice Mulford, *Your Forces and How to Use Them, II* (New York: F. J. Needham, 1890), p. 7.

8. Mulford, "A Plea for Laziness," in Prentice Mulford's *California Sketches* (San Francisco: Book Club of California by J. Nash, 1935), pp. 92, 93, 95.

9. Mulford, "The Church of Silent Demand," in his *Your Forces and How to Use Them, III* (New York: F. J. Needham, 1892), pp. 2, 8.

10. Huber, pp. 152–53.

11. O. S. Marden, *Prosperity: How to Attract it* (New York: Thomas Y. Crowell Co., 1922), pp. 4–5.

12. Ella Wheeler Wilcox, as cited in Marden, *How to Get What You Want* (New York: Thomas Y. Crowell Co., 1917), p. 237.

13. Napoleon Hill, *Think and Grow Rich* (New York: Crest Books, 1937), p. 27.

14. *Ibid.*, 37.

15. *Ibid.*, 248.

16. *Ibid.*, 215.

17. Norman Vincent Peale, *The Power of Positive Thinking* (New York: Prentice-Hall, 1952), p. 13.

18. *Ibid.*

19. *Ibid.*, 24, 65, 66.

20. *Ibid.*, 16, 3, 119, 120.

21. *Ibid.*, 57, 210, 211.

22. Donald B. Meyer, "The Confidence Man." In *The American Gospel of Success: Individualism and Beyond,* ed. Moses Rischin (Chicago: Quadrangle Books, 1965), p. 420.

23. Albert Bandura, "Self-efficacy Mechanism in Human Agency," *American Psychologist* 37 (1982): 123.

24. Paul Tillich, *The Courage to Be* (New Haven: Yale University Press, 1967).

25. Stephen Gottschalk, *The Emergence of Christian Science in American Religious Life* (Berkeley: University of California Press, 1973), p. xxviii.

26. Mary Baker Eddy, *Science and Health with Key to the Scriptures* (Boston: Christian Science Publishing Society, 1910), p. 128.

27. Eddy, *Miscellaneous Writings, 1883–1896* (Boston: Christian Science Publishing Society, 1896), pp. 15–17.

28. Eddy, *Science and Health*, p. 368.

29. Gottschalk, p. 121.

30. Mark Twain, *Christian Science* (New York: Harper and Brothers, 1907), pp. 4–7.

31. H. L. Mencken, in *Bulletin of the Freethinkers of America* (n.d.), as quoted in Gottschalk, p. 66.

32. Robert Schuller, *The Be (Happy) Attitudes* (Waco: Word Books, 1985), pp. 21–25.

33. *Ibid.*, 39.

34. *Ibid.*, 71.

35. *Ibid.*, 76.

36. *Ibid.*, 95.

37. *Ibid.*, 147 ff.

38. *Ibid.*, 198–99.

39. Maxwell Maltz, *The Search for Self-Respect* (New York: Grosset & Dunlap, 1973), p. 187.

40. *Ibid.*, 132–33, 231.

41. *Ibid.*, 230–49.

42. *Ibid.*

43. Joe Greene, as quoted in Roy Blount, Jr., "He Does What He Wants Out There," *Sports Illustrated* 81 (September 5, 1994), 148.

Chapter 4. The Personality Ethic

1. Huber, *American Idea of Success*, pp. 226–30, 264, 271.

2. Christopher Lasch, *The Culture of Narcissism* (New York: Warner Books, 1979), pp. 114–15, 116.

3. Dale Carnegie, *How to Win Friends and Influence People* (New York: Simon & Schuster, 1936).

4. Huber, *American Idea of Success*, pp. 231–34.

5. Carnegie, *How to Win Friends*, pp. 12–13.

6. *Ibid.*, 24.

7. *Ibid.*, 71.

8. *Ibid.*, 72.

9. John G. Cawelti, *Apostles of the Self-Made Man* (Chicago: University of Chicago Press, 1965), p. 216.

10. Huber, *American Idea of Success,* pp. 201, 203–5.

11. *Ibid.*, 207–9.

12. Ronald Hayman, *Arthur Miller* (New York: Frederick Ungar, 1972), pp. 37–38.

13. Arthur Miller, *Death of a Salesman,* in *Arthur Miller's Collected Plays* (New York: Viking Press, 1957), p. 134.

14. *Ibid.*, 146.

15. *Ibid.*, 180.

16. *Ibid.*, 138.

17. Norman A. Graebner, "Eisenhower's Popular Leadership." In *Eisenhower as President,* ed. Dean Albertson (New York: Hill and Wang, 1963), pp. 154–55.

18. Gary Wills, *Reagan's America: Innocents at Home* (Garden City, N.Y.: Doubleday, 1987), p. 2.

19. See Kevin McCann, *Man from Abilene* (Garden City, N.Y.: Doubleday, 1952); and Elmo Richardson, *The Presidency of Dwight D. Eisenhower* (Lawrence: Regents Press of Kansas, 1979), pp. 2–4.

20. See Wills, *Reagan's America,* chs. 1–5, 11–15.

21. See William Lee Miller, *Piety Along the Potomac: Notes on Politics and Morals in the Fifties* (Boston: Houghton Mifflin, 1964), pp. 59–72.

22. Graebner, "Eisenhower's Popular Leadership," p. 155.

23. Wills, *Reagan's America,* p. 296.

24. Sherman Adams, "At Work in the White House," in Albertson, *Eisenhower As President,* p. 2.

25. Samuel Lubell, "Ye Compleat Political Angler," in *ibid.,* 24–25.

26. *Ibid.*, 26.

27. *Ibid.*, 28.

28. Paul D. Erickson, *Reagan Speaks: The Making of an American* Myth (New York: New York University Press, 1985), p. 100.

29. Wills, *Reagan's America,* p. 387.

30. *Ibid.*, 198.

31. Peter Steinfels, "'America's Pastor': At 74, Billy Graham Begins to Sum Up, Regrets and All," *New York Times* (October 3, 1992): A14. See also William Martin, *A Prophet With Honor* (New York: Morrow, 1991).

32. Donald B. Meyer, "Billy Graham." In *The American Gospel of Success: Individualism and Beyond,* ed. Moses Rischin (Chicago: Quadrangle Books, 1965), p. 427.

33. *Ibid.*

34. Paul W. Chapman, *Your Personality and Your Job* (Chicago: Science Research Associates, 1944), p. 8.

35. *Ibid.*, 17–19.

36. Eugene J. Benge, *You — Triumphant: A Guide to Effective Personal Living* (New York: Harper & Brothers, 1946), p. 200.

37. *Ibid.*, 203.

38. David Riesman, Nathan Glazer, and Reuel Denney, *The Lonely Crowd: A Study of the Changing American Character* (Garden City, N.Y.: Doubleday, 1950), pp. 35–38, 151–52.

39. John B. Watson, *Behaviorism: An Introduction to Comparative Psychology* (New York: Henry Holt, 1924), p. 303.

40. Huber, *American Idea of Success*, p. 377.

41. Riesman, Glazer, and Denney, *The Lonely Crowd*, p. 153.

42. Matthew B. Miles, "The Training Group." In *The Planning of Change: Readings in the Applied Behavioral Sciences*, ed. Warren G. Bennis, Kenneth D. Benne, and Robert Chin (New York: Holt, Rinehart and Winston, 1961), p. 717.

43. Bryan Burrough and John Helyar, *Barbarians at the Gate: The Fall of RJR Nabisco* (New York: Harper Collins, 1990), pp. 12–13, 22–24.

44. *Ibid.*, 38–39.

Chapter 5. The Service Ethic

1. Robin M. Williams, Jr., "Values and Beliefs in American Society." In *The Character of Americans: A Book of Readings,* ed. Michael McGiffert (Homewood, Ill.: Dorsey Press, 1964), p. 183.

2. *Ibid.*

3. John Steinbeck, *Cannery Row* (New York: Viking Press, 1945), p. 150.

4. Vernon L. Parrington, *Main Currents in American Thought* (New York: Harcourt, Brace and Company, 1930), Book III, p. xxiii.

5. Jonathan Messerli, *Horace Mann: A Biography* (New York: Alfred A. Knopf, 1972), pp. 175, 219, 232–33, 238.

6. Horace Mann, as quoted in *ibid.*, 524.

7. Lawrence A. Cremin, *The Transformation of the School: Progressivism in American Education, 1876–1957* (New York: Alfred A. Knopf, 1961), pp. vii–ix, 3–22. See also his *The Genius of American Education* (New York: Vintage Books, 1965).

8. Gary K. Clabaugh and Edward G. Rozycki, *Understanding Schools: The Foundations of Education* (New York: Harper & Row, 1990), p. 379.

9. Michael B. Katz, *The Irony of Early School Reform: Educational Innovation in Mid-Nineteenth Century Massachusetts* (Cambridge, Mass.: Harvard University Press, 1968), pp. 27–49.

10. Colin Greer, *The Great School Legend: A Revisionist Interpretation of American Public Education* (New York: Viking Press, 1972), p. 152.

11. Richard Pratte, *Ideology and Education* (New York: David McKay, 1977), p. 122.

12. David Moberg, *The Church as a Social Institution: The Sociology of American Religion* (Englewood Cliffs, N.J.: Prentice-Hall, 1962), p. 180.

13. Cecil E. Greek, *The Religious Roots of American Sociology* (New York: Garland Publishing, 1992), p. 6.

14. *Ibid.*, 7.

15. Horace Bushnell, *Views of Christian Nurture* (Delmar, N.Y.: Scholar's Facsimiles and Reprints, 1847; 1975), p. 149.

16. Richard D. Knudten, *The Systematic Thought of Washington Gladden* (New York: Humanities Press, 1968), p. 8.

17. *Ibid.*, 52.

18. *Ibid.*, 65.

19. Washington Gladden, *Present Day Theology* (Columbus: McClellan and Company, 1913), p. 75.

20. Gladden, *Social Facts and Forces* (New York: G. P. Putnam's Sons, 1897), p. 95.

21. Gladden, *Applied Christianity: Moral Aspects of Social* Questions (New York: Houghton Mifflin, 1886), p. 212.

22. Greek, *The Religious Roots of American Sociology,* pp. 66–67.

23. Frederick Sontag and John K. Roth, *The American Religious Experience: The Roots, Trends, and Future of Theology* (New York: Harper & Row, 1972), pp. 129–30, 137. See also Walter Rauschenbusch, *Christianity and the Social Crisis* (New York: Macmillan, 1907), pp. 143, 220.

24. *Ibid.*, 361.

25. Rauschenbusch, *Christianizing the Social Order* (Boston: Pilgrim Press, 1912), pp. 235, 404.

26. Rauschenbusch, *Christianity and the Social Crisis,* p. 209.

27. Greek, *The Religious Roots of American Sociology,* p. 65.

28. Sontag and Roth, *The American Religious Experience,* pp. 141–42.

29. Christopher Lasch, *The New Radicalism in America, 1889–1963: The Intellectual as a Social Type* (New York: Vintage Books, 1965), pp. 7, 12.

30. Ellen Condliffe Lagemann, *Jane Addams on Education* (New York: Teachers College Press, 1985), p. 22.

31. Lasch, *The New Radicalism in America,* p. 25.

32. Richard Hofstadter, *The Age of Reform* (New York: Alfred A. Knopf, 1955), pp. 151–52. Cf. Lasch, *The New Radicalism in America,* pp. 31–32.

33. For this consensus perspective, see Lawrence A. Cremin, *The Transformation of the School;* and Lagemann, *Jane Addams on Education,* pp. 46–47.

34. Lasch, *The New Radicalism in America,* pp. 145–47.

35. Paul C. Violas, "Jane Addams and the New Liberalism." In *Roots of Crisis: American Education in the Twentieth Century,* ed. Clarence J. Karier, Paul C. Violas, and Joel Spring (Chicago: Rand McNally, 1973), pp. 66–83.

36. Lagemann, *Jane Addams on Education,* p. 33.

37. Nel Noddings, "An Ethic of Caring." In *Women, Culture and Morality: Selected Essays,* ed. Joseph L. DeVitis (New York: Peter Lang, 1987), p. 335.

38. Eleanor Roosevelt, *The Autobiography of Eleanor Roosevelt* (New York: Harper & Brothers, 1958), pp. xvi, 12, 41, 411–12.

39. *Ibid.*, 66.

40. *Ibid.*, 178, 208–9.

41. *Ibid.*, 413.

42. Noddings, "An Ethic of Caring," p. 370.

43. Olga L. Skorapa, *Feminist Theory and the Educational Endeavor of Mary McLeod Bethune,* doctoral dissertation, Atlanta, Georgia State University, 1989, p. 43.

44. Betty Powell, in "Charlotte Bunch and Betty Powell Talk about Feminism, Blacks, and Education as Politics." In *Learning Our Way: Essays in Feminist Education,* ed. Charlotte Bunch and Sandra Pollak (Trumansburg, N.Y.: The Crossing Press, 1983), p. 304.

45. Skorapa, *Feminist Theory and the Educational Endeavor of Mary McLeod Bethune,* p. 65.

46. *Ibid.*, 52–53, 67–68. See also Lagemann, *Jane Addams on Education,* pp. 49–62.

47. Rackham Holt, *Mary McLeod Bethune: A Biography* (Garden City, N.Y.: Doubleday, 1964), pp. 293–94.

48. B. Joyce Ross, "Mary McLeod Bethune and the National Youth Administration: A Case Study of Power Relationships in the Black Cabinet of Franklin D. Roosevelt." In *Black Leaders of the Twentieth Century,* ed. John Hope Franklin and August Meier (Urbana: University of Illinois Press, 1982), p. 196.

49. Holt, *Mary McLeod Bethune,* p. 43.

50. Mary McLeod Bethune, "Loyalty or Conformity," *Chicago Defender* (August 4, 1951), Mary McLeod Bethune Foundation Archives, Bethune-Cookman College, Daytona, Florida.

51. On the origins of King's intellectual sources, see Keith D. Miller, *Voice of Deliverance: The Language of Martin Luther King, Jr. and Its Sources* (New York: Free Press, 1992), ch. 6.

52. James H. Cone, *Black Theology and Black Power* (New York: The Seabury Press, 1969), p. 108.

53. James P. Hanigan, *Martin Luther King, Jr. and the Foundations of Nonviolence* (Lanham, Md.: University Press of America, 1984), p. 312.

54. Rosemary Carter, "Justifying Paternalism," *Canadian Journal of Philosophy* 7 (March 1977): 133.

55. John Stuart Mill, *On Liberty* (Indianapolis: Library of Liberal Arts, 1956), p. 71.

56. Rudolf Dreikurs, *Social Equality: The Challenge of Today* (Chicago: Regnery, 1971), p. viii. See also Alfred Adler, *The Nervous Character: Fundamentals of a Comparative Individual Psychology and Psychopathology,* 4th ed. (Munich: Bergmann, 1928), pp. iv–vi.

Chapter 6. Education, the Success Ethic, and the American Dream

1. Dale Carnegie, *How to Win Friends and Influence People* (New York: Simon & Schuster, 1936).

2. Andrew Carnegie, *The Empire of Business* (Toronto: Wilhaim Briggs, 1902), p. 110.

3. Frederick Rudolf, *The American College and University: A History* (New York: Vintage Books, 1965), pp. 338–39.

4. *Ibid.*, pp. 116–17.

5. Lawrence Cremin, *American Education: The National Experience, 1783–1876* (New York: Harper & Row, 1980), pp. 306–7.

6. Cremin, *American Education: The Metropolitan Experience, 1876–1980* (New York: Harper & Row, 1988), pp. 445–46.

7. Robert W. Ott, "Museums." In *Encyclopedia of Educational Research,* 5th ed. (New York: Macmillan, 1982), Vol. 3, 1284–87.

8. Joseph E. Gould, *The Chautauqua Movement* (Albany, N.Y.: State University of New York Press, 1972).

9. Cremin, *National Experience,* pp. 353–60.

10. Marvin Lazerson and W. Norton Grubb, eds., *American Education and Vocationalism: A Documentary History, 1870–1970* (New York: Teachers College Press, 1974).

11. Ellwood P. Cubberley, *Public Education in the United States* (Boston: Houghton Mifflin, 1934).

12. Merle Curti, *Social Ideas of American Educators* (Paterson, N.J.: Pageant Books, 1959).

13. Harvey C. Minnich, *William Holmes McGuffey and His Readers* (New York: American Book Co., 1936), ch. 3.

14. John H. Westerhoff III, *McGuffey and His Readers* (Nashville: Abingdon Press, 1978), pp. 104–5.

15. Richard D. Mosier, *Making the American Mind* (New York: King's Crown Press, 1947), p. 123.

16. McGuffey, *Eclectic Second Reader* (Milford, Mich.: Mott Media, 1982). Originally published in 1836.

17. *Ibid.*, Lesson XXIII.

18. *Ibid.*, Lesson XXII.

19. *Ibid.*, Lesson XXIV.

20. McGuffey, *Eclectic Third Reader* (Milford, Mich.: Mott Media, 1982). Originally published in 1837.

21. Mosier, *Making,* p. 122.

22. W. W. Charters, *The Teaching of Ideals* (New York: Macmillan, 1927), p. 33.

23. Hugh Hartshorne, *Character in Human Relations* (New York: Charles Scribner's Sons, 1932).

24. Harry C. McKown, *Character Education* (New York: McGraw-Hill, 1935), ch. 4.

25. Hartshorne, *Character,* ch. 6.

26. McKown, *Character Education,* ch. 3. For a recent criticism of the character trait approach, see Lawrence Kohlberg, *The Philosophy of Moral Development* (San Francisco: Harper & Row, 1981).

27. Hugh Hartshorne and M. A. May, *Studies in the Nature of Character: Studies in Deceit,* Vol. 1; *Studies in Service and Self-Control,* Vol. 2; *Studies in the Organization of Character* (New York: Macmillan, 1928–30).

28. S. M. Gross, "The Effect of Certain Types of Motivation on the 'Honesty' of Children," *Journal of Educational Research* 40 (1946): 133–40.

29. C. R. Stendler, "A Study of Some Socio-moral Judgments of Junior-High School Children," *Child Development* 20 (1949): 15–28.

30. Urie Bronfenbrenner, "The Role of Age, Sex, Class, and Culture in Studies of Moral Development," *Religious Education* 14 (1962): 104–15.

31. David Tyack and Elizabeth Hansot, *Learning Together: A History of Coeducation in American Public Schools* (New York: Russell Sage Foundation, 1992), ch. 1.

32. John Demos, "Images of the American Family, Then and Now." In *Changing Images of the Family,* Virginia Tufte and Barbara Meyerhoff, eds. (New Haven: Yale University Press, 1979), pp. 43–60.

33. Benjamin Rush, "Thoughts upon Female Education, Accommodated to the Present State of Society, Manners, and Government in the United States." In *Essays on Education in the Early Republic,* Frederick Rudolf, ed. (Cambridge, Mass.: Harvard University Press, 1965), pp. 230, 25–40.

34. Barbara Miller Soloman, *In the Company of Educated Women* (New Haven: Yale University Press, 1985), ch. 3.

35. *Ibid.,* ch. 8.

36. Harold Innis, *The Bias of Communication* (Toronto: University of Toronto Press, 1971).

37. Innis, *Empire and Communication* (London: Clarendon Press, 1950).

38. Marshall McLuhan, *Understanding Media* (New York: McGraw-Hill, 1964).

39. See Wilbur Schramm, ed., *Mass Communication* (Urbana: University of Illinois Press, 1949), pp. 387–429.

40. Examples of research guided by social categories perspective: Paul F. Lazarfeld, "Communications Research," *Current Trends in Social Psychology* (Pittsburgh: University of Pittsburgh Press, 1949), pp. 233–48; Wilbur Schramm and David White, "Age, Education, and Economic Status as Factors in Newspaper Reading." In Schramm, ed., *Mass Communication,* pp. 402–12.

41. Elihu Katz, "The Two Step Flow of Communication: An Up-to-Date Report on an Hypothesis," *Public Opinion Quarterly* 21 (Spring 1957): 61–78.

42. Harold L. Wilensky, "Mass Society and Mass Culture: Interdependence or Independence?" *American Sociological Review* 29 (April 1964): 173–97.

43. Bradley G. Greenberg, "The Content and Context of Violence in the Mass Media." In *Violence and the Media,* eds. Robert K. Baker and Sandra J. Ball (Washington, D.C.: Government Printing Office, 1969), pp. 423–49.

44. Michael Wood, *America in the Movies* (New York: Basic Books, 1975), p. 77.

45. *Ibid.,* 10–11.

46. Brian Neve, *Film and Politics in America: A Social Tradition* (New York: Routledge, 1992), ch. 8.

47. Leonard Quart and Albert Auster, *American Film and Society Since 1945,* 2nd ed. (New York: Praeger, 1991), ch. 5.

48. *Ibid.,* 10–11.

49. Michael Medved, *Hollywood vs. America* (New York: Harper Perennial, 1993), ch. 13.

50. Quart and Auster, *American Film,* p. 6.

51. Garth Jowett and James M. Linton, *Movies as Mass Communication,* 2nd ed. (Newbury Park, Calif.: Sage Publications, 1989), p. 83.

52. Michael A. Oliker, "On the Images of Education in Popular Film," *Educational Horizons* 71 (Winter 1993): 72–75.

53. Paul Farber and Gunilla Holm, "A Brotherhood of Heroes: The Charismatic Educator in Recent American Movies." In *Schooling in the Light of Popular Culture,* Paul Farber, Eugene F. Provenzo, Jr., and Gunilla Holm, eds. (Albany: State University of New York Press, 1994), pp. 153–72.

54. John Dewey, *Democracy and Education* (New York: Macmillan, 1916), p. 107.

Chapter 7. Psychological Perspectives

1. Michael Walzer, *The Company of Critics: Social Criticism and Political Commitment in the Twentieth Century* (New York: Basic Books, 1988), pp. ix, 232.

2. Cf. Sigmund Freud, "New Introductory Lectures on Psychoanalysis." In *The Standard Edition of the Complete Psychological Works of Sigmund Freud,* ed. James Strachey (London: Hogarth Press, 1960), 22:166; and Elizabeth Janeway, *Cross Sections: From a Decade of Change* (New York: William Morrow, 1982), pp. 78–79.

3. See Calvin S. Hall and Gardner Lindzey, *Theories of Personality,* 3rd ed. (New York: John Wiley & Sons, 1978), pp. 54–58.

4. Freud, "Character and Anal Eroticism." In Sigmund Freud: *Collected Papers,* ed. Ernest Jones (London: Hogarth Press, 1956), 2: 45–50; and James A. Knight, *For the Love of Money* (Philadelphia: Lippincott, 1968).

5. Michael Schneider, *Neurosis and Civilization: A Marxist/Freudian Synthesis* (New York: Seabury Press, 1975), p. 133.

6. Alfred Adler, *Co-operation Between the Sexes: Writings on Women and Men, Love and Marriage, and Sexuality,* ed. Heinz L. Ansbacher and Rowena R. Ansbacher (New York: W. W. Norton, 1978), pp. 49, 147–48, 168–69.

7. Adler, *The Nervous Character: Fundamentals of a Comparative Individual Psychology and Psychotherapy,* 4th ed. (Munich: Bergmann, 1928), pp. iv–vi.

8. Adler, *Social Interest: Challenge to Mankind* (New York: Capricorn, 1938).

9. Carl Jung, *The Integration of the Personality,* tr. S. M. Dell (London: Kegan Paul, 1940), p. 106. Jung is critical of the Western penchant to "overdifferentiate" consciousness. He was more hopeful that non-Western cultures would offer a more compensating balance between the conscious and the unconscious.

10. Jung, *Psychological Types — Or The Psychology of Individuation,* tr. H. G. Baynes (London: Kegan Paul, 1923), p. 547. Jung's typological theory is still used in modern psychological practice, particularly in career and vocational assessment, e.g., the Myers-Briggs inventory.

11. Jung, *Modern Man in Search of a Soul,* tr. C. F. Baynes (London: Kegan Paul, 1933), p. 99.

12. Jung, *Two Essays on Analytical Psychology,* tr. H. G. Baynes and C. F. Baynes (London: Bailliere, 1928), p. 266.

13. Jung describes his idealized "self-actualized" person as one who is "excellent in knowledge" and "excellent in will," but who is "no arrogant superman." *Ibid.,* 264.

14. Erich Fromm, *Man for Himself: An Inquiry into the Psychology of Ethics* (New York: Henry Holt, 1947), pp. 62–63.

15. *Ibid.,* 64–65.

16. *Ibid.,* 65–67.

17. *Ibid.,* 87–88, 92, 229.

18. Karen Horney, *Our Inner Conflicts* (New York: W. W. Norton, 1945), p. 41.

19. Horney, *The Neurotic Personality of Our Time* (New York: W. W. Norton, 1937), pp. 123–34.

20. *Ibid.,* 107–14.

21. Hall and Lindzey, *Theories of Personality,* p. 177. Cf. Horney, *Our Inner Conflicts.*

22. Horney, *The Neurotic Personality of Our Time,* pp. 163, 171.

23. Horney, *Our Inner Conflicts,* p. 196.

24. Horney, *The Neurotic Personality of Our Time,* pp. 162–87.

25. *Ibid.,* 189.

26. Carl R. Rogers, *On Becoming a Person* (Boston: Houghton Mifflin, 1961), p. 170.

27. *Ibid.*, 105.

28. Albert Ellis, "Rational-Emotive Therapy." In *Current Psychothera-pies,* ed. Raymond Corsini (Itasca, Ill.: F. E. Peacock, 1973), p. 167.

29. Epictetus, *The Enchiridion,* as quoted in *ibid.*

30. Adler, *Superiority and Social Interest,* ed. Heinz L. Ansbacher and Rowena R. Ansbacher (Evanston, Ill.: Northwestern University Press, 1964), as cited in *ibid.*

31. *Ibid.*, 171–72.

32. Ellis. "An Impolite Interview with Albert Ellis," *The Realist* (1983), 4.

33. *Ibid.*, 6, 9.

34. *Ibid.*, 13.

35. Nicholas Lemann, "Is There a Science of Success?" *Atlantic Monthly* 273 (1994) 2:86.

36. David C. McClelland, *The Achieving Society* (Princeton, N.J.: D. Van Nostrand, 1961), pp. 71 ff.

37. *Ibid.*, 6, 16, 140, 295, 321, 340, 356–64.

38. Lemann, 88.

39. *Ibid.*, 92.

40. *Ibid.*, 98.

41. David G. Winter, David C. McClelland, and Abigail J. Stewart, *A New Case for the Liberal Arts: Assessing Institutional Goals and Student Devel-opment* (San Francisco: Jossey-Bass, 1981), p. 43.

42. McClelland, *The Achieving Society,* p. 229.

43. Kenneth D. Benne, "The Process of Re-Education: An Assessment of Kurt Lewin's Views," *Groups and Organizational Studies* 1 (1976): 33.

Chapter 8. Philosophical Perspectives

1. Rosemary Carter, "Justifying Paternalism," *Canadian Journal of Philos-ophy* 7 (March 1977): 133.

2. Donald Van De Veer, *Paternalistic Intervention: The Moral Bounds on Benevolence* (Princeton, N.J.: Princeton University Press, 1986), p. 346.

3. Dan Brock, "Paternalism and Promoting the Good." In *Paternalism,* Rolf Sartorius, ed. (Minneapolis: University of Minnesota Press, 1983), p. 239.

4. Aristotle, *Nicomachean Ethics,* Book I. In *Introduction to Aristotle,* Richard McKeon, ed. (New York: Random House, 1947).

5. *Ibid.*, Bk. II.

6. *Ibid.*, Bk. X.

7. Immanuel Kant, *Groundwork of the Metaphysic of Morals* (New York: Harper & Row, 1964), p. 88.

8. *Ibid.*, 95.

9. Martin Buber, *I and Thou* (New York: Charles Scribner's Sons, 1958).

10. Buber, *Between Man and Man* (Boston: Beacon Press, 1955), pp. 87–88.

11. *Ibid.,* 98.

12. *Ibid.,* 104.

13. Friedrich Nietzsche, *Beyond Good and Evil,* trans. by Walter Kaufmann (New York: Random House, 1966).

14. Walter Kaufmann, ed., *The Portable Nietzsche* (New York: Viking Press, 1954), p. 305.

15. *Ibid.,* 306.

16. John Stuart Mill, *Utilitarianism* (New York: Liberal Arts Press, 1949).

17. Brian Medlin, "Ultimate Principles and Ethical Egoism." In *Value and Obligation,* ed. Richard Brandt (New York: Harcourt, Brace and World, 1961), pp. 150–57.

18. Richard B. Brandt, *Ethical Theory* (Englewood Cliffs, N.J.: Prentice-Hall, 1959), pp. 369–75.

19. Karl Marx, *Theses on Feurerbach,* VI (New York: International Publishers Co., 1939), 148.

20. Marx, Preface to *A Contribution to the Critique of Political Economy* (Chicago: Charles H. Kerr and Co., 1904).

21. Lewis S. Feuer, ed., *The German Ideology in Marx and Engels: Basic Writings in Politics and Philosophy* (Garden City, N.Y. : Doubleday, 1959), p. 254.

22. John Dewey, *Freedom and Culture* (New York: G. P. Putnam's Sons, 1939), pp. 117–18.

23. *Ibid.,* 75–76.

24. Dewey, *The Public and Its Problems* (Chicago: Gateway Books, 1946), pp. 13–14.

25. *Ibid.,* 15.

26. *Ibid.,* 64.

27. Dewey, *Individualism, Old and New* (New York: Minton, Balch, and Co., 1930), pp. 11–12.

28. *Ibid.,* 18.

29. Reinhold Niebuhr, *Christianity and Power Politics* (New York: Charles Scribner's Sons, 1940), pp. 156–57.

30. Reinhold Niebuhr, *The Nature and Destiny of Man,* Vol. I (New York: Charles Scribner's Sons, 1943), p. 16.

31. Reinhold Niebuhr, *Discerning the Signs of the Times* (New York: Charles Scribner's Sons, 1946), pp. 120–21.

32. Reinhold Niebuhr, *The Irony of American History* (New York: Charles Scribner's Sons, 1952), p. 84.

33. Reinhold Niebuhr, *The Children of Light and the Children of Darkness* (New York: Charles Scribner's Sons, 1946), p. 54.

34. Reinhold Niebuhr, *Beyond Tragedy* (New York: Charles Scribner's Sons, 1937), pp. 165–66.

35. Paul Tillich, *The Courage to Be* (New Haven: Yale University Press, 1967), p. 66.

36. In addition to *The Courage to Be,* see Tillich's *Dynamics of Faith* (New York: Harper & Brothers, 1957).

37. For discussion of these ethical issues, see Kurt Baier, *The Moral Point of View: A Rational Basis of Ethics* (Ithaca: Cornell University Press, 1958); and Richard B. Brandt, *A Theory of the Good and the Right* (New York: Oxford University Press, 1979).

Chapter 9. Social Perspectives

1. Pitirim A. Sorokin, *Society, Culture and Personality* (New York: Harper & Row, 1947), pp. 700, 703.

2. Georg Simmel, *The Philosophy of Money,* ed. D. Frisby and trans. T. Bottomore and D. Frisby (London: Routledge, 1907), pp. 510–11.

3. Karl Marx, *Frühe Schriften,* ed. Hans-Joachim Lieber and Peter Furth, vol. 1 (Stuttgart: Cotta, 1962), pp. 599/B159, 482/B34, as cited in Richard Schact, *Alienation* (Garden City, N.Y.: Doubleday, 1970), pp. 108–10.

4. Simmel, *The Sociology of Sociability,* as quoted in David Riesman, Nathan Glazer, and Reuel Denney, *The Lonely Crowd: A Study of the Changing American Character* (Garden City, N.Y.: Doubleday, 1950), p. 151.

5. Philip Slater, *The Pursuit of Loneliness: American Culture at the Breaking Point,* rev. ed. (Boston: Beacon Press, 1976), p. 171.

6. *Ibid.,* 184.

7. Riesman, et al., *The Lonely Crowd,* pp. 30, 59, 62.

8. *Ibid.,* 139.

9. *Ibid.,* 77–79.

10. *Ibid.,* 149.

11. *Ibid.,* 37.

12. *Ibid.,* 122, 124–25, 132.

13. William H. Whyte, Jr., *The Organization Man* (Garden City, N.Y.: Doubleday, 1956), p. 7.

14. *Ibid.,* 37–42, 57, 64–65.

15. *Ibid.,* 66, 78–79, 85.

16. *Ibid.,* 116, 88, 102.

17. *Ibid.,* 146–47.

18. *Ibid.,* 281.

19. *Ibid.,* 282.

20. *Ibid.,* 310, 344.

21. *Ibid.,* 395.

22. Vance Packard, *The Status Seekers: An Exploration of Class Behavior in America and the Hidden Barriers That Affect You, Your Community, Your Future* (New York: David McKay, 1959), p. 7.

23. C. Wright Mills, *White Collar* (New York: Oxford University Press, 1956), p. xvii, as quoted in Packard, *The Status Seekers,* p. 124.

24. Packard, *The Status Seekers*, pp. 294–99.

25. *Ibid.*, 301, 306.

26. Herbert Marcuse, *Reason and Revolution: Hegel and The Rise of Social Theory* (New York: Oxford University Press, 1941), p. 246.

27. Marcuse, *One-Dimensional Man: Studies in the Ideology of Advanced Industrial Society* (Boston: Beacon Press, 1964), pp. 10–11, 23, 228.

28. *Ibid.*, 11, 48–55.

29. Joseph C. Flay, "Alienation and the Status Quo," *Man and World* 2 (1969) 2:248.

30. Marcuse, *One-Dimensional Man*, p. 144. Cf. Jacques Ellul, *The Technological Society*, trans. John Wilkinson (New York: Vintage Books, 1964) for an absorbing survey of how technology has developed into an institutional frame of reference — one that conditions human value orientations as well as strategies for social planning.

31. Marcuse, "The Realm of Freedom and the Realm of Necessity: A Reconsideration," *Praxis* 5 (1960) 1–2:21.

32. Marcuse, "Remarks on a Redefinition of Culture," *Daedalus* (Winter, 1965), p. 201.

33. See Katherine S. Newman, *Declining Fortunes: The Withering of the American Dream* (New York: Basic Books, 1993).

34. Robert N. Bellah, Richard Madsen, William M. Sullivan, Ann Swidler, and Steven M. Tipton, *Habits of the Heart: Individualism and Commitment in American Life* (Berkeley: University of California Press, 1985), p. 149.

35. John Winthrop, "A Model of Christian Charity." In *Puritan Political Ideas, 1558–1794*, ed. Edmund S. Morgan (Indianapolis: Bobbs-Merrill, 1965), p. 139, as quoted in Bellah, et al., *Habits of the Heart*, p. 29.

36. *Ibid.*, 34.

37. Walt Whitman, *Complete Poetry and Prose* (New York: Library of America, 1982), p. 297, as quoted in Bellah, et al., *Habits of the Heart*, p. 34.

38. Bellah, et al., *Habits of the Heart*, pp. 28–35.

39. Robert N. Bellah, Richard Madsen, William M. Sullivan, Ann Swidler, and Steven M. Tipton, *The Good Society* (New York: Alfred A. Knopf, 1991), pp. 90, 101, 104.

Chapter 10. The Future Success Ethic in American Culture

1. Gayle Reaves, "Report: U.S. Becoming More Dangerous for Youths," *American Statesman* (September 26, 1993): A4.

2. "Violence in Schools," *U.S. News & World Report* (November 8, 1993): 30–32, 34–35, 37.

3. James Patterson and Peter Kim, *The Day America Told the Truth* (New York: Prentice-Hall, 1991).

4. *Ibid.*, chs. 4, 5, 8, 22, 31.

5. *Ibid.*, 55.

6. Benjamin R. Barber, "America Skips School," *The National Times* 3 (February/March 1994): 38.

7. John Dewey, *Democracy and Education* (New York: Macmillan, 1916/1966), ch. 7.

8. R. S. Peters, *Ethics and Education* (Atlanta: Scott, Foresman, 1967), ch. 10.

9. Amitai Etzioni, *The Spirit of Community: Rights, Responsibilities, and the Communitarian Agenda* (New York: Crown Publishers, 1993), pp. 31, 34.

10. Richard Pratte, *The Civic Imperative: Examining the Need for Civic Education* (New York: Teachers College Press, 1988).

11. *Ibid.*, ch. 1.

12. Benjamin R. Barber, *An Aristocracy of Everyone: The Politics of Education and the Future of America* (New York: Ballantine Books, 1992), ch.6.

13. Pratte, *Civic Imperative*, ch.4.

14. Ernest L. Boyer, *High School* (New York: Harper & Row, 1983), p. 210.

15. Barber, *An Aristocracy of Everyone*, ch.7.

16. Daniel Bell, *The Coming of Post-Industrial Society* (New York: Basic Books, 1973).

17. Daniel Bell, "The Social Framework of the Information Society." In Michael L. Dertouzos and Joel Moses, eds., *The Computer Age: A Twenty Year View* (Cambridge, Mass.: MIT Press, 1979), p. 163.

18. Charles Jencks, "The Post-Modern Agenda." In Jencks, ed. *The Post-Modern Reader* (New York: Academic Editions, 1992), pp. 10–39.

19. Stanley Aronowitz and Henry A. Giroux, *Postmodern Education: Politics, Culture, and Social Criticism* (Minneapolis: University of Minnesota Press, 1991), 60–67.

20. Jean-François Lyotard, *The Postmodern Condition: A Report on Knowledge* (Minneapolis: University of Minnesota Press, 1984), Appendix.

21. Fredric Jameson, "Postmodernism or the Cultural Logic of Late Capitalism," *New Left Review*, 146 (1984): 53–93.

22. Wolfgang Isser, "The Reading Process: A Phenomenological Approach." In Philip Rice and Patricia Waugh, eds. *Modern Literary Theory: A Reader*, 2nd ed. (New York: Edward Arnold, 1992), pp. 77–83.

23. Jacques Derrida, *Of Grammatology*, trans. O. C. Spivak (Baltimore: Johns Hopkins University Press, 1976); and the essay, "Différance," in his *Margins of Philosophy*, trans. Alan Bass (Chicago: University of Chicago Press, 1982), pp. 3–27.

24. Immanuel Wallerstein, "Culture as the Ideological Battleground of the Modern World System." In Mike Featherstone, ed. *Global Culture* (London: Sage Publications, 1990), p. 42.

25. J. W. Guthrie, "Globalization of Educational Policy and Reform." In *International Encyclopedia of Education*, eds. T. Husen and T. N. Postelwaite (New York: Pergamon, 1983), vol. 5, pp. 2945–50.

26. Gerald Celente with Tom Hamilton, *Trend Tracking* (New York: Warner Books, 1991), pp. 202–4.

27. Joseph I. Lipson and Kathleen M. Fischer, "Technologies of the Future," *Education and Computing* 1 (1985): 11–23.

28. Robert B. Reich, "American Society in a Global Economy," *Society* 28 (November–December 1990): 66–71.

29. Lester Thurow, *Head to Head* (New York: Warner Books, 1993), pp. 51–55.

30. Paul Kennedy, *Preparing for the Twenty-First Century* (New York: Vintage Books, 1993), pp. 304–15.

31. Benjamin R. Barber, "America Skips School," p. 37.

32. Lester Thurow, *Head to Head*, p. 274.

33. Robert B. Reich, "American Society in a Global Economy."

34. Lester Thurow, *Head to Head*, pp. 275–79.

35. Advisory Task Force, Council on Learning, *Education and the World View: Final Task Force Report and Recommendations* (New Rochelle, N.Y.: Change Magazine Press, 1981).

36. Quoted in "A Look Ahead: Education and the New Decade," *Education Week* (January 10, 1990): 31.

37. Austin H. Kiplinger and Knight A. Kiplinger, *America in the Global 90s* (Washington, D.C.: Kiplinger Books, 1989), p. 157.

38. "Best Business Schools," *U.S. News & World Report* (March 19, 1990): 55–56.

39. The Race is On to Ready Students for Globalization," *New York Times* (March 26, 1990): 85.

40. *Arthur C. Clark's July 20, 2019* (New York: Macmillan, 1986), p. 76.

41. "A Look at the Economy," *The Washington Spectator* (April 15, 1990): 2.

42. John Naisbitt, *Megatrends* (New York: Warner Books, 1982), pp. 95–96.

43. Kiplinger and Kiplinger, *America*.

44. R. F. Dearden, *Problems in Primary Education* (London: L. Routledge & Kegan Paul, 1976), pp. 69–74.

45. A. L. Costa, ed. *Developing Minds: A Resource Book for Teaching Thinking*. (Alexandria, Va.: Association for Supervision and Curriculum Development, 1985).

46. *Nichomachean Ethics*, Bk. I, Ch. 7.

47. "Composed by the Sea-shore." In Thomas Hutchinson, ed. *Wordsworth: Poetical Works* (New York: Oxford University Press, 1969), p. 360.

Index

211